A pleasure to read. At last a practical approach, written by a passionate leader, which reflects first hand the issues facing business today.

In this ever changing environment Fabian has managed to provide real solutions for managers and workers alike. A quality read!

JOCK MCLEAN - MANAGING DIRECTOR, JARDINE RESTAURANTS VICTORIA (PIZZA HUT)

This book is a vital and challenging as well as psychologically sound approach to change in business. Fabian Dattner is provocative in challenging assumptions about the business process. An ardent advocate of managing employees in the change process, she stresses the importance of democratic human values in business. This book provides us with powerful lessons that will persist into and beyond the twenty-first century.

DR SANDRA NEIL - DIRECTOR-AT-LARGE, INTERNATIONAL COUNCIL OF PSYCHOLOGISTS

A leader whose company has adopted the correct strategy for ensuring its long term future would do well to take note of the contents of this book in his or her day to day operations. Good leadership involves generating the sort of internal 'ecology' - which this author teases out so well. Naked Truth is an engaging book and very worthwhile reading.

PHIL RUTHVEN - EXECUTIVE CHAIRMAN, IBIS BUSINESS INFORMATION

Naked Truth

AN OPEN LETTER TO THE AUSTRALIAN WORKING COMMUNITY

FABIAN DATTNER

WOODSLANE PRESS

Published by
Woodslane
Unit 7/5 Vuko Place
Warriewood, NSW 2102

First Published by Woodslane Press 1996

Designed by Yolande Gray
Typeset by Taninka Visuals

National Library of Australia
Cataloguing–in–Publication data:

Dattner, Fabian, 1954-
Naked Truth: an open letter to the Australian working community.
ISBN 1 875889 06 X
1. Personnel management - Australia. 2. Business enterprises - Australia. I. Title.
650.0994

Printed and bound in Australia.

10 9 8 7 6 5 4 3 2

Distributed in Australia by Woodslane Pty Ltd. Woodslane Press books are available
through booksellers and other resellers across Australia. For further information contact
Woodslane Pty Ltd on (02) 9970 5111.

To Ken, my soul mate in life;
to Dib, who teaches me the power of unfettered freedom;
to Kess, who can truly touch the stars
if he but stretches his arms;
to KD who has courage in abundance

&

to people everywhere fighting
their way to a better place.

Contents

PART ONE: WHAT DO YOU THINK IS GOING ON?

PART TWO: MYTH BUSTERS

Acknowledgments

This page is about people who give a great deal, expecting little in return.

To all those people, many unknowingly, from whom I have stolen (and continue to steal) inspiration and energy; to employees who in their every action exemplify the value of dignity and respect; to leaders whose humility and curiosity inspire those they come into contact with to try harder (myself included). Just in case you don't think I am talking about you, here's a few names I would mention: Jock, Niamh, Jim, Brian, Greg, Bob, Ron, David, Bill, Susie, Maurie, Geoff, Denni, Rubin, Mike, John, Hugh, Simon, Linda, Phil, Tassos and Nick.

To Tim and the team at Woodslane - for all the good laughs and being old-fashioned publishers with your heads in the future.

To Paul, for being a bloody pedant, and for improving the manuscript enormously.

To Jerry B Harvey, the author of *The Abilene Paradox*. We've never met but I hope a lot of people go out and buy your book!

And last but not least, to my family in its eccentric and delicious nest of non-conformity: what magic is woven there!

Introduction

They say that at any one time, some thirty people around the world will be working on the same idea at the same time. Well, I don't know who the other twenty-eight are, but I do know that while the idea for this book was rumbling around in my head, it was also rumbling around in the head of a like-minded publisher. Having heard of the work I was doing, Tim Edwards (the publisher in question) contacted me to see if I was interested in writing the very book that I was struggling with — a book which would be a survival manual for people in business in the late twentieth century.

The motivation for this particular story goes back a few years for me, I guess to the time I lost my own business and had some of the most poignant lessons as a leader I have ever had. That was early in 1990. As many Australians will vividly remember, it was the time of the "recession we had to have," in its early infancy. I was then Managing Director and Chief Executive Officer of the Stephen Dattner Group, known by many Australians for its leather and fur products. Behind the scenes we had diversified into an extraordinary array of business areas. I won't go into the details of all that we did, all the crazy adventures I managed to lead my dedicated team into throughout the nineteen-eighties. What I will say here is that I led a group of variously 150 to 250 people — full-time employees, management, part-timers, contract workers, external chamber manufacturers, cleaners and the not infrequent dog or child. In the majority, these were people with skills, expertise, ideas, passion and vision. Many of them had worked in the business far longer than I, most of them had a level of expertise that exceeded mine in one of several areas.

I headed the Stephen Dattner Group throughout the major part of the nine-teen-eighties. I was creative, passionate, excited and excitable. I loved business — retailing, manufacturing, importing, exporting, negotiating, managing people, learning, experimenting. I was a street fighter — a leader empowered by adversity. I loved a challenge and rarely felt defeated. I charged into unknown territory with all the courage of a bull fighter — always for good reasons, but ultimately with expensive and almost terminal outcomes.

In theory the way I ran the business was highly consultative. We had no apparent hierarchy. It was a predominantly young work force. People were responsible for their own decisions and although we didn't like mistakes, we expected and accepted them as part of the process of learning. I thought myself a good mentor, coach, friend. I was approachable, nice even. I thought I fitted the bill of the ideal, modern transformational leader, working with an enlightened, informed, empowered work force. Unfortunately, reality did not match my perceptions as neatly as I thought it should.

In January 1990, faced with the imminent closure of the Dattner Group, I acknowledged a reality that I had been avoiding — not only was this a business whose time had come but also I was not the crash hot leader I had thought myself to be. I was not as enlightened as I imagined and didn't listen well: if I was determined to get something done, then incoming information which might dissuade me from my course simply did not register. I believed that it was my job to come up with all the answers, to be the problem solver. I was too caught up in my own cleverness and was only marginally aware of the talent around me. I affected the lives of people every day yet I had little genuine thought for the long term impact of my actions.

Nevertheless, I did get a few things round the right way. I genuinely liked people. I was not seduced by hierarchy or status, politics or chicanery — and I had a sense that there might be a more enlightened way to conduct business than the old world style, which to my eyes was all profit and no people.

In the process of experimenting, I had drawn only from my own limited experiences — with family, leaders I had known, during academic training, from personal experience. I did not facilitate the generation of wisdom in our business — if it happened, it was by happenchance. Staff education was arranged only as the need arose. Planned education that ensured continuous and progressive development of all staff was something that we were going to set in motion when there was more time — but time was never available. We were always rushing into the future.

And this future we rushed into? Whose design was it? Who really understood it, owned it, was passionate about it? Too few, despite a belief to the contrary. Although I involved a large number of people in designing the future, the truth was that too many people were on the outside, wearing the consequences of our actions but not really understanding their purpose.

The result? Not enough input from the many talented people in the business about how we could do things better, differently, more wisely. Too often, our actions were at cross purposes. We would be ignorant of what each other had to offer; there was a lack of quality time spent communicating and coordinating our objectives. Although people were raising concerns, I wasn't listening or, if I was, I wasn't hearing what was being said. In fact, I could be so overpowering in my intent that, despite protesting open communication ("my door is always open"), I could just be too much of a challenge. Even with the best will in the world, people gave up.

So, no matter how much I might try to justify the position of the Dattner Group in early 1990 by referring to the state of the economy, our lack of capital or the death of an industry, the truth was that by far the greater ills were caused by my lack of skills as a leader. I might have been clever and capable in certain areas, but my skills alone were nowhere near enough to steer a large business through the increasingly changeable and chaotic waters of business in the nineteen-nineties. The company needed the empowered thinking of all its people; to achieve that, it needed a wise leader, without ego, facilitating excellence at every turn.

In early January 1990, at the end of the worst retailing two weeks on record for our group (and for many other Australian retailers), the ANZ Bank decided that we were no longer a secure risk. In fact, technically we were insolvent. At a very sober meeting at the regional head office in Melbourne, at 4 pm on the second Thursday in January, the ANZ asked me to fully repay all outstanding loans. They knew and I knew that this was not possible. That same meeting, they appointed receiver managers to oversee the winding up of the Stephen Dattner Group. It was to be the final curtain for an old business — and a very interesting new beginning for a then thirty-six-year-old chairman.

In the two weeks following the appointment of receiver managers, we conducted a very highly publicised closing down sale. In essence, it was straightforward — stock was priced to sell, come hell or high water, and there was an advertising blitzkrieg in the media. Along with this, we made an honest appeal to the public, telling them the truth about the company and how we had arrived at our current predicament.

I think, in some part because of our honesty, we found ourselves at the end of January 1990 in the unexpected position of having experienced in just one month the two most extraordinary retailing periods in the history of our business. If the first two weeks were memorable for the appalling lack of turnover, the second two were memorable for their record-breaking sales figures. We were actually in the entirely unexpected position of being able to repay all secured creditors and, with the sale of our family home, return to the bank one hundred cents in the dollar. Bankruptcy, which had seemed inevitable at the bank's meeting on that Thursday afternoon, was relegated to the land of nightmare. Certainly, we lost ninety-five percent of our family money and a very beautiful home — but we didn't have to live with the stigma of bankruptcy and we had honourably been able to meet all of our commitments to creditors.

This unexpected outcome also meant we actually had the option to restart the business. We had no debts, thousands of Victorians had registered their support for the business by coming to the wind-up, we had managed to hold our head above water and were respected for the way we had managed the crisis. Having placed ourselves in a far stronger position than we had been in for over a decade, everything was in our favour to restart Dattners.

However, as the Chief Executive Officer, the final decision lay in my hands, I knew that I actually had much to learn. It was time for me to move on. By closing Dattners down I gave myself the chance to begin a new voyage. Though I wanted to stay in business, I wanted to take my experience and study the world of business. I wanted to learn about leading, following, discovering, inventing; I wanted to see how other businesses did it, how other leaders worked, how other employees felt. I wanted to explore the notion of leadership and discover how different the world of business might be if all those involved in it are valued, united and passionate about the future.

I made a series of critical decisions after the closure of Dattners. Firstly, I became committed to my own education. I sought an honest appraisal of what it was that I needed to do differently, drawn not only from insights solicited from the people I worked with, but also from reading and study. Secondly, I decided to learn how to listen to people — not just their words, but the meaning behind them. I committed myself to developing an understanding of the diversity of perspectives that surrounded me — and to allowing myself the luxury of experimenting with that diversity. Thirdly, I decided to study leadership, both good and bad, based not only on the leader's perspective but on the quality of feedback given by the people who are led. Fourthly and finally, I vowed to hold true to my driving values as a leader in business — integrity, honesty, compassion — above and beyond the pursuit of profit.

So when all is said and done, who am I to be talking about the way we participate in business? What happened between the closure of the Stephen Dattner Group and now that puts me in a position to write a hundred thousand words on the topic? Well, for starters, I've talked to people — all sorts of people.

I have worked with many hundreds of leaders as their strategic partner — sometimes on major projects (working to reinvigorate the company's sense of the future) or sometimes in preparation for an appearance on behalf of the company as a speaker at a major event. I have interviewed and worked with well over 5,000 Australian employees, supervisors and managers alike. They come from many fields — in small ventures and large. Here's a smattering of business sectors in which their businesses operate:

– primary (agriculture and mining);

– government (federal, state and local);

– retail (clothing, whitegoods, music, hardware and general);

– service (education, management consultants);

– service, industrial (building, electrical, plumbing and transport);

– industry bodies (representative bodies for retailing, small business, farming, recruitment and career counselling);

– import-export specialists; and

– research and development (technical, medical and scientific).

About four-fifths of the people I have spoken to — usually in an interview situation — were "ordinary" employees. About one-fifth were in management. My definition of "management" extends to include leading hands or first-line supervisors as much as it refers to senior management, the Managing Director, the Chief Executive Officer or the Board of Directors.

I have accumulated thousands of stories about both good and bad business practices — about good and bad leadership — and I have amassed an almost limitless supply of stories that reflect the frustration of those working at "the business coalface". All these stories are the fuel for this book. What you are reading is a percolation of all these people's experiences. (Actually, what fascinates me is that most people raise *all* the primary issues covered in this book.)

Some discoveries that I've made have been exhilarating, but sadly they've been more than counterbalanced by realisations that have been distressing and debilitating — if not for me then for the people I have learnt from. I have met leaders too afraid to admit they don't have the answers but are arrogant and bullish enough to continue in their pursuit of political or personal gratification at the expense of sometimes hundreds of employees. I have met employees so cynical of leadership in Australia that they have long since given up any commitment to personal responsibility and, no matter what the rhetoric of leadership might be, have adopted the nine-to-five mentality. I have met inspired and highly motivating leaders, characterised by compassionate humility, decency and a genuine liking of humanity — and I have met coalface workers whose business acumen and instinct for "right" action has stopped me dead.

I am not suggesting that all leaders are bad or inadequate or poorly equipped for the position of responsibility to which they have been appointed, nor am I saying that all employees are undiscovered saints. I am not saying that "profit" is a dirty word or that sometimes, in order for a business to survive, critical and sometimes painful decisions must be taken. What I am suggesting is that in pursuit of profit none of us has the right to diminish the sense of worth of another human being. The foremost responsibility of leadership is to be considerate of the people who are being lead — and in business, that consideration should not occur in isolation from the pursuit of growth and profit.

It is time for employees to value their concerns. It is time for leaders to listen, without fear or favour, and act upon what they hear. To this end, this book is an exposé of what has been said to me in an enormous number of one-on-one confidential interviews with both leaders and employees about the difficulties and challenges of being in business in the late twentieth century. I will try to be balanced and present both the leader's and the employee's "sides". I will also suggest how you might get people talking, contributing and ultimately caring for one another in business. My sincere hope is that by conducting this sort of discussion, we might learn how to make the workplace a more decent and enjoyable place to be.

MAKING SENSE OF THE STRUCTURE OF THIS BOOK

I have read much of the available literature that addresses change in business and other issues of concern to those in business in the late twentieth century. That reading has led me to some odd conclusions — not so much about the content of the books, but more about their style of presentation.

For instance, my concentration span for facts and figures is not long. I get bored and daydream. For me, many of the facts and figures become disconnected from the 'real' world. I have assumed, in writing this book, that there are many other readers who share my lack of concentration. To address this, I have peppered the book with anecdotes, stories and theatrical representations of events that have either occurred to me personally or that I have been told about.

There are two parts to this book. I begin by sharing with you the issues that principally concern people right now. Then I share with you quite specific strategies that I have successfully helped people use to make the changes they so dearly sought.

Part One, *What do you think is going on?* reviews major issues of concern about business life today. By looking at the causes of those concerns, fresh solutions for the problems can be identified. Part Two, *Myth busters,* brings this newly learnt critical approach to bear on some commonly held perceptions and, in the process, exposes them as myth. *Myth busters* is exactly what it sounds like it's going to be — if you don't read something in this section which has you vigorously nodding your head in agreement, I will be surprised.

In *What do you think is going on?* each chapter begins with stories that underline the sentiment of the chapter. Though the stories are meant to make the task of reading more enjoyable — after all, storytelling is a time-honoured and ancient tool for sharing learnings — they are dramatisations of real events. They carry meaning. After the stories, the topic is explored in depth.

Each chapter concludes with an action section, in which I provide recommendations for courses of action. These recommendations have been trialled in many different companies by many different people. They *do* work.

The action sections are generally divided between recommendations for employees and suggestions for leaders. Such a division is not meant to deter you from reading one action plan instead of the other. On the contrary, the divisions between leader and employee have really changed: all of us can be both leader and follower — in the course of a day, a week, or a year. The change in position more and more has to do with function rather than hierarchy, it is fluid rather than fixed, and is more consultative than dictatorial. So read all sections because they are relevant to all of us — if not obviously now then perhaps more plainly tomorrow.

In *Myth busters,* the topics are more about perception. I have heard from enough people in enough different industries to be confident that certain behaviourial habits and certain assumptions about the way things are supposed to work in business prevail *regardless of the nature of business.* But more than that, I contend that these widely accepted practices are questionable. Some of them are merely fashionable; all of them are entrenched. *Myth busters* tries to unclothe them in order to discover if there is any underlying 'truth'.

Overall, the reading is designed to be of general interest, for people who are curious about business, how it is done now and how it might be done in the future. I trust you find the style down to earth, entertaining, engaging and, of course, challenging.

My hope is that as you read this book there will be times when the content hits home for you, when it describes a dilemma you are dealing with, a frustration that makes your work life challenging. If I could wish for any outcome from your reading, it is that you understand that your experience is not isolated. You are one of many. If we understood this better, then we might be able to do something to change things.

This is a book for the silent majority. My dearest hope is for that majority to break its silence.

Part One

WHAT DO YOU THINK IS GOING ON?

The world we live in – are we having fun yet?

I don't know too many people who are entirely happy with the rate of change nowadays. Most agree that you have to be on the ride to survive, but the speed is a killer and controlling it takes just about all the energy we've got.

Let's be clear about something before we get into the nitty gritty of this book: I am sick of pretending that everything around me is okay. I am uncertain about the journey I'm on, particularly as it affects my working life and the working lives of people around me. I want to use this beginning chapter to talk about how the world of work affects our enjoyment of life, and see if the things that I am not sure about are also things that you are not so sure about, either. If you have a grip on my gripes, you have a hold of my vision.

So, listen up a bit. See what you think.

1

SPEED...

Do you know that each year Christmas is arriving earlier? Without checking my calendar, I have the impression that we are up to about June or July. In terms of what I have achieved and what remains to be done in the year, that would seem reasonable. Time would be manageable; I would be satisfied. But it is not to be: in fact, at the time I write, it is, this very day, 1 November. Seven and a half weeks to Christmas. Commercial decorations are already being put up. Some retailers have been playing for at least three weeks those loathsome Christmas carols that we all look forward to during the Yuletide festival. As a result of all this premature jollity, I (like many others, I suspect) have gone into blind panic... "Not Christmas, not yet, *I'm not ready*!!"

If you haven't already experienced this phenomenon, ask anyone you like, man, woman or child. They'll confirm the truth of what I say. Even the diehards who passionately love Christmas are surprised at the speed with which this year's festivities are looming. Children, God bless their little dollar signs, are (delightedly) every bit as amazed at the rapidity with which their key bargaining opportunity of the year rolls round. The citizens of the mortgage belt — every broken unit of 2.5 kids and separated parents — are in exhausted denial: "It's best just to assume that it isn't happening." Old people have gone into shock and are seen walking — slower than usual — on our suburban streets muttering, in barely audible whispers... "It wasn't like this when I was young!" And they are right, it wasn't.

Everything we do is being done faster and faster. Often, I find myself (figuratively) spinning in one spot, having a sense of what I should be doing, but so overwhelmed at the need for speed and efficiency that I am unable to do anything but spin. People have less and less time to do more and more. Diaries groan with entries, double bookings and overlaps. Schedules are so tightly packed that a Monday morning traffic jam can cause a bottleneck in plans for the whole working week.

People are leaving earlier for work and arriving home later. Evenings are a frenzy of feeding, weeding, reading and sleep. Sex, that wonderful, elusive thing we once did when we were too young to worry or too in love to stop, has been put onto the backburner. The sum total of our erotic undertakings, married or otherwise, is a quick kiss good night and a barely audible "I love you!" as sleep claims our weary souls.

Arranging workable schedules increasingly makes us borderline manic. No longer is it possible to get executives to meet without secretaries speaking to each other five or six times to try and co-ordinate diaries: "How about 4 pm Monday?" "No, Jim's in Sydney." "10 am Tuesday." "No, Jennifer's in a teleconference link up." "What about Wednesday 12 noon." "Actually, Sam's attending a buyers' conference in Tasmania." "What about Thursday 3 pm." "No, Sandra's interviewing staff." "What about Friday 11 am." "No, Gail is doing a stress management course."

Once a meeting is organised, it is bound to be postponed at least three times because of sudden demands placed upon people to go here or there, speak to this or that person, produce the final draft of such-and-such or make a sudden plane trip to wherever… so a meeting that was harder to organise than a private session with the big "G" himself goes repeatedly back to the drawing board. Time again for the secretaries to play diary volleyball — and hope, patient beasts of burden that they are, that the second, third or fourth attempt will be successful.

And as for the peaceful coalface where all is planned, quiet, predictable action? Humph! Now we have quality circles, customer focus groups, increasing cost efficiencies, productivity gains, changing systems, new team evaluations, rush orders this month for X, biggest order on record for Y. We have management challenges to produce this month's quota with a zero defect record and higher levels of profitability — with less staff, less essential resources and a shorter amount of time. So go to it! It's a case of head down, arse up. Laughter? What's that? We have work to do, and if you're not serious about being a productive part of the team, well, there are a lot of people out there looking for a job.

Anyone with children knows that respite on the weekend is an illusion. Two or three kids will keep you dog-trotting from 6 pm Friday until the Sunday movie creaks into action some 50 hours later: basketball, football, gymnastics, netball, swimming, cricket, parties, haircuts, train trips, take me here, take me there. Somewhere between a 12-year-old's birthday party and a quick dash to the hairdresser, the week's shopping is squeezed in. Maybe a night out is managed, but most people I know are just too damned tired.

Certainly, having friends over has become much more simplified. I can remember that I used to actually *cook* for people if I asked them over for a meal. Now, my idea of cooking is a few chops on the barbeque — and I always look for a volunteer to work the fire while I collapse into a director's chair and gasp for oxygen.

People everywhere seem to have more to do, are doing it all to tighter deadlines, under more pressure and with less time for common decencies. In business, we are dealing with escalating change processes, restructures, takeover bids, new leadership teams, reconfigured work groups. The work-place is fiercely competitive, jobs are hotly contested, qualifications need to be better and better (soon you will need a Phd in advanced physics to be a dispatch clerk).

People are inventing, developing, researching, experimenting, merging everywhere, for a zillion business reasons. Strategic alliances and commercial partnerships are blossoming. The business amoeba is dividing and multiplying at a formidable speed. In the open marketplace all hell has broken lose. To the faint-hearted it seems as though the business world has become a seething tide of hungry piranha.

We talk about quality, committing to customer service and committing to people, but when competition is hotting up, values have a way of disappearing out the business back door. And boy, has it hotted up. No one can predict trends with any degree of certainty; patterns change with kaleidoscopic rapidity. Things are being invented, the purpose of which has yet to be revealed, whose commercial potential is evolving, even as the research is being finalised. And for every product, idea, service, anyone invents — anywhere on the planet — remember, there are probably twenty-nine others inventing it at exactly the same time. And they're all racing to see who can get it to the consumer first.

Phew!

Over the last decade we have talked endlessly about changing work practices, improving the processes of empowerment, valuing human beings, looking after each other, adding value in the business journey. We have talked about the rise of quality and the demise of the cheap and nasty, we have talked about the changing requirements of leaders — out with dictators, in with visionary motivators, mentors, coaches and friends. We have talked about education and enlightenment.

Talking so much, we are in danger of believing our own rhetoric. But damn it, I think we are all going so fast that all we have time for is talk and, with rare exceptions, we are not really improving things a whole lot. We're just doing what we basically always did — but we're doing it a lot faster.

I am worried that we might have reached terminal velocity. In the pursuit of profit, with passionate dedication to the idea of endless growth, in fear of a competitor lurking around the corner, business is on a rocket ride, travelling at incomprehensible speed. The outcome is anyone's guess.

I have a wonderful book in my library called *The Abilene Paradox and other meditations on management,* by Jerry B Harvey (Lexington Books:

New York, 1988). Early in the book, Jerry tells the story of going to visit his in-laws in West Texas on a particularly hot summer's day:

That July afternoon in Coleman, Texas (population 5,607), was particularly hot — 104 degrees according to the Walgreen's Rexall's thermometer. In addition, the wind was blowing fine grained West Texas topsoil through the house. But the afternoon was still tolerable — even potentially enjoyable. A fan was stirring the air on the back porch; there was cold lemonade; and finally, there was entertainment. Dominoes. Perfect for the conditions. The game requires little more physical exertion than an occasional mumbled comment, "Shuffle 'em," and an unhurried movement of the arm to place the tiles in their appropriate positions on the table. All in all, it had the makings of an agreeable Sunday afternoon in Coleman. That is, until my father-in-law suddenly said, "Let's get in the car and go to Abilene and have dinner at the cafeteria."

I thought, "What, go to Abilene? Fifty-three miles? In this dust storm and heat? And in an unairconditioned 1958 Buick?"

But my wife chimed in with, "Sounds like a great idea. I'd like to go. How about you, Jerry?" Since my own preferences were obviously out of step with the rest, I replied, "Sounds good to me," and added, "I just hope your mother wants to go."

"Of course I want to go," said my mother-in-law. "I haven't been to Abilene in a long time."

So into the car and off to Abilene we went. My predictions were fulfilled. The heat was brutal. Perspiration had cemented a fine layer of dust to our skin by the time we arrived. The cafeteria's food could serve as a first-rate prop in an antacid commercial.

Some four hours and 106 miles later, we returned to Coleman, hot and exhausted. We silently sat in front of the fan for a long time. Then, to be sociable and to break the silence, I dishonestly said, "It was a great trip, wasn't it?"

No one spoke.

Finally, my mother-in-law said, with some irritation, "Well, to tell the truth, I really didn't enjoy it much and would rather have stayed here. I just went along because the three of you were so enthusiastic about going. I wouldn't have gone if you all hadn't pressured me into it."

I couldn't believe it. "What do you mean 'you all'?" I said. "Don't put me into the 'you all' group. I was delighted to be doing what we were doing. I didn't want to go. I only went to satisfy the rest of you. You're the culprits."

My wife looked shocked. "Don't call me a culprit. You and Daddy and Mama were the ones who wanted to go. I just went along to keep you happy. I would have had to be crazy to want to go out in heat like that."

Her father entered the conversation with one word: "Shee-it." He then expanded on what was already absolutely clear: "Listen, I never wanted to go to Abilene. I just thought you might be bored. You visit so seldom I wanted to be sure you enjoyed it. I would have preferred to play another game of dominoes and eat the leftovers in the icebox."

After the outburst of recrimination, we all sat back in silence. Here we were, four reasonably sensible people who — of our own volition — had just taken a 106-mile trip across a godforsaken desert in a furnace-like heat and a dust storm to eat unpalatable food at a hole-in-the-wall cafeteria in Abilene, when none of us had really wanted to go. To be concise, we'd done just the opposite of what we wanted to do. The whole situation didn't make sense.

At least it didn't make sense at the time. But since that day in Coleman, I have observed, consulted with, and been a part of more than one organisation that has been caught in the same situation. As a result, the organisations have either taken side trips or, occasionally, terminal " journeys to Abilene," when Dallas or Houston or Tokyo was where they really wanted to go. And for most of those organisations, the negative consequences of such trips, measured in term of both human misery and economic loss, have been much greater than for our little Abilene group.

I now call the tendency for groups to embark on excursions that no group member wants "the Abilene Paradox." Stated simply, when organisations blunder into the Abilene Paradox, they take actions in contradiction to what they really want to do and therefore defeat the very purposes they are trying to achieve.

Call me crazy if you want, but something tells me that the rate of change we are caught up in, the speed at which we now live our lives, the brevity of interaction between human beings, the absence of any quality reflective time in business, the blurring of what I call busyness (the sometimes madly hectic and unproductive activity of any given day) and business (the soundly planned and reasonable pursuit of clear business objectives), is the ultimate example of the Abilene Paradox.

I don't know too many people who are entirely happy with the rate of change nowadays. Most agree that you have to be on the ride to survive, but the speed is a killer and controlling it takes just about all the energy we've got. I have always loved change, fast and furious. I am one of those curious beasts who actually prosper in the face of rapid change but I am honest enough to admit that (a) I am not typical and (b) just because I happen to like it doesn't mean that it's okay to drag everyone else along with me.

I have learnt this lesson expensively as a leader. I don't want to stop the ride; the outcome is bound to be exciting and unpredictable. It will take us to places no one has dared to go before — bar the Star Trek team — and that is all as it should be. I just want to suggest that maybe it's time to think about slowing down, just a bit, to make space for the things that matter to us. It's time to look around and appreciate what we have, what we make, where we are going — before it passes by so fast that it's gone before we even knew it was coming.

TECHNOLOGY

I am going to be very honest with you, right now, and tell the truth, spit it out, purge myself, admit my madness, lay my cards on the table. I am writing on a Power Macintosh 6100/66. Oh, I got seduced very artfully by a good-looking young smooth-talker. He saw me coming a mile off. Quite clearly I knew very little about computers. Quite clearly I thought I could learn much. Being ever-so-helpful, he persuaded me (and it wasn't hard), on behalf of my business, to spend some $13,000 on the new Mac, two Performas, a Umax Vista-T630 (for photo production), Quark Express (a hot desktop publishing program), Adobe Photoshop (software that allows me to do all sorts of fancy things with photos) and Macromedia Freehand (which allows me to do all sorts of fancy things with drawings). I also got the 6.01 update of Word from Microsoft — all in the space of four working weeks. I now have the computer power to publish my own magazines, books, brochures, advertising material, pamphlets, letter drops, handouts, educational material. In fact, I have the gear to produce just about anything that can be printed.

Of course, there is a little glitch to this investment. I now have to spend the next 12 months swatting with an intensity that leaves university study for dead. I have neither the time nor the motivation to do this. So, what I am actually doing is badgering my secretary to learn all the necessary skills. I am also badgering anyone else that works with me — my husband, children, visiting guests, distant important persons, the dog, even my blue point Siamese.

I am overwhelmed by what I can do with all this hot equipment and under-whelmed at my individual capacity to put it to use. Personally, I actually use this very expensive gear as a glorified typewriter. I know what it can do for me, I just can't/won't/don't/haven't done it yet myself.

And that seems to sum up the relationship a lot of us have with technolog-ical wizardry. Yet we can sense the complexity of the wizard's world. We listen, mouths agape, to the latest story on *Beyond 2000* about what the latest computer-driven technology can do for us — see minutiae, voyage through the human body, create worlds on film that are so convincing we can hardly tell the real from the constructed, use credit facilities as part of our daily lives, book airline tickets, eat food the mix of which is driven by a computer, purchase paints the combination of which is driven by a computer… and on and on.

Personal computers have changed forever the art of writing, communi-cating, calculating, packaging. School children use portable PCs the way earlier generations used slide rules. The Internet has created a global community whose heartbeat is computer-driven communication. Every day, in a thousand different ways, our world touches the surface of the wizard's world… but that is all.

(There are exceptions to the rule, of course. There are those whose lives are entwined in this world — the software engineers, systems analysts, programmers — the people whose expertise and personal addiction have drawn them to a world where today's toying becomes tomorrow's megabucks. But for the most part, they are remote from us mere mortals: their eyes are turned to screens of endless code, their minds are performing complex acts of logic that are not part of the day-to-day parry and thrust of ordinary human commerce.)

Yet we are led, relentlessly, on a journey over which few have any control and on which we all, it seems, must go. Few today would dare challenge the place the computer has in our lives. The computer is here to stay. It is transforming the way we do things. That there is an ever-increasing rate of exploration and invention, fuelled by an increasingly sophisticated and awe-inspiring computer-led technological revolution, is undeniable.

Some say the evolution of computer-driven technology has historical parallels — the advent of the printing press, the invention of the telephone, the introduction of electricity. They argue that, in their time, these were earth-shattering, world-changing inventions. But I think such inventions pale in comparison. Computer-driven exploration has become its own self-fulfilling prophecy; it is self-generative. Technological outcomes spring from our limitless imaginations; we can have no real sense of where this particular revolution will take us. We are in the midst of a transformation, the outcome of which is unknowable.

Recently, I watched Bill Gates, Chief Executive of the Microsoft empire, interviewed on the ABC. I was delighted by his precocity, his child-like wonder of his product and his world. I was haunted by his voracious appetite for the future, for the business opportunities to expand computer technology. This one human being may be having a greater influence on my destiny and on the destiny of many millions of others than any leader since the dawn of time. Like it or not, I can do little about it except watch and, where possible, exercise wisdom and personal responsibility in the choices I make. I am not seduced by the twinkle in his eye; I do not sympathise with the cry of anger from competitors who feel that this modern Ghengis Khan has cut them off from their vital supplies. If Bill Gates weren't determining the course of this particular battle, there would be someone else. The world of computers, of a racing, rampant technology, breeds giants who will, in their five minutes of fame, change the face of their and our world, through the technology over which they are briefly emperor.

This is my world, your world. I take a deep breath and try not to be intimidated by it all. I take small comfort from a Telstra commercial that kindly says its role is to provide a level of service that is driven by a technology that the consumer need never understand. I have used for a long time objects the functioning of which I am unable to fathom (God alone knows, I cannot live without a mobile phone — and I am still looking for the wires) and I *tell* myself that the computer and its wedded technology are just more of the same... but I am not sure.

Talking to ordinary souls from all walks of life, I sense a similar bewilderment. Few adults genuinely understand the technology that surrounds them, although most have an inkling of what is coming in science, medicine, education and the like. Many adults use computers at home, shopping or at work but few speak with any confidence about the technology that drives it.

I don't know that there are easy answers but surely part of the process is to acknowledge the uncertainty. We should check to see how much of our journey is a reflection of the Abilene Paradox. I love the promise of where we are going, but I don't think that we have the right to leave people behind. I don't want a world which is alien to the majority, no matter how clever or entertaining that world may be.

THE ENVIRONMENT

Very recently, feeling world-weary and burnt out after eight of the hardest working months of my business career, I headed off to Kakadu with my family. We didn't want to do a three day flying visit. We wanted to take our time and gain some small taste for the Northern Territory. Over the years I have seen documentaries of the north and had come to yearn for its wide open spaces and its dramatic intensity. Nothing prepared me for the wonderful reality. After four weeks of exploring — walking, smelling, gazing, listening — I want little more than to go back again, and soon. What a very beautiful country Australia is — and the north has some of the most breathtaking land of all.

One experience, however, stands out above the others and continues to haunt me in my waking hours. We were on top of Ubirr rock — ancient landscape around us, 360 degree views of breathtaking, awe inspiring, unparalleled magnificence. This escarpment with its grey and tumbling rocks has been a meeting place for the Gagudju people for many thousands of years and you can see everywhere evidence of their passage, in the stone artefacts, in their art work — if you look. Speechless, atop this place of beauty, with only a ranger and a Texan sharing our experience, we gazed in what we took to be respectful silence. Then, out of the blue, the Texan said with his long and commanding drawl, "You know they left us nothing!". "Pardon?" said the ranger. "The Aboriginals — left us nothin' — 40,000 years, no buildings, no tools, no food, nothin'." We thought he was joking, but he wasn't. Finally, drawing a weary breath, the ranger responded. "That's curious," he said, "I thought they left us all this and I would have thought, considering how we've dirtied the planet, polluted the cities, transformed the natural world with our buildings, our industries in the last 200 years alone, it was a pretty priceless gift. I just hope we have the wisdom and foresight to manage our inheritance and not squander it."

My husband and I left the rock, distressed, lost for words to express the fear that can be inspired by such stupidity, such short-sightedness. On the way back to our car, we came across a plaque on which the following words were written:

> EARTH...
> LIKE YOUR FATHER OR BROTHER OR MOTHER,
> BECAUSE YOU BORN FROM EARTH,
> YOU GOT TO COME BACK TO EARTH.
> WHEN YOU DEAD...
> THAT'S YOUR BONE,
> YOUR BLOOD.
> IT'S IN THIS EARTH.
>
> MY PEOPLE...
> NOT MANY.
> WE GETTING TOO OLD.
> YOUNG PEOPLE...
> I DON'T KNOW IF THEY CAN HANG ONTO THIS STORY.
> BUT, NOW YOU KNOW THIS STORY
> YOU RESPONSIBLE NOW.
> YOU GOT TO GO WITH US TO EARTH.
> MIGHT BE YOU CAN HANG ONTO THIS STORY
> TO THIS EARTH.

The words belonged to one of the most respected of the Gugudju elders, Bill Neidjie. They haunted me then and they haunt me still.

You know, there is no 'them' and 'us' in this journey. Let's face it, we've all either become or will become 'greenies', 'environmentalists'. We simply don't have a choice, not if humans want a future. We might not be willing to chain ourselves to trees or throw ourselves in front of bull-dozers; we might not join a tent-in to save a remote site from mining, or dress ourselves in black to protest nuclear testing. We might not recycle everything in the house or think carefully about all that we purchase — plastics, recyclable bottles, pressure packs, food dyes — but we know about it all, and we're less and less comfortable ignoring it.

We read about the damage occurring to our rivers, on our land, in the air we breathe. We might do little, but we've been touched, and we know that there's no going back to the happy days of ignorance and apathy.

Most of the time, most of us manage to live our lives as we have always lived them, only marginally affected by the evolving environmental crisis. But this is changing: I, for one, look around at what we're doing, and get an uncomfortable feeling somewhere in my chest, as if I were watching something terribly important to me die. There is an increasingly large part of us that is becoming genuinely worried about the final outcome of this rampant, technology-driven, revolutionary transformation of the world.

We used to keep this issue out of our workplace — we debated it around the dinner table, with children over homework assignments, after watching a particularly harrowing documentary on television, after reading a disturbing press article. Today, this has changed. The environmental debate is alive and well in business, and more and more of us want it to take an even more prominent place. I understand the critical importance of making a profit (you won't be in business for long with out it) but I think the days of the economists lauding it over everyone are gone. We *have* to think of the bigger picture. It has to be okay to debate these issues and to question business practices so that we can be sure that what we do genuinely sustains the wellbeing of the people in the business, the community in which we live and, ultimately, the planet on which we are taking this precarious journey.

I don't think it is acceptable, under the guise of affordability, economic rationale or business common sense to continue practices in business which place any part of our environment at risk. Together, we have already done enough damage. Now, without fighting one another, without labelling this person a 'greenie' or that person a 'mindless profiteer', we have to defend what we have, this irreplaceable resource on which our future depends, all of us.

A BAG OF ISSUES

There are many issues that are beginning to creep their way into boardrooms, factory floors, tea rooms and toilets. Issues that were once cut and dried are not so clear any more, and more of us are feeling a responsibility towards considering them, not just at home, but increasingly in the workplace. Where once business was isolated from the range of human issues that concerned thinking people, it is now, in many instances, leading change or is pivotal to change. By bringing to the workplace dilemmas not traditionally tackled by business, we highlight them and, hopefully, begin the process of change.

Australians, from dockside workers to engineers, from urban junkies to outback recluses, are recognising that while we accelerate our world, fill it with extraordinary inventions, create more toys to play with, more things to make life easier, more profitable and more efficient, there are victims aplenty. It is no longer alright just to let these people fall by the wayside. The Good Samaritan is no longer walking the dusty road. He or she is now standing by a lathe, negotiating a forklift, working at a computer screen, debating in a boardroom. The issues that concern us cover the full range of human needs.

THE POVERTY CYCLE: Is it acceptable that so many have so little? That the gulf between educated and uneducated is increasing? That while some decide on the latest technological toy, others are struggling for food in their bellies? We worry that the world we are inventing will alienate, disenfranchise and disempower so many.

YOUTH UNEMPLOYMENT: We've heard a lot about this, it's been thrust under our noses almost daily for the last ten years or so. We've blamed it on this or that political party, but don't let's kid ourselves: youth unemployment has little to do with politics and much to do with the world in which we live. The issue has come home to roost and it is everybody's issue. We should think carefully about how we can change this phenomenon, in business and in the broader community.

THE RISE OF VIOLENCE: Is our world getting more dangerous? When old people are attacked and young people abused, when gang warfare is common news, when unresolved religious differences explode into widespread and sustained warfare, what future can we expect? At our own back door, violence has become so commonplace that only the most ugly and extreme catches our attention. It doesn't seem right, but we are unsure how to change what is happening.

CHANGES IN FAMILY DYNAMICS: Divorce is commonplace, many parents are at odds with their teenagers, the elderly are isolated. Many of us want something more from family life, but the 'more' that we want seems to be less and less attainable. We see films or read books about the extended families of old and we wonder what has changed so profoundly that today such families are a rarity.

CONFUSION OVER ROLES: Men and women are less clear today than they have been in a long time over acceptable behaviour between the sexes — and never more so than in business. We know that there are nowhere near enough women in senior or decision making positions, but most of us don't really understand why this is so, let alone how to go about reversing the imbalance; we feel uncomfortable with the politics of discrimination but we are not sure how to change it.

DEATH OF POLITICS: The one institution that once held out the promise of resolving so many debates is nowadays, it seems, an embarrassment. We don't like the mud-slinging that goes on in Parliament; we feel that too many politicians have lost contact with real people; once upon a time we used to say "I'm a Liberal voter" and understand why this was so, or "I'm a Labor voter" and feel totally confident in the reasoning for our decision. Today we get the impression, more and more, that may be we should be voyaging out into the unknown together. The politics of division are no longer serving us.

Conflict and confusion in the house of commerce!

As each of us has experienced in one way or another, people in business — whether they are the managing director of a multi-national, an accounts clerk in the local grain warehouse, head of finance for a large corporation or a part-timer working for a fast food chain — have a creeping sense that there has to be more to life than what we are all experiencing.

As the rate of change exceeds even our most adventurous predictions, the workplace seems to be less and less satisfying — yet we are spending more and more time there! Leader and employee alike find themselves on a voyage, the returns of which are, in too many instances, diminishing even despite increased effort. People in business feel less and less confident of their ability to sustain their market share, their growth, their profitability. Planning seems shaky at best, almost impossible at worst. Predictions are held with little conviction and there seems to be a pervasive nervousness among decision makers.

As individuals become more concerned about the environment and start to ask whether or not enough is being done to manage a sustainable life on the planet, environmental issues are raised more frequently in the workplace. Debates in business now embrace most of the greater debates that concern humanity. Values and ethics, the teaching of which was once the preserve of esoteric university courses, have found their way into business. Where business actions run counter to commonsense environmental remedies or responses, values and human hearts are being torn in half.

Honesty and integrity are becoming catchwords, keys to sustainability and profitability. Fifty years ago you would have been laughed out of the boardroom if you had raised such concepts. In the second half of the nineteen-nineties, 'business' is no longer strictly defined by what it *does*, but *how and why it does it*. Perhaps it is not so far-fetched to suggest that business today might, for the first time, be spearheading human emotional evolution — rather than ignoring it in pursuit of profit.

How we treat each other is important for a thousand and one reasons. If we can't trust each other, who can we trust? If we can't dignify and respect human endeavour, why are we doing what we are doing? If we cannot care for our planet, then when and where will our journey come to a conclusion? These issues, and many more, are crowding in on all of us, individually and collectively. As our frustration and anger about what we are doing to ourselves, each other and our environment grows, we might finally turn to the most powerful vehicle at our disposal to effect the changes that we genuinely crave. That vehicle is the vehicle of business. In the next decade, businesses small and large will lead the change processes — *because they must*, if they and the people who make them work, are to survive.

These change processes will not be about efficiencies, profit levels, customer service, quality management. They will be about care, compassion, decency, integrity, honesty — towards each other and towards the physical world which sustains our existence.

I am sure that the outcome of our endeavour will, to our delight, reward us beyond our expectations. As collectively we learn to care more, individually the rewards will be greater.

In the following chapters, I talk about issues that are of immediate concern to many Australian employees and to many Australian leaders. The issues are not exclusive to this part of the world, although their elaboration reflects Australian thinking. The topics are simple and, in many different ways, have been addressed by other thinkers and writers. However, in this instance, I have a journey in mind: I want us to reach a place that we know is the truth not because it is someone else's theory, but because it has become so glaringly apparent. The journey is commenced only when these key issues are tackled by leaders and employees alike.

Practical help

SOME THINGS TO PONDER...

WHAT ISSUES MOST CONCERN YOU TODAY? HOW DO THEY RELATE TO THE ISSUES WHICH CONCERN FAMILY, FRIENDS AND PEOPLE YOU WORK WITH?

HAVE YOU NOTICED A CHANGE IN THE SPEED AT WHICH THINGS ARE CHANGING OR DEVELOPING AROUND YOU?

ARE YOU COMPUTER LITERATE? IF YOU ARE, DO YOU KNOW AS MUCH AS YOU WANT, OR NEED, TO KNOW? IF YOU DON'T, DOES IT CONCERN YOU?

DO YOU THINK MUCH ABOUT WHAT IS HAPPENING TO THE ENVIRONMENT? DO YOU DISCUSS IT WITH FAMILY AND FRIENDS? DOES DISCUSSION ABOUT THE ENVIRONMENT TAKE PLACE IN YOUR WORKPLACE?

ARE YOU AWARE OF THE IMBALANCE BETWEEN MEN AND WOMEN IN TERMS OF DECISION MAKING AS IT AFFECTS YOUR LIFE? DOES IT WORRY YOU? HOW WOULD THINGS BE DIFFERENT IF THERE WAS A BALANCE OF THE SEXES IN LEADERSHIP POSITIONS?

ARE YOU HAPPY WITH YOUR WORKING ENVIRONMENT? DO YOU FEEL YOU ARE PERSONALLY PROGRESSING AS YOU WOULD WISH?

HOW DO YOU RELATE TO PEOPLE WHO WORK WITH OR FOR YOU? DO YOU SEE CHANGES IN THE WAY BUSINESS IS BEING CONDUCTED? ARE THERE MORE ENLIGHTENED WORK PRACTICES, OR DO CHANGES MERELY HERALD MORE OF THE SAME?

DO YOU SENSE THAT THERE MIGHT BE A BETTER WAY TO CONDUCT BUSINESS — A WAY THAT WOULD IMPROVE THE QUALITY OF LIFE FOR YOU AND THE PEOPLE AROUND YOU? WHAT CHANGES WOULD YOU LIKE TO SEE? WHAT DO YOU THINK IT WOULD TAKE TO GET THEM?

Is anyone clear on where we are going?

"Nobody he know what she do!"

2

'Vision without action is dreaming; action without vision merely fills the day. But action with vision can change the world.' I don't know who said this, but…

TALL TALES AND TRUE FROM THE COALFACE

I was in the suburbs doing some shopping. It was a pleasant spring day, Melbourne was at its best. I had parked my car in a side street and was walking towards my targeted shopping centre. Along the way, I had to cross a second street. At this small but nonetheless strategically important crossroads, a number of council workers were gathered around two excavated manholes at diagonally opposing corners.

I stood and watched. One group were slowly feeding a large black hose down one hole, while the other group was (I assumed) waiting for it to arrive up the other. There must have been twelve or so people hard at their labours. Actually, there were more like three who were hard at their labours, the rest were watching and, periodically, vouchsafing opinions on how to do the job more effectively.

I watched this activity for some fifteen minutes. Nothing appeared to be happening, but there was a lot of swearing and head scratching and brow wiping. Eventually, from somewhere underground, a deep, slow voice rumbled to the surface: "No body he know what she do!"

There was a lot of embarrassed laughing, a bit more head scratching — but nothing changed.

Smiling to myself, I thought it was a good example of the absence of vision. As I ambled off to spend some money, I wondered who was responsible for the absence of a clearly articulated purpose and design — a councillor? A town planner? A city engineer? A supervisor? A leading hand? In the end, of course, it didn't matter who was responsible; the net effect was a job badly done, resources wasted and a comedic performance in full view of an already cynical ratepayer.

TALL TALES AND TRUE FROM THE TOP

It was an immense task. The huge organisation was seriously adrift. Profits had been falling steadily for the last three years. Signs of mismanagement were evident everywhere. Staff levels were inordinately high, yet productivity was almost non-existent. The acquisition trail of the late nineteen-seventies and early nineteen-eighties had produced a breadbasket of loosely affiliated businesses. This ensured that the capacity of leadership to concentrate was fractionated. Yet to everyone's disbelief, the organisation had retained a loyal customer base. Why? Because of an unparalleled brand name and the absence of quality competition. However, despite two potent strengths, the Company was dangerously close to extinction.

Wheel in the new leadership team! Bright, astute, highly educated, broadly experienced. They are quickly renamed the "Razor Gang". Within eight months, the working population is reduced by twenty percent. Thirty percent of the acquired businesses have been sold off, a radical debt reduction plan is well under way. The Managing Director has piloted a well publicised, radical restructure.

Twelve months after taking on the appointment, things are, superficially, looking good. The shareholders are feeling more reassured, the banks are more content.

But the head hunters are watching. Clearly, the new MD knows what he's doing. Eventually, 18 months after taking up the job, the right opportunity arrives and an offer is made to the 39 year old executive. A million dollar salary, a guaranteed share portfolio and all the usual perks are used to seduce him to a new opportunity in another country. So he leaves.

A new Managing Director is appointed. To everyone's surprise (with the exception of people working in the business), the new MD finds that the business is riddled with problems. he appoints a new leadership team. They, too, restructure; there is much yet to be done. Fundamentally sales are not improving, discontent is still evident in the workplace, efficiencies are not what they should be, union problems are brewing, there is still a lack of expertise in the business.

The cycle repeats itself — twice more, in fact. Another leader is head hunted, another has a heart attack. Eventually, some ten years after the rot first set in, a young leader is appointed to take up the position of Managing Director and, by accident rather than design or delibera-tion, the young leader manages to break the stranglehold that tradition had over this large organisation. The young leader continues to do what has been done by predecessors — rule of restructure, change the lead-ership team, retrenchment — but somewhere in his heart there is a nagging doubt about the process. So he does something that no one has done before him: he goes and speaks, firsthand, to the people of the business.

What he hears is anger, cynicism and doubt about leaders and what they try to do. He hears about how business fundamentals have been ignored. He sees evidence of stupid decisions, lack of consultation, brutality even. He is appalled. But what shocks him most is that absolutely no one knows what the business is trying to achieve, its purpose for being in business. By far the majority of the employees believe the organisation has no future.

He goes through a harrowing month of listening. He is the first leader to realise that the future of this industry giant is in the very hands of people who do not even believe that it actually has a future. Their lack of faith is not the product of a collapsing marketplace or the redundancy of the service provided by the business; it is the product of a leadership who have failed, completely, to build a sense of future, to share it with its people and to commit itself absolutely to seeing plans eventuate.

He makes a range of critical decisions. He commits himself to a term of not less than five years with the Company. He sets in train a process that will ensure that all the people of the business understand and have ownership over the future direction of the organisation. He gains the absolute commitment of the Board to support him and to stay informed of and personally involved with the business, rather than to dictate decisions from afar. And finally, he sets a rule, the breaking of which means immediate termination. It is this: no decision will be taken in the business without a clear sense of its repercussions for the Company's vision, nor without feedback, from all the people it affects, about the initiative's strengths and weaknesses.

Within eighteen months of this Managing Director's appearance, the people are, for the first time in over a decade, talking about the future of the organisation. That is to say, the company's future success was in the very hands of people who now believe it actually had a future.

This is a true story.

"VISION" AND "BUSINESS PLANS": PINNING DOWN THEIR MEANINGS

Although detailed materials are provided at the end of this chapter, let's get some simple definitions agreed before we get into the nitty gritty of this chapter.

A vision is an exciting, motivating, commonly owned sense of the future — of something that does not yet exist, but towards which a person or group of people are moving. A vision is not a bunch of words thought up in an isolated boardroom and handed down to the masses on a piece of paper or pasted up behind reception for customers to look at. If it is not exciting and motivating, people won't fight for it. If it is not commonly owned, it will rely on the capacity of one or two key people to see it through (which is dangerous) or it simply will not turn into a reality (which is true in ninety-five percent of cases).

Without an agreed sense of the future, planning tends to be short term, actions often at cross purposes, ambitions personal rather than unified. Certainly, today's vision may be superseded tomorrow, but that's okay: visions are not absolute statements of purpose. They are like the architectural plans for a building. Any number of changes may occur (including not actually building the original design), but the plans remain the focus for activity. The principal value of a vision is to ensure that today's actions work towards an agreed purpose.

A business plan is a clear, agreed, empowering summary of how exactly a vision will be achieved, including long term, medium and immediate agreed actions. Plans come in a multitude of shapes, but whichever their form, simplicity, clarity and common ownership are more important than anything else. Everyone contributes to the plan according to their responsibilities, to produce a tiered tool, with connected and flexible cascading actions (that is, each of us focuses on, helps the design and implement, that portion of the plan that is relevant to what we do or to which we feel able to contribute).

There are two common forms of business plan: one is cast to persuade the bank, the board, the financiers and all the others we approach to lend the business money, leave the business alone, trust the people running it; the other plan (the real one) is for all the people of the business and is simple, practical and usable. It is a day-to-day tool for guiding decisions.

Experimenting with the business plan is essential. It is the territory of action, and action is the tool for learning how to do things better. Constant feedback is critical.

WHY ON EARTH DO WE BOTHER?

People think that developing a vision of the future and a workable plan for a business is difficult; you have to be an MBA or an entrepreneur just as a starting point. Certainly, many have tried and failed — coming up with something so dull it wouldn't motivate a starving dog to get up for a chunk of roast lamb! But I believe every human being is capable of creating the future — the trick is to simplify the process and be motivated.

Do you remember your first kiss? That hot moment behind the bicycle shed at school or in the dark on the porch by the front door to your parents' house or in the garden with a group of friends playing 'spin the bottle' …I will if you will? You know where it happened, I'm sure — you can't be that old!

Well, take yourself back to that kiss and think for a moment on what it was like. Was it everything that it had been cracked up to be? Was it sensual, delightful, enticing, perfect in every respect? Hmmm?

No? What a surprise! Let's face it, that first kiss was bloody awful. No one told you that your noses would get in the way. No one said that breathing would be a challenge. No one explained about the dangers of connecting dental bands. No one said (oh yuk) that the other person might try sticking their tongue in your mouth!! Oh, how gross.

A simple question for you: has *that* first kiss stopped you experimenting? No, of course not! You had a vision of possibility that way exceeded *that* kiss and you sure as hell weren't going to let such a minor glitch get in the way of such magnificent opportunity, were you!

I came away from *that* first kiss in a state of absolute shock. Naturally, I then went and discussed the experience, in minute detail, with my best friend. A great deal of giggling later, and much poking and prodding when the said male next walked passed me, led to a conclusion very different from the one that this particular episode in my life should — on the 'face' of it — have led to.

There's got to be more than this!

Now, at the age of 41, I can only say I am still experimenting! That, my friends, is the power of vision in the hands of someone empowered to do something with it, working to a plan which has changed many times, thanks to all that I have learnt in a lifetime of experimenting, practising and recalibrating what it is that I need to do differently next time round.

If you want something badly enough, if you are willing to get a lot wrong on the way, then in the end, whatever you dream of having will be yours. It only relies on some very basic ingredients:

– what you want you need to want pretty badly;

– what you want needs to be something that you think you can get;

– you need to be willing to make a lot of mistakes as you work towards getting what you want;

– as you make mistakes, you have to reflect on what you have learnt and what you will do differently next time to move you a little closer.

Remember this as you read on.

COMING UNSTUCK: THE ABSENCE OF AGREED VISION AND PLANNING

It can be easy to get a vision up and running for ourselves, whether it is a first kiss and all that subsequently follows, or when and where we are going to take our next holiday, or what sort of car we are going to buy. Maybe it's about what flowers we want to plant in the garden this spring, maybe it's about the question of putting an extension on the house. We can have a vision of the type of schooling we want our kids to have, what to wear in the morning, what to cook for breakfast, who to invite to a dinner party. All simple, straightforward, achievable, doable stuff.

Why then is it so hard to work up a vision in business? Managers go away on retreats, lock themselves in boardrooms, sit around tables, put butcher's paper up on walls, debate, argue, pace, struggle, think. And then, after all that work, too often come up with something so banal, so puerile that everyone is embarrassed:

"We will commit to outstanding quality in all that we do — our customer service will be second to none!"

"We will exceed our customers' expectations."

"We will be the leaders in the field."

"We will have a dedicated team of people committed to excellence in all we do."

"We will be market leaders based on a fair return to our shareholders, respect for the people who work in our business and honest commitment to our customers' needs."

Sometimes leaders commit such visions to plaques and place them behind reception desks. Others decide to make sure the people of the business can't miss it, so put it on to great big posters and slap them up on the factory or canteen wall. Sometimes visions are put onto business cards so they can be handed out to customers and service providers alike.

A large number of Australian employees, including a large number of leaders, regard the whole exercise as a monumental waste of time. We ask ourselves: Do we really need a vision? Haven't we been doing without one for quite a while? Isn't it just part of another Harvard or Stanford MBA fad?

Even if we do have a vision we might find that, when push comes to shove, shifting priorities will quickly put paid to our original plans. A sudden cash flow crisis is a great destroyer of visions — when the bank is breathing down your neck or share prices are plummeting because of huge debt to financial institutions, visions are forgotten and leaders turn to the perennial strategy of retrenchment and restructure! Just as there appears to be little commitment to visions (apparently irrespective of how much work went into their formulation), there is certainly almost no passion behind them. Ownership is either non-existent or is isolated to the boardroom or the small team responsible for the words that have been stuck on the canteen wall.

Now, if you add to this apparent lack of commitment and passion the insecurity and uncertainty behind any kind of planning (reflecting, in part, the chaotic and changeable world in which the visioning process is occurring), then perhaps it is no wonder that no one really believes that today's vision is going to stick.

So why then is the absence of a vision of the future such a sticking point for so many of us? If we are so cynical about its effectiveness, why are we so hungry to have a clear sense of the future to be working towards? Why are we so frustrated by its absence? What should we make of this apparent paradox in business?

WHY WE NEED A SENSE OF THE FUTURE AND WHY WE ARE SO CYNICAL ABOUT GETTING IT — THE PEOPLE'S PERSPECTIVE

Let's face it, life can be a bitch. The journey from womb to grave can be a crazy, sometimes pretty lonely journey. Too often, the dreams of child-hood, the wild and exotic ambitions of teenager-hood, the passionate conviction of our early twenties fades into oblivion in our thirties and forties. We develop an aching uncertainty. We love our families, enjoy our home time, perhaps playing golf, jogging, gardening, reading, television, videos. But beyond this, many of us become more and more puzzled by the purpose of it all. Where do we fit in? Why are we here?

Of course, since the dawn of time, we've questioned the nature of our exis-tence and the part we play in a seemingly purposeless yet God-filled universe. I don't want to get into a theological debate about the existence of God here, but it is important to acknowledge that having a reason for existence has driven us to explore everything around us in order to ratio-nalise ourselves, our purpose. Along the way, hundreds of religions have blossomed to comfort us, give us a sense of belonging, a belief in the reason behind life that has taken away the questioning. But for as many as find comfort in religion, there are many, many more who find it wanting. They simply come around to the same question which the religion sought in its origins to address: There has to be more to this?

In the late twentieth century, particularly in the West, people are struggling to live in a morass of invention and sensory indulgence. It should be marvellous, the ultimate toy shop, but it's not. We've sped up our world and given ourselves a lot of new things to play with, sure, but we're working harder and harder to have it all. Business has become more competitive but, thanks to our hard play and constant invention, needs fewer of us than before.

Employers demand a more informed and better educated workforce. Competition everywhere is hotting up and we all know that if we don't perform, there are plenty of hungry others waiting to prove they are a better investment for the business.

We are taught the spirit of capitalism, the notion of free enterprise and the practice of so-called 'healthy' competition. But over time, we are moved to question what we are doing. Yet again, the elusive 'why?' is cropping up. Why do we have to put so much energy into our work, why so much time? Our families are challenging the moods we bring back from the office and the factory. We seem to have less and less time to do the things we love, with the people we love. A lot of us are getting tetchy, frustrated, distressed even. Work, which was once, perhaps, a place which fed our dreams, has become a dream robber. Do you remember your first job — the first one that would be a passage from one place to another? Didn't you expect to go in at one point and gather knowledge, skill and recognition, so that you'd end up somewhere better? You didn't have to be the local genius, the resident Einstein. You didn't have to be wildly ambitious, want to be a supervisor or a managing director. It was enough that you understood the process of improving, of learning, of going somewhere. You could join a company, an industry, that was on the move, building something, making something, changing something, and your journey would contribute to the whole. But that's just not the way it is any more, is it?

Everything is up in the air — up for grabs. The rules of the game keep changing. It might once have been Aussie Rules, but the goalposts have disappeared and the ball seems to get higher and higher, the crowd noisier, and the outcome more and more confusing. Despite our input, our energy, our time — despite running faster than ever — we are covering less and less ground every day.

In such an environment, is it any wonder that we find it frustrating to work for an organisation without understanding where the business is heading or what part we have to play in the process. If we are working harder, putting in more time and energy, committing ourselves to all sorts of extra education to keep pace with demand, is it any wonder that we want to know why we are doing it? We might not be able to fully comprehend the purpose of our existence, but we sure as hell want to know where our workplace is heading. And really, if we can't even get purpose there, we might as well chuck the whole lot.

People are tired and demoralised. Our faith in everything is being challenged — in work, in families, in ourselves. Our chaotic world has given us toys aplenty, but the price has been exorbitantly high.

As our world has sped up, leaders have clutched at all sorts of concepts, fads, ideas and opportunities to help them work through the maze of decisions that daily present themselves. And out of this, the restructure epidemic was born.

I know people who have weathered up to *seven* restructures in companies they have worked for. Amazed to have survived the process, they are deeply cynical of the thinking behind restructuring. Far too often, there is no evidence of the supposed benefits of management-led restructures, so fuel is added to the fires of discontent burning brightly in many chests.

We still can't see the future, we still don't know where we are heading, we still don't really understand the purpose of our businesses, our restructures, our own life's endeavours. Our need for vision is great, because it isn't being satisfied either at home, in a place of worship or in the office. And so, it's hardly surprising that in business, the single biggest issue raised is the need for a sense of the future — and our single biggest doubt is that we'll get it.

WHY WE NEED A SENSE OF THE FUTURE AND WHY WE ARE SO CYNICAL ABOUT GETTING IT — THE LEADER'S PERSPECTIVE

It is a challenging, some would say tough, time to be a leader in business. The game plan is, as we have acknowledged, changing dramatically from day to day; the skills required today for good leadership are dramatically different from those required even a short time ago. A leader or manager can be vulnerable to many things — failure, being wrong, changes from on high, revolution from below.

It is time for some honesty. I do not meet a lot of leaders who are entirely happy with the way things are going at the moment. They might embrace personal responsibility with their title, but they are no longer confident of the direction their businesses are taking. They, too, are suffering from the fire of discontent in the belly.

I know many leaders who have been victims of a restructure or a major change process. They were victims in that they suddenly found themselves out of a job or had to implement a plan they did not agree with. Managers themselves are having to respond to demands from other managers and boards, and all too often these demands can seem unreasonable and disassociated from the substance of the business they will affect.

Despite the best intentions, many leaders become separated from their employees, frustrated by the increasing void and unable to bridge the gap. I know leaders who have fought hard to put integrity, honesty and decency back into the workplace, only to find that for the sake of the change, restructure, acquisition or merger, they have had to lie to the people they have worked alongside. Caught between the exigencies of commercial necessity and the heartbeat of decency, they tear themselves apart, on the inside, far from sight.

They don't get retrenched or fired. They get sick.

Sometimes leaders feel that the process of democratising the workplace has diminished the role of leadership. It is not uncommon to hear leaders voice concern with their roles in the changing work environment. They ask: "If all the planning is in the hands of the people in the business, where do I fit in?" They feel vulnerable, open to a level of scrutiny with which they are unaccustomed. They are aware that they may be lacking certain skills: "I'm a damn good engineer. It used to be my job to tell people what to do. Now I'm meant to teach them, motivate them, facilitate their work. I wasn't trained to do any of that. I don't even know if I can."

Once-healthy egos are feeling challenged and fragile.

On top of all this — the changing demands of the commercial environment, the changing requirements of leaders — we are asking leaders to be seers, fortune tellers, futurists. We ask them to initiate, envision (clearly) the future direction of the businesses that they head, and to then help us all plan how to reach this future nirvana. Oh, if only it were that straightforward.

The neediness of the workplace has become, for many leaders, an overwhelmingly oppressive weight on their shoulders. Many try their hardest to get it right, but they are doing it in isolation, frustrated often at the outcomes that are produced. In their view of the world, many have done all they can to produce quality communication in the workplace, consultative work practices, empowered workforces. They have committed to quality management, signed off on millions of dollars worth of education, taken ideas from the coalface, listened to demands of customers, re-educated themselves and kept abreast with competition. But it is never enough. More is better and for a lot of leaders, the process of trying to satisfy the needs of business and staff is killing them. The demands of the future are on the doorstep, but they are shrouded in such a heavy fog it is impossible to discern any detail.

I have sat in on a very considerable number of visionary processes, watched leaders struggle to articulate the future in a meaningful way. Producing a useful outcome often depends on two things: firstly, dropping the rhetoric of business and reminding themselves that they are engaged in a human activity with a lot of other humans and, secondly, dropping politics and their own egos, reminding themselves that powerful outcomes are produced by united individuals, not by individuals alone.

THE ROAD AHEAD

If all this experimenting has taught us anything, it is that there are no simple or easy answers to getting business right, just a slow accumulation of experience from our endeavour. We've had lots of fads: "MBO" — management by objectives, "MBWA" — management by walking around (as if we needed reminding!), "TQM" — total quality management (and all its offshoots, including the obsession with 'manualising' quality — more on that later). We've talked about empowerment of the workforce and we've entered into enterprise bargaining with great fervour. Although many of these ideas have sometimes produced outstanding short term results, by far the greater number have produced little if any tangible change at all.

Despite best intentions, much that we have tried to do in business has fallen well short of expectations. We are diverted: a merger changes the game plan, a new leadership team wants to do it differently, short term cash flow sidelines commitment to guiding principles, and so on. Too often, leaders and the businesses they lead end up back at square one. Frustrations mount, cynicism becomes entrenched, and our hunger for a sense of the future remains.

We need to go back (or forward, if you like) to basics. Because of the complexity of the world we live in, because of the rate of change, we need (for sanity's sake, let alone good commercial reasons) to involve people much more in designing the future of their business. To do this, leaders, managers and employees need to learn honest, to-the-point, and straight-forward communication — a mechanism for building vision, and the plans to support it — that can be sustained by all, not just the few with specific titles.

As Victor Frankl noted in *Man's Search For Meaning*, his tender and moving account of life in the German concentration camps of the Second World War, when people have a 'why' for their existence, they can deal with almost any 'how'.

In business, vision is the 'why'. With a clear vision, people can intelligently manage the crazy, unpredictable and constantly changing 'how' of getting business right.

Through clearly articulated and commonly shared vision, we have to realise that we do have the power to make part of life more satisfying for everyone, employee and employer alike.

Practical help

THE FOLLOWING MATERIALS ARE TOOLS FOR HELPING EMPLOYEES AND LEADERS ALIKE TO REFLECT ON THE WAY WE CAN CHANGE THE WAY WE DO BUSINESS. THE FOCUS IS SPECIFICALLY ON THE WAY THAT A VISION, OR SENSE OF THE FUTURE, CAN BE DEVELOPED AND IMPLEMENTED.

THE QUESTIONS — ONE FOR EMPLOYEES AND ONE FOR LEADERS — WILL HELP DETERMINE WHETHER OR NOT YOU NEED TO TAKE ACTION ON THE VISION OF YOUR BUSINESS AND THE PLAN THAT SUSTAINS IT.

QUESTIONS FOR EMPLOYEES

1. DO YOU KNOW THE VISION OF THE BUSINESS YOU WORK FOR? IF YOU CLOSED YOUR EYES AND IMAGINED YOUR BUSINESS FIVE YEARS FROM NOW, COULD YOU OUTLINE WHAT IT WILL HAVE ACHIEVED THAT WOULD BE DIFFERENT FROM OR AN IMPROVEMENT UPON TODAY?

2. WOULD YOUR ANSWER MATCH THAT OF THE MAJORITY OF PEOPLE WHO WORK IN YOUR BUSINESS?

3. IF YOU KNOW YOUR COMPANY'S VISION, ARE YOU EXCITED AND COMMITTED TO IT, OR IS IT A BIT 'HO HUM'? DOES IT FIT THE BILL OR DOES IT NEED FURTHER WORK? ARE YOU INSPIRED TO FIGHT FOR IT?

4. IF YOU ARE CLEAR ON THE PURPOSE OF YOUR BUSINESS (THE 'WHY' FOR ITS EXISTENCE), ARE YOU AWARE OF A CLEAR BUSINESS PLAN WHICH SETS OUT HOW THE VISION WILL BE ACHIEVED?

5. IF YOU ARE AWARE OF THE BUSINESS PLAN, HAVE YOU ACTUALLY BEEN INVOLVED IN CONTRIBUTING TOWARDS ITS EVOLUTION? HAS YOUR EXPERTISE BEEN RECOGNISED, AND HAVE YOU BEEN ASKED TO PROVIDE INPUT?

6. LASTLY, IF YOU DO KNOW YOUR COMPANY'S VISION AND HAVE PARTICIPATED IN THE BUILDING OF A BUSINESS PLAN FOR ACHIEVING THAT VISION, DO YOU REGULARLY REVISIT THE PLAN (SAY MONTHLY) WITH A VIEW TO REVIEWING OR CHANGING IT?

QUESTIONS FOR LEADERS

1. DO YOU HAVE A VISION FOR YOUR BUSINESS THAT YOU PERSONALLY FEEL IS EXCITING, MOTIVATING AND PASSIONATE?

2. DID YOU DEVELOP THIS VISION WITH A TEAM OF MANAGERS?

3. DID YOU GIVE THE PEOPLE WHO WORK IN THE BUSINESS THE CHANCE TO HAVE THEIR INPUT INTO THE VISION? DID MANAGEMENT PRESENT THE PEOPLE OF THE BUSINESS WITH A DRAFT VISION AND ALLOW THEM TO PROVIDE FEEDBACK?

4. IF MANAGEMENT WAS INVOLVED, DID IT FEEL CONFIDENT ABOUT INVITING PEOPLE TO PARTICIPATE IN REVIEWING, CHANGING, OR CHALLENGING THE VISION? HAVE THEIR RECOMMENDATIONS BEEN INCORPORATED INTO THE VISION?

5. IF OTHER PEOPLE PARTICIPATED IN BUILDING THE VISION, ARE THEY STILL CLEAR ON WHAT THAT VISION IS? IF YOU WENT OUT AND ASKED TWENTY PERCENT OF THE STAFF WHAT THEY THOUGHT THE VISION OF THE ORGANISATION IS, WOULD THEY AGREE WITH MANAGEMENT AND WITH EACH OTHER?

6. IF THE VISION IS COMMONLY SHARED AND CLEARLY UNDERSTOOD, IS IT BACKED BY A CLEAR PLAN WHICH EVERYONE HAS CONTRIBUTED TO, EACH ACCORDING TO THEIR CAPACITY AND KNOWLEDGE?

7. DO MANAGEMENT INVITE REGULAR REVIEWS OF THE VISION AND PLAN BY MANAGEMENT AND STAFF?

THINGS ABOUT A BUSINESS VISION THAT MAKE IT WORK

1. IT MAKES SENSE IN TERMS OF WHAT THE BUSINESS DOES AND IS NOW

THE VISION IS A BELIEVABLE AND ACHIEVABLE EXTENSION OR DEVELOPMENT OF WHAT THE BUSINESS DOES AND IS NOW.

2. IT HITS THE HEART AS WELL AS THE HEAD

THE VISION APPEALS TO OUR CORE VALUES, OUR BELIEFS; OUR HEARTS BEAT FASTER AT THE THOUGHT OF ACHIEVING THE VISION. MOTIVATING VISIONS ELEVATE OUR SENSE OF WORTH, MAKE US FEEL EXCITED. WE WANT TO COMMIT OURSELVES.

3. IT IS SINGLE-MINDED AND DAMNABLY CLEAR OF PURPOSE

THERE'S NO ARGUMENT IN THE INTENTION. IT DOESN'T MEAN WE WON'T DO ALL THE OTHER THINGS WE WANT TO DO, BUT THE VISION IS OVERRIDING; IT IS THE MOST IMPORTANT AMBITION OR PURPOSE WE CAN HAVE. IT FOCUSES OUR DAY-TO-DAY ACTIONS.

4. IT SKIPS THE BUSINESS LINGO

THE WORDS OF VISIONS WITH THE POWER TO INSPIRE ARE SIMPLE, MEMORABLE, HUMAN, EMOTIVE. THERE ARE PLENTY OF ADJECTIVES, DESCRIPTIVE WORDS. GET THE GOOSE BUMPS UP THE BACK OF THE NECK AND YOU ARE CLOSE.

5. IT EXPRESSES THE EXCEPTIONAL

A POWERFUL VISION TELLS ALL THE PEOPLE OF THE BUSINESS WHAT IT IS THAT EVERYONE CAN AIM FOR THAT WILL BE SPECIAL, UNIQUE, INSPIRING (AND LEAVE THE COMPETITORS FOR DEAD!).

6. IT GIVES FORM TO OUR COMBINED POTENTIAL

A MOTIVATING VISION TELLS PEOPLE WHAT THEY ARE CAPABLE OF ACHIEVING OR BECOMING, BOTH INDIVIDUALLY AND COLLECTIVELY. IT ENSURES THE ACTIONS OF ONE ADD VALUE TO AND ARE PART OF THE ACTIONS OF MANY.

7. IT IS OWNED, FELT AND FOUGHT FOR BY ALL THE PEOPLE OF THE BUSINESS

WHILE PLANNING DOES AND SHOULD CASCADE INTO AN ORGANISATION, EACH ACCORDING TO HIS OR HER ABILITY AND AREA OF RESPONSIBILITY, EVERYONE IN THE BUSINESS NEEDS TO HOLD THE VISION AS THEIR OWN.

8. IT WORKS AS A GUIDE FOR GOOD RECRUITMENT

USED IN THE SELECTION PROCESS, A POWERFUL VISION WILL HELP ENSURE THE RIGHT SELECTION OF NEW STAFF BY MATCHING VALUES AND BELIEFS TO THE ORGANISATION AND ENSURING THAT THE AMBITIONS OF THE BUSINESS MATCH THE AMBITIONS OF THE INDIVIDUAL.

9. IT LASTS

WHILE A BUSINESS MAY HAVE ANY NUMBER OF SHORT-TERM GOALS, A VISION THAT WORKS IS SUSTAINABLE; IT IS NOT TIED TO THIS OR THAT LEADER, AND IT GUIDES — RATHER THAN DISAPPEARS — DURING THE PROCESS OF MERGER, RESTRUCTURE OR SALE.

DESPITE THE VALUE OF SUSTAINABILITY, VISIONS CAN AND DO EVOLVE OVER TIME AS CERTAIN THINGS ARE ACHIEVED. SOMETIMES (ALTHOUGH RARELY) THEY MAY EVEN CHANGE COMPLETELY AS A RESULT OF MARKET CHANGES. HOWEVER, THAT IS NOT WHY SO MANY SO-CALLED VISIONS NEVER GET OFF THE GROUND. IF YOU'VE BEEN INVOLVED IN A 'VISIONARY' PROCESS AND IT HAS FAILED TO DELIVER THE DESIRED RESULTS, CONSIDER WHICH OF THESE NINE POINTERS WERE IGNORED.

THINGS THAT POISON A BUSINESS VISION

HERE ARE SOME THINGS THAT KILL A VISION STONE DEAD:

1. IT IS A MASSIVE HIKE ON WHERE THE BUSINESS IS NOW

IF THE FACTORY FLOOR RESPONDS TO THE VISION WITH A CRY OF "YEAH, SURE!" THE VISION IS PROBABLY UNREALISTIC OR INAPPROPRIATE. A BUSINESS HAS BEEN THROUGH FIVE RESTRUCTURES IN AS MANY YEARS IS UNLIKELY TO SUCCEED BY SUDDENLY DECLARING "WE WILL COMMIT OURSELVES TO OUTSTANDING CUSTOMER SERVICE!" — IT'S BETTER TO GO FOR SOMETHING LIKE "WE WILL EMBRACE CHANGE AND EMPOWER OUR PEOPLE TO THRIVE ON IT."

2. IT'S A DEAD VISION

THE LANGUAGE OF THE VISION IS DEAD. THE SLOGAN "WE WILL HAVE QUALITY CUSTOMER SERVICE, DELIVERED ON TIME, EVERY TIME." IS AMBIGUOUS AND NO ONE, LEAST OF ALL THE WRITERS, IS INSPIRED. THERE IS A NOTICEABLE ABSENCE OF ANY DESCRIPTIVE WORDS. NO ONE SEEMS TO HAVE HEARD OF ROGET'S THESAURUS.

3. IT TRIES TO DO EVERYTHING FOR EVERYONE

INSTEAD OF AGREEING ON THE MOST IMPORTANT FOCUS OF ATTENTION, THE WRITERS COVER ALL THEIR OPTIONS, THEREBY TURNING THE VISION INTO A PRESCRIPTION FOR BEING IN BUSINESS: "WE WILL HAVE OUTSTANDING CUSTOMER SERVICE, WE WILL CARE FOR OUR PEOPLE, WE WILL COMMIT TO QUALITY IN ALL WE DO, WE WILL BE EFFICIENT, WE WILL INVEST IN TECHNOLOGY...". THE VISION FAILS TO DISCRIMINATE FOR PEOPLE BETWEEN WHAT CAN BE DONE AND WHAT MUST BE DONE.

4. IT EXPRESSES WHAT EVERYONE ELSE IS EXPRESSING IN THEIR VISION

A VISION THAT TELLS EVERYONE WHAT THEY ALREADY KNOW, WHAT THEY ARE ALREADY TRYING TO DO OR WHAT THEY BELIEVE THE COMPETITION ARE TRYING TO DO IS DESTINED FOR THE BIN. IF THE VISION COULD BE — OR ALREADY HAS BEEN — WRITTEN BY THE COMPETITION, IT IS GARBAGE.

5. **IT FAILS TO MAXIMISE THE POTENTIAL OF THE PEOPLE AND THE BUSINESS**

A DUD VISION INSPIRES NO ONE TO AIM FOR MORE THAN WHAT THEY ARE ALREADY ACHIEVING. SUCH VISIONS ARE OFTEN A MORE ACCURATE DESCRIPTION OF WHAT THE BUSINESS IS NOW. FOR INSTANCE, A DECLARATION THAT "WE WILL DELIVER EXCEPTIONAL CUSTOMER SERVICE" WHEN THE BUSINESS IS ALREADY DELIVERING EXCEPTIONAL CUSTOMER SERVICE FAILS TO ELEVATE AMBITIONS. THIS TENDENCY IS TYPICAL OF MATURE BUSINESSES; IT OFTEN EXPLAINS WHY PEOPLE FEEL THEY ARE IN BECALMED WATER, GOING NOWHERE. AND THE FIRST PEOPLE TO LEAVE? THE YOUNGEST AND BRIGHTEST — THE PEOPLE HUNGRY FOR A CHALLENGE.

6. **IT IS WRITTEN BY SENIOR MANAGEMENT ON RETREAT AND USES NO FEEDBACK FROM OR INTERACTION WITH THE PEOPLE OF THE BUSINESS**

SUCH VISIONS ARE RECEIVED WITH SCEPTICISM BY THE WORKFORCE — THEY'VE "SEEN IT ALL BEFORE". MANAGEMENT END UP PUSHING THE VISION RATHER THAN ALLOWING THE COMBINED ENERGY OF THE PEOPLE TO PULL IT FORWARD.

7. **IT'S ONLY KNOWN BY THE PEOPLE AROUND AT THE TIME OF WRITING**

THESE VISIONS AREN'T FOLLOWED EXCEPT IN THE FEEDING FRENZY FOLLOWING THE ORIGINAL COMPOSITION. CERTAINLY, THEY ARE NEVER ADEQUATELY USED IN THE RECRUITMENT OR INDUCTION PROCESSES.

8. **IT'S GOT A SHELF LIFE OF EIGHTEEN MONTHS, MAXIMUM**

A VISION THAT ONLY VAGUELY MOTIVATES THE PLANNING PROCESS FOR THREE TO SIX MONTHS IS DESTINED TO FADE COMPLETELY WITHIN TWELVE TO EIGHTEEN MONTHS. BY THEN, NO ONE BUT THE MANAGING DIRECTOR CAN REMEMBER WHAT IT WAS (AND ANYWAY, ANOTHER RESTRUCTURE IS ON THE WAY — SO WHO CARES?).

NECESSITIES IN A BUSINESS PLAN

BUSINESS PLANS COME IN ALL SHAPES AND SIZES. THERE ARE ZILLIONS OF REFERENCE BOOKS. TOO MANY BUSINESS PLANS ARE COMPLICATED AND DISASSOCIATED FROM THE DAY-TO-DAY PARRY AND THRUST OF THE BUSINESS. WHICHEVER PLANNING METHOD IS USED, THE KEY TO THEM ALL IS NOT STYLE, BUT SIMPLICITY AND OWNERSHIP. THE BASIC CRITERIA FOR AN EFFECTIVE BUSINESS PLAN ARE:

— EVERYONE CAN USE IT;

— IT IS SIMPLE AND EASILY UNDERSTOOD;

— IT CASCADES INTO THE ORGANISATION; AND

— IT EMBRACES ABSOLUTELY THE VISION.

PLANNING WHICH CASCADES FROM POISONED VISIONS HAS NO CHOICE BUT TO BE REACTIVE. HERE ARE SOME INSIGHTS INTO BUSINESS PLANS THAT WORK.

1. THE BUSINESS PLAN MUST REFLECT THE VISION

WHATEVER STYLE OF PLAN YOU CHOOSE, THE PLAN MUST REFLECT, CONSTANTLY, IN EVERY WAY, THE INTENDED VISION OF THE BUSINESS.

2. THE PLAN MUST CASCADE INTO THE BUSINESS

THOUGH THIS NECESSITY SEEMS SELF-EVIDENT, MANY PLANS ACTUALLY FAIL TO MEANING-FULLY WORK THEIR WAY INTO THE BUSINESS. GOOD PLANNING IS NOT JUST FOR MANAGERS, IT HAS TO BE UNDERSTOOD BY EVERYONE. IF SOMEONE CAN SAY "I DON'T REALLY UNDERSTAND WHY I HAVE TO DO THIS" THE CASCADING ISN'T WORKING.

3. THE PLAN MUST INVOLVE ALL PEOPLE, ACCORDING TO THEIR AREA OF RESPONSIBILITY

CASCADING IS ALSO ABOUT LETTING PEOPLE DETERMINE THEIR OWN PLANS FOR THEIR AREA OF THE BUSINESS, INSOFAR AS IT IS IN ACCORDANCE WITH THE MAIN PLANS OF THE ORGANISATION. THEY SHOULD BE ACCOUNTABLE FOR THEIR RESULTS AND BE RESPONSIBLE FOR HOW THEY GO ABOUT ACHIEVING THEM.

4. PLANS SHOULD BE SUBJECT TO DAILY, WEEKLY, MONTHLY REVIEW

PLANS ARE ORGANIC, DAY-TO-DAY TOOLS FOR MEASURING OUTCOMES AND DETERMINING ACTIONS. IF THEY ONLY COME OUT OF THE DRAW EVERY SIX MONTHS AT THE BUSINESS PERFORMANCE REVIEW, THEY ARE PROBABLY TOO COMPLICATED AND OUT OF TOUCH WITH THE REALITY OF THE BUSINESS.

5. PLANS MUST REFLECT CRITICAL SUCCESS FACTORS

A CRITICAL SUCCESS FACTOR (REFERRED TO AS A CSF) TELLS PEOPLE HOW TO DETERMINE THE MOST IMPORTANT ASPECTS OF A VISION. THERE CAN BE DIFFERENT LEVELS: CSFs FOR THE BUSINESS MAY BE BROAD AND GENERALISED; CSFs FOR TEAMS CAN BE VERY SPECIFIC.

6. OUTCOMES FOR A PLAN MUST BE MEASURABLE

TEAMS, INDIVIDUALS AND MANAGEMENT NEED TOOLS (FOR INSTANCE, KEY PERFORMANCE INDICATORS) TO GAUGE THE SUCCESS OF THEIR PLANS. MEASURED OUTCOMES SHOULD NOT BE USED TO INTIMIDATE BUT TO ELEVATE; THEY SHOULD BE CAST SO THEY ASK HOW THINGS MIGHT BE DONE BETTER.

7. A PLAN MUST HAVE ACTIONABLE POINTS FOR EVERYONE

IN A GOOD PLAN, EVEN THE 16-YEAR-OLD PART-TIMER KNOWS WHAT CONTRIBUTION THEY MAKE, SPECIFICALLY, TO THE OVERALL PLAN.

8. A PLAN MUST MEASURE LEARNING

GOOD PLANS TAKE INTO ACCOUNT THE LEARNING CYCLE. THEY RECOGNISE THAT IN DEVELOPING DAY-BY-DAY ACTIONS FOR PEOPLE, MISTAKES WILL BE MADE. SUCH MISTAKES SHOULD BE EMBRACED, NOT USED TO INTIMIDATE.

POISON IN A BUSINESS PLAN

THE FOLLOWING THINGS KILL A BUSINESS PLAN STONE DEAD.

1. THERE IS NO VISION

IF EVERYONE BECOMES BORED WITH THE IDEA OF A VISION OR FAILS COMPLETELY TO UNDERSTAND ITS PURPOSE, THERE IS NO VISION. WORSE, IT IS LIKELY TO BE SO BANAL IT FAILS ALTOGETHER TO GUIDE THE PLAN. THE PLAN IS JUST A REFLECTION OF WHAT THE MANAGERS BELIEVE HAS TO BE DONE.

2. THERE IS TOO MUCH TO DO

PLANS THAT TRY TO BE EVERYTHING TO EVERYONE OVER-PROMISE AND UNDER-DELIVER — TO THE PEOPLE WHO FORMULATED THE PLAN AND TO THE BUSINESS. INSTEAD OF DISCRIMINATING BETWEEN THE MUST-DO AND WOULD-LIKE-TO-DO, EVERYTHING GOES IN. IN THE FACE OF SUCH A PLAN PEOPLE ARE OVERWHELMED AND CANNOT DECIDE WHAT TO DO.

3. ONLY MANAGERS CONSTRUCT AND SEE THE PLAN

IF PLANNING IS THE PRESERVE OF MANAGEMENT ONLY, EVERYONE ELSE IS OPERATING "BLIND" — ON INSTRUCTIONS LACKING RATIONALE OR CONTEXT. IN SUCH INSTANCES, BUSINESSES FAIL COMPLETELY TO MAKE MAXIMUM USE OF THE INTELLIGENCE OF THE WORKING POPULATION.

4. THE PLAN ONLY INVOLVES OBVIOUS SECTIONAL HEADS

IN SUCH A PLAN, NO CASCADING OCCURS. PEOPLE CANNOT MAKE USEFUL DECISIONS ON THEIR DAY-TO-DAY ACTIONS WHICH GENERATE AN ACCUMULATION OF BENEFITS TOWARDS THE VISION. THE PLAN TYPICALLY SEES MOST DECISIONS REVERTING BACK TO SENIOR MANAGEMENT. THERE ARE HIGH STRESS LEVELS, AND PERSONAL RESPONSIBILITY AND ACCOUNTABILITY IS LIMITED TO SENIOR MANAGEMENT.

5. THERE IS LIMITED REVIEW OF THE PLAN

IF MAJOR PLANS ARE ONLY REVIEWED EVERY SIX TO TWELVE MONTHS, AS PART OF A DIVISION'S REVIEW OR AS PART OF AN APPROACH TO THE FINANCIAL INSTITUTIONS FOR THE COMING YEAR, DAY-TO-DAY ACTIVITIES ARE LEFT TO BE DECIDED IN THE HEAT OF THE

MOMENT. THE RESULT IS 'BUSYNESS' VERSUS 'BUSINESS'. SUCH ORGANISATIONS SPEND THEIR ENERGY MANAGING SPOT FIRES AND CONSTANTLY BATTLING CASH FLOW CRISES.

6. THERE ARE NO CRITICAL SUCCESS FACTORS

WHEN PEOPLE DO NOT KNOW THE CRITICAL SUCCESS FACTORS OF THE BUSINESS, THEY ARE LEFT TO GUESS — AND THEIR GUESSES OFTEN DIFFER FROM OTHER STAFF AND FROM LEADERS.

7. THE OUTCOMES CANNOT BE MEASURED

IF PEOPLE DON'T KNOW HOW TO MEASURE PERFORMANCE OR DON'T KNOW WHAT TO MEASURE, LITTLE OR NO MEASUREMENT OCCURS. WITHOUT MEASUREMENT, HOW DO YOU KNOW PROGRESS IS OCCURRING OR, PERHAPS MORE IMPORTANTLY, HOW CAN YOU AGREE ON PROGRESS?

8. THERE IS A 'JUSTIFICATION' CLAUSE

A SECTION IN THE PLAN THAT EXPLAINS AWAY THINGS THAT WERE COMMITTED TO IN THE LAST PLANNING SESSION BUT WHICH DIDN'T HAPPEN CAN INDICATE SIGNIFICANT WEAKNESS IN THE ORIGINAL OBJECTIVES.

ACTION FOR EMPLOYEES

HERE ARE SOME IDEAS ON DEVELOPING A UNITED SENSE OF THE FUTURE.

1. GATHER AVAILABLE INFORMATION ON WHAT HAS BEEN DONE SO FAR

— AT THE NEXT MOST APPROPRIATE BREAK, OR BEFORE THE WORKDAY STARTS, HAND OUT SHEETS OF PAPER TO PEOPLE YOU WORK WITH AND ASK THEM TO WRITE DOWN WHERE THEY THINK THE BUSINESS IS HEADING, AND WHAT THEY BELIEVE IS THE TRUE PURPOSE OR VISION OF THE BUSINESS. LOOK AT THE RESPONSES. DO PEOPLE KNOW WHERE THE BUSINESS IS HEADING? DO THEY AGREE?

— FIND ANY (AND ALL) PUBLICATIONS THAT HAVE BEEN PUT OUT BY MANAGEMENT WHICH OUTLINE THE COMPANY'S FUTURE PLANS. LOOK AT ANNUAL REPORTS, MANAGEMENT STRATEGIC PLANNING STATEMENTS, PUBLIC PUBLICATIONS, INTERNAL MEMOS, ETC.

— CHECK WITH THE PEOPLE YOU WORK WITH AS TO WHO HAS SEEN THESE PUBLICATIONS — AND WHO HASN'T. OF THOSE WHO HAVE SEEN THEM, HOW MANY FEEL THAT THE BUSINESS IS BEING RUN ACCORDING TO THIS VISION OR STRATEGIC PLAN? DO THEY THINK THAT IT KEEPS CHANGING? SEE IF YOU CAN DETERMINE WHY THE CHANGES ARE OCCURRING.

WHY?

TOO MANY PEOPLE SHOOT FROM THE HIP WHEN TRYING TO BRING ABOUT CHANGE OR WHEN COMPLAINING ABOUT THE ABSENCE OF FOCUSED DIRECTION. THE LETTING-OFF-STEAM CONVERSATIONS THAT TAKE PLACE IN THE TEAROOM, AT A BREAK AROUND A COFFEE MACHINE, OR SIDE BY SIDE ON A PRODUCTION LINE ARE USEFUL, BUT THEY CAN BE COUNTER-PRODUCTIVE IF THEY ARE REGURGITATED AS 'TRUTH' IN MEETINGS OR IN CASUAL CONVERSATIONS WITH MANAGERS. THE CRY "NOBODY AROUND HERE KNOWS WHAT WE ARE MEANT TO BE DOING!" MAY BE TRUE FOR SOME, BUT NOT FOR ALL.

TALKING TO PEOPLE, FINDING OUT THEIR PERCEPTIONS OF THE TRUTH, GETTING THEIR SENSE OF HISTORY, LOOKING AT PUBLICATIONS, MEMOS, E-MAILS AND THE LIKE ALL HELP BUILDS A COMPOSITE PICTURE OF 'REALITY' WHICH AMOUNTS TO MORE THAN THE OPINIONS OF ANY INDIVIDUAL. THIS TYPE OF RESEARCH ARMS YOU WITH THE ABILITY TO BE FLEXIBLE WHEN TALKING TO MANAGERS. THERE IS NOTHING WORSE THAN BEING IN A DEBATE WITH SOMEONE EMPOWERED TO MAKE A DIFFERENCE AND BEING UNABLE TO DRAW UPON GOOD FACTS AND

FIGURES. YOU MIGHT NOT HAVE ALL YOU NEED, BUT A STARTING POINT IS GETTING WHAT YOU CAN AND MAKING DAMN SURE THAT YOU PRESENT MORE THAN JUST YOUR OWN OPINION.

2. DETERMINE WHAT YOU NEED AND WHY

- IN THE LIGHT OF WHAT YOU HAVE READ, CONSIDER WHETHER THE BUSINESS LACKS A CLEAR PICTURE OF THE FUTURE. DOES IT HAVE AN AGREED PLAN FOR GETTING THERE THAT EVERYONE HAS CONTRIBUTED TOWARDS AND UNDERSTANDS?

- NOTE DOWN HOW YOU COULD DO THE JOB BETTER AS A RESULT OF THIS INFORMATION, AND WHAT IT WOULD MEAN TO YOU AS AN INDIVIDUAL.

- REFLECT ON YOUR EXPERIENCES AND THE EXPERIENCES OF FELLOW WORKMATES, AND NOTE THE PROBLEMS THAT DEVELOP IN RELATION TO THE LACK IN THE BUSINESS OF A CLEAR SENSE OF THE FUTURE OR A PLAN FOR GETTING THERE.

- NOTE DOWN BENEFITS FROM ENVISIONING OR PLANNING THAT YOU HAVE EXPERIENCED.

WHY?

THIS IS THE WAY YOU KINDLE PASSION, BEGIN THE PROCESS OF OWNING A FUTURE WHICH WILL FILL A NICHE, SERVICE A NEED, SOLVE A PROBLEM. IT DEMONSTRATES TO YOU AND YOUR WORKMATES THE TANGIBLE, MEASURABLE OUTCOMES THAT MIGHT REASONABLY BE EXPECTED TO COME FROM A CLEAR SENSE OF THE FUTURE THAT IS SUPPORTED BY A PLAN.

IN ADDITION, WHEN DISCUSSING YOUR NEEDS WITH SENIOR MANAGEMENT, YOU WILL BE WELL ARMED WITH PERSUASIVE MATERIAL TO SUPPORT YOUR REQUESTS. MANAGEMENT MIGHT ONLY SEE THE NEEDS FROM THEIR OWN PERSPECTIVE AND MAY NOT HAVE FULLY THOUGHT THROUGH THE REPERCUSSIONS FOR EMPLOYEES. IN FACT, SENIOR MANAGEMENT OFTEN DEVELOPS VISIONS OF THE FUTURE BASED ON SUCH SELECTIVE PICTURES OF REALITY THAT THEY END UP MISMATCHING THEIR OWN ORGANISATIONS: THEY AIM FOR SOMETHING WHICH IS TOO FAR FROM THE REALITY OF THE DAY-TO-DAY RUNNING OF THE COMPANY OR SIMPLY DOES NOT ACCOUNT FOR THE NEEDS OF THE PEOPLE. YOUR ARGUMENTS MAY WELL TURN THE TABLE AND GIVE THEM INSIGHTS INTO DIFFERENT ASPECTS OF THE BUSINESS AND THE THINKING OF THE PEOPLE WHO WORK THERE.

3. MEET FORMALLY WITH MANAGEMENT

— First, get a group of fellow employees together. Your objective is to have two or three people who understand — as you do — the need for a clear direction in the business. These people should be willing to articulate that need to management.

— See the appropriate manager and put your needs forward. The person you approach might be a manager close to you, it might be someone very senior.

— Don't be confrontational or create a 'them and us' situation. Think carefully about how you set up the meeting. Think about the location, who should attend, the time of day, the informality of the setting.

— At the meeting, ask the manager to respond both informally (at the meeting) and formally (in writing, with a recommended response or action plan). And make it clear to the manager that you are willing to help.

WHY?

There are too many people who could make a difference but don't because they are waiting for the action to come from someone more senior. I have spoken to many hundreds of people who say things like "Well I mentioned this to so-and-so and nothing happened" or "I bought it up at our weekly sales meeting and there was no follow-up". A passing conversation in the corridor about "We really need to clarify where we are heading" will not produce the results you want. People give 'snatch and grab' responses which are rarely well considered and almost never turn into action.

Dedicating a meeting to a matter (particularly when it is backed by thoughtful research) gives an appropriate level of 'seriousness'. When you ask leaders for a formal response, you can also reasonably ask for a time frame and an indication of what the content will be.

Don't let fear of reprisal stop you from taking action. I have spoken to plenty of leaders who wish staff would take such action; only once have I come across a leader who would have punished someone for it. If you have a leader who fits into the latter category, believe me, it is time for them (or you) to move on!

4. BRAINSTORM WITH MANAGERS ON CLARIFYING THE DIRECTION OF THE BUSINESS AND THE PLANS FOR GETTING THERE

– GIVE COPIES OF THE NECESSITIES AND POISONS FOR VISIONS AND BUSINESS PLANS TO THE RELEVANT MANAGERS AND TO YOUR TEAM.

– ORGANISE A 'THINK TANK' OR 'BRAINSTORM' SESSION.

– IDENTIFY WHAT IS MISSING AND DISCUSS THE IMPLICATIONS.

– WORK OUT HOW AND WHEN YOU CAN TOGETHER ADDRESS THE IMBALANCE.

– AGREE UPON A TIMETABLE FOR YOUR AGREED ACTIONS.

– GAIN THE COMMITMENT OF EVERYONE TO FOLLOW THROUGH.

WHY?

BECAUSE A LOT OF MANAGERS WON'T ACTUALLY KNOW WHAT TO DO! THEY WILL AGREE WITH YOU THAT THE COMPANY REALLY NEEDS TO HAVE A SENSE OF THE FUTURE AND A PLAN TO BACK IT, BUT THEY MAY NOT KNOW WHERE TO BEGIN. LIKE YOU, THEY MAY HAVE HAD A BAD PRIOR EXPERIENCE: THEY MAY HAVE BEEN ON TIME-WASTING VISIONARY RETREATS, FOR INSTANCE. HOWEVER, I WOULD SAY TO BOTH PARTIES, JUST BECAUSE IT DIDN'T WORK AS EXPECTED LAST TIME, DON'T GIVE UP!

BRAINSTORMING IS A GREAT WAY TO BREAK PREVIOUS THINKING PATTERNS AND COME UP WITH NEW STRATEGIES WHICH REFLECT A TEAM'S THOUGHTS RATHER THAN ONE PERSON'S EXPERIENCE. IF YOU USE THE NECESSITIES AND POISONS LISTS AS A GUIDE, YOU WILL HAVE AN EXCELLENT AND VERY SIMPLE TOOL FOR WORKING TOWARDS A PRODUCTIVE OUTCOME.

5. KEEP IT SIMPLE AND TAKE ACTION

– MAKE SURE THE ACTIONS THAT YOU, YOUR TEAM OR MANAGEMENT COMMIT TO TAKING ARE SIMPLE, BELIEVABLE AND ACHIEVABLE. SET A DEADLINE OF A WEEK TO THREE MONTHS FOR YOUR GOALS.

– WRITE THE ACTIONS DOWN, AND BE SURE THAT EVERYONE HAS RECORDED THE DATE FOR COMPLETION AND WHO, EXACTLY, IS RESPONSIBLE.

HAVE THE COURAGE TO DO YOUR OWN FOLLOW-UP WHEN DEADLINES ARE APPROACHING.

WHY?

TOO MANY PEOPLE OVER-PROMISE AND UNDER-DELIVER TO THEMSELVES AND THE PEOPLE AROUND THEM. WHEN THE GROUP THINK AN ACTION IS EASILY DONE, THEN IT IS PROBABLY A GOOD ACTION. IT IS CRITICALLY IMPORTANT TO TAKE ACTION IMMEDIATELY RATHER THAN WAIT. AS EVERY ACROBAT KNOWS, THE LONGER YOU WAIT TO ACT, THE HARDER IT BECOMES. ACTIONS FOR IMPROVEMENT ARE, POTENTIALLY, INFINITE. SO THE ACTIONS YOU ARE LOOKING FOR ARE THE NEXT MOST APPROPRIATE ACTIONS, NOT ALL THE ACTIONS THAT COULD BE TAKEN. BY 'NEXT MOST APPROPRIATE ACTIONS' I MEAN ACTIONS THAT SHOULD BE TAKEN IN THE NEXT ONE TO THREE MONTHS.

FINALLY, BE WILLING TO CHECK ON PROGRESS YOURSELF RATHER THAN WAIT FOR THE RESULTS. IF SOMEONE DOESN'T MEET AN AGREED TIMELINE, FIND OUT WHY AND DEVELOP AN ALTERNATIVE TIMELINE. OR, IF THE PERSON LOOKS LIKE THEY CAN'T OR WON'T TAKE ACTION, FIND A MANAGER WHO WILL.

POINTERS FOR LEADERS

IDEAS ON DEVELOPING A UNITED SENSE OF THE FUTURE.

1. WHAT VISIONARY WORK HAVE YOU DONE SO FAR? ARE YOU HAPPY WITH IT?

— HAVE YOU OR OTHER SENIOR MANAGEMENT SAT DOWN TOGETHER TO THINK ABOUT OR DETERMINE THE FUTURE DIRECTION OF THE BUSINESS, OR IS IT ASSUMED THAT EVERYONE ALREADY KNOWS ABOUT IT?

— IF YOU HAVE A VISION WHICH YOU FEEL IS CLEAR AND APPROPRIATE, HOW WELL DOES IT FIT WITH THE NECESSITIES OF VISIONING? HOW DOES IT RATE AGAINST THE POISONS LIST?

WHY?

BECAUSE THE FIRST STEP OF REVIEW STARTS WITH THE MANAGEMENT TEAM! IT'S TIME FOR HONESTY: DO YOU LIKE WHAT YOU'VE GOT, OR IS IT MEANINGLESS TWADDLE AND SOMETHING YOU'VE AGREED TO IN ORDER TO GET ON WITH THE DAY-TO-DAY RUNNING OF THE BUSINESS? DO YOU REALLY UNDERSTAND WHAT A VISION IS FOR? HAVE YOU ASKED FOR EVIDENCE OF WHERE, IN OTHER BUSINESSES, ENVISIONING HAS BEEN SUCCESSFUL? YOU SHOULD HAVE. IN MY EXPERIENCE, TOO MANY MANAGERS DO NOT REALLY UNDERSTAND WHAT A VISION IS AND SO ARE CYNICAL OF ITS FUNCTION. YOU ARE ENTITLED TO BE SUPPORTED WITH EDUCATION IF YOU ARE BEING ASKED TO DEVELOP A VISION OR ENSURE AN EXISTING VISION IS SUCCESSFULLY ACHIEVED.

2. WHO WAS INVOLVED IN DEVELOPING THE VISION?

— WHEN WAS THE VISION DEVELOPED? WHO DEVELOPED IT? HAVE STAFF GIVEN YOU AND OTHER MANAGEMENT FEEDBACK ON THE VISION? IF YOU HAVEN'T HAD FEEDBACK FROM STAFF, GIVE THEM THE OPPORTUNITY TO TELL YOU WHAT THEY THINK ABOUT THE VISION, WHAT THEY WOULD CHANGE AND WHY. USE QUESTIONNAIRES, PERSONAL INTERVIEWS, GROUP DISCUSSIONS, QUALITY CIRCLES ETC.

— BRAINSTORM HOW TO BRING THE VISION ALIVE. STAGE A BARBEQUE SESSION, USE BUTCHER'S PAPER, WHATEVER, BUT BE SURE TO POSE THE QUESTION: "HOW CAN WE BRING THE VISION ALIVE?" GET PARTICIPANTS TO CHOOSE THE TEN BEST IDEAS.

— WHATEVER TECHNIQUE YOU USE, SET UP A FORMAL FEEDBACK PROCESS THAT ALLOWS STAFF TO TALK ABOUT THE VISION AND WHAT THEY KNOW OF THE BUSINESS AT THIS TIME IN, PREFERABLY, CROSS FUNCTIONAL GROUPS. THIS CAN BE DONE ALMOST ANY TIME BUT REQUIRES SOME PREPARATION: THINK ABOUT THE VENUE, CATERING, SEATING, WHO SHOULD ATTEND AND WHY. GET PEOPLE INTO BREAKOUT GROUPS OF, SAY SIX TO EIGHT INDIVIDUALS, AND LET THEM DISCUSS THE EXISTING VISION AND WHAT IT MEANS TO THEM. ASK STAFF TO WRITE THEIR COMMENTS DOWN ON PAPER.

— WORK THROUGH STAFF'S COMMENTS WITH OTHER MANAGEMENT AND SEE HOW AND WHERE YOU CAN IMPROVE WHAT YOU'VE GOT. THEN LET STAFF KNOW ABOUT CHANGES SO THEY CAN 'SEE' EVIDENCE OF THEIR INPUT.

WHY?

TWO CRITICAL KEYS TO SUCCESSFUL ENVISIONING ARE 'OWNERSHIP' AND 'PASSION'. OWNERSHIP MEANS THAT EVERY INDIVIDUAL HAS A PERSONAL SENSE OF WHAT THE VISION MEANS TO THEM AND HOW THEY INFLUENCE ITS SUCCESSFUL REALISATION. PASSION IS ABOUT HOW EXCITED AND COMMITTED PEOPLE ARE. THE VISION IS A WASTE OF TIME IF IT IS TOP-DIRECTED: PEOPLE WON'T SPEAK UP AND THE COMPANY WILL LOSE THE BENEFIT OF INDIVIDUAL THOUGHTFULNESS IN THE DAY-TO-DAY OPERATION OF THE BUSINESS.

PEOPLE NEED TO BE CLEAR ON THE PURPOSE OF THEIR BUSINESS. IT HELPS THEM DETERMINE HOW BEST TO ACT IN ACCORD WITH THE VISION. AND THOSE WHO HAVE A HAND IN DESIGNING A VISION AND DEVELOPING THE PLANS FOR MAKING IT HAPPEN WILL HAVE A MUCH HIGHER LEVEL OF COMMITMENT TO A SUCCESSFUL OUTCOME.

3. WHAT PLANNING HAVE YOU DONE AND HOW EFFECTIVE HAS IT BEEN?

— IF YOU'RE NOT SURE OF A PARTICULAR PLANNING FORMAT THAT COULD BE APPROPRIATE TO YOUR BUSINESS, GET ON YOUR BIKE AND HEAD FOR THE NEAREST BUSINESS OR TECHNICAL BOOKSHOP. A QUICK BROWSE WILL FIND AT LEAST TEN BOOKS THAT WILL HELP YOU WITH PLANNING. CHOOSE THE SIMPLEST METHOD YOU CAN FIND.

— DISCUSS YOUR PLANNING FORMAT WITH YOUR MANAGEMENT TEAM.

— DISCUSS CASCADING THE PLANNING PROCESS INTO THE BUSINESS: WHAT WILL WORK, WHAT WON'T. GAIN COMMITMENT FROM ALL MANAGERS TO FOLLOW THROUGH ON THE PLANNING PROCESS AND TO CASCADE IT INTO THE BUSINESS. AT THE SAME TIME, ENSURE THE PROCESS IS CONTINUOUS AND TWO-WAY. (THAT IS, ENSURE (A) EVERYONE — INCLUDING PART-TIMERS — UNDERSTANDS THE OVERALL BUSINESS PLAN; AND (B) THAT CONTINUOUS FEEDBACK ON ROADBLOCKS OR WEAKNESSES OR MISSING SEGMENTS CAN COME BACK TO MANAGEMENT FROM ALL STAFF.)

— ESTABLISH A TIMETABLE FOR THE CASCADING PROCESS — SET A TIME FRAME OF A MAXIMUM OF 12 WEEKS.

— ONCE THIS HAS BEEN DONE, REMEMBER TO REVIEW THE WORKING PLAN MONTHLY AND REINVIGORATE IT — UPDATE IT — NOT LESS THAT QUARTERLY.

WHY?

TOO MANY PLANS STAY IN THE HANDS OF SENIOR MANAGEMENT. THE COMPANY WILL ONLY HAVE THE BENEFIT OF THE THINKING OF A VERY SMALL NUMBER OF PEOPLE IF IT STAYS THIS WAY. THE MORE PEOPLE WHO UNDERSTAND WHERE WE ARE GOING AND HOW WE INTEND TO GET THERE, THE MORE CHANCE OF THEM PUTTING THOUGHT INTO MAKING SURE WE GET THERE EFFICIENTLY, EFFECTIVELY AND ENJOYABLY.

A CRITICAL RESPONSIBILITY OF LEADERSHIP IS THE MANAGEMENT OF THE STRATEGIC PROCESS AS DISTINCT FROM THE DAY-TO-DAY BUSYNESS OF RUNNING A COMPANY. LEADERS NEED GOOD PEOPLE SKILLS AND A WILL TO LISTEN AND ACT ON FEEDBACK.

WHEN THINKING ABOUT THE PROCESS OF CASCADING THE PLAN INTO THE BUSINESS, BE CLEAR ABOUT WHO CAN CONTRIBUTE TO THE PLANS, AND FOR WHAT REASONS. REMIND YOURSELF HOW DISEMPOWERED YOU FEEL WHEN SOMEONE TELLS YOU TO DO SOMETHING WHEN THERE IS NO ACCOMPANYING EXPLANATION AS TO WHY. CONSIDER THE LEVEL OF OWNERSHIP YOU HAVE OVER A PLAN WHEN YOU HAVE EITHER DESIGNED THE PLAN OR HAVE PLAYED AN IMPORTANT PART IN ITS DESIGN.

4. PROCESS OF OWNERSHIP — TAKING FEEDBACK

- DON'T BE FEARFUL OF TAKING FEEDBACK ON THE VALIDITY OF THE BUSINESS PLAN. STAFF WILL RESPECT AND VALUE A LEADER WHO TAKES FEEDBACK. MORE IMPORTANTLY, THE BUSINESS PLAN WILL VASTLY IMPROVE.

- WHEN YOU TAKE FEEDBACK, DON'T TRY TO JUSTIFY WHY YOU DIDN'T THINK OF IT ORIGINALLY OR WHY YOU THINK IT IS WRONG.

WHY?

BEING ATTENTIVE TO FEEDBACK IS THE BEST TOOL WE KNOW OF FOR ACCELERATING LEARNING. STAFF WILL APPRECIATE THE OPPORTUNITY AND ARE MORE LIKELY TO BE THOUGHTFUL IN THEIR RESPONSES.

FEEDBACK IS ABOUT DECENCY. NO DOUBT YOU LIKE TO HAVE THE OPPORTUNITY TO VOUCHSAFE AN OPINION YOURSELF? SO DOES EVERYONE ELSE — EACH ACCORDING TO THEIR LEVEL OF RESPONSIBILITY AND KNOWLEDGE. YOU DON'T WANT TO CREATE AN ENDLESS CONSULTATIVE PROCESS, BUT YOU DO WANT TO HEAR WHAT PEOPLE HAVE TO SAY ABOUT BOTH THE VISION AND THE PLAN FOR ACHIEVING IT.

God is in his heaven but does anyone trust him anymore?

The water is murky, but of one thing I am certain: the whole concept of leadership in business has fundamentally changed. The question is, however, have the leaders?

Don't be mistaken into thinking leadership is something bestowed by other leaders or Boards. It may appear so, but nothing is more powerless than a leader with a title who the troops do not respect.

A FRAME OF REFERENCE

Once upon a time there was a young man who thought it might be good to go for a walk. He needed to stretch his muscles and get some fresh air.

3

Fortunately, close to his office there was a coastal walk that meandered along a cliff face which towered hundreds of metres above the pounding surf of the Pacific Ocean.

It was a wonderful walk, invigorating and meditative.

Unfortunately, after walking rhythmically for some twenty minutes, the young man was so deep in thought that he stopped paying attention to where he was going and, in one of those awful moments when everything can and does go wrong, he tripped over a root that ran across his path. Before he could save himself, he tumbled over the edge of the cliff, to his sure and imminent death on the rocks below.

Marvellously and magically, about halfway down the cliff face, the young man managed to throw his arm out and grab just about the only outcropping of growth on the entire cliff face — one strong, dry, isolated tree root! Holding on for dear life, the young man assessed his predicament. Towering above him was a fifty-metre unscalable wall. Falling away below him was another hundred or more metres of craggy, impassable rock face, finishing in a pounding, surging, unhappy wash of surf and granite.

The young man looked up and then down, searching for some possible purchase — but none was apparent. Finally, recognising his position was impossible, he started to call desperately for help.

"Help", he cried, "HELP! Somebody, ANYBODY HEEEELLLPPPP!"

He called and called and when he thought his luck was done, he heard an extraordinary voice from above. "My son", the voice spoke, deep and sonorous, "I am here, I will help you. Trust in me. Let go of the root and I will save you!"

The young man listened carefully. He looked up and he looked down. "Look," he said, respectfully, "I don't mean to be rude, but who are you?"

"It is your father, my son, God The Almighty! Let go and I will save you, trust in me. LET GO!" His voice boomed loudly above the pounding surf.

The young man looked up again and, once more, down at the surf and rocks below him. He shook his head, closed his eyes and whispered to himself and then said...

"Look, please understand me, I don't mean to be rude... but is there anyone else up there?"

You see, the Gods might be in their heavens still but the question is — do we trust their judgment anymore?

TALL TALES AND TRUE FROM THE COALFACE

It was (in fact, still is) a very successful organisation. The Managing Director was (dare it be said, still is) a charismatic, good looking, ambitious man. In fact, to be honest, he was the sort of leader that women met and then thought very few business-related things about! He was charming, funny, creative, talented, immensely informed, had great connections and had a brilliant track record in the industry.

Apart from all this, as a leader, he was a total nightmare. He had a 'drama hook' — he actually thrived on, was goaded to higher action by, nothing less than unmitigated disaster. On numerous occasions you could see him make otherwise intelligent, capable people genuinely frightened — or reduced almost to automatons — in response to this 'leader's' storm of sighs and accusations, passionate speeches, rushed requests and ill-considered, frantic last-minute demands. If it wasn't happening naturally (rape, pillage, fire, pestilence, black acrid smoke falling from the sky) he would manufacture it. His skill at precipitating disaster was, like most of his skills, outstanding. While some people have a capacity to cope, with equanimity and a sense of positive purpose, the loss of every cent they have, the bombing of their house, or even the death of all their domestic pets, this man could foresee dire consequences arising from the tiniest of events.

This is no exaggeration! If in a meeting someone were to spill a glass of water, he would — despite the presence of a dozen other people — call the perpetrator of such a mistake stupid. He would then connect that episode of idiocy to a dozen others, and use that fabricated 'leverage' as evidence of the potential to lose a multi-million dollar account. Later, when his predictions of disaster were averted only after some extraordinarily brilliant initiative led by either himself or his hero of the day, he would smile with smug satisfaction.

It sounds funny, but for Joe and Jill Blow, it was a waking nightmare. On the one hand people really liked him. He was endearing, funny, sometimes very generous, life of any party, genuinely friendly with all his staff. On the other hand, he could paralyse people with his capacity for generating tension, panic and blame. It was indeed a miracle that anyone survived, and few did. He managed single-handedly to ensure that staff turnover ran at about 80% per annum, not because "good staff are hard to find" but because the legion of good staff who walked in through his reception area (and then out again some months later) were unable to live in the frenetic, stress-packed, hysterical environment that he generated.

Interviewing some of the staff, I heard them, one after the other, express distress and frustration with his style of managing problems. Each person echoed what others had said only minutes before. They all complained, in their own way, that the man robbed people of their ability to think, to contribute, to resolve, to innovate, to imagine.

Eventually, when I found the right opportunity, over a very good bottle of red, I broached the topic of his leadership style, as gently as I knew how... something like "Why are you such a prick with your staff when something looks like it might go wrong?" My query was met with stunned silence. He looked his beguiling and innocent best — quite clearly failing, even in small part, to comprehend what I was saying. I then gave him, in some detail, feedback from his people, how they saw him, his leadership style, the impact of his drama hook, what they wished he would do instead.

Nearly an hour later I drew breath and waited for his response. He shook his head and sighed; "Jesus, the bastards, I do everything for them. I can't believe they would say all that. How else do they expect to get anything done around here. You've got to put a spike up people's arses in this business or nothing happens. I pay 'em enough to do that! Christ, all this time I thought they liked being in the industry. It's adrenaline that counts, and if they don't like it they should piss off!"

He grinned at me at the end of his speech and winked. I now knew what drove him, gave him pleasure, made him make the world turn over and do his bidding. I said nothing more, then or subsequently. I am not a psychiatrist. One day, perhaps, he will understand why his company, despite his brilliance and the brilliance of the people he keeps hiring and losing, remains in the top twenty of its kind in Australia when everyone, myself included, sees the potential for it to be in the top five.

There is no arguing that he makes a great deal of money, as do many of the people who (temporarily) work with him, but I sense, as do those closest to him, that the money is less and less rewarding. He wants more, although he won't articulate it easily. He is increasingly hurt by the sometimes bitter and vitriolic comments thrown at him by a finally courageous but nonetheless creative director. He is confused by the sudden tears that erupt from a writer under fire, or the increasing level of sick leave in the accounts department. He doesn't understand yet, but his people do. He doesn't know how to listen or learn yet, but his people do — and they mark their learning by leaving.

Some things are hard won.

TALL TALES AND TRUE FROM THE TOP

The company had recently 'merged' with its only competitor in the industry. Some three hundred men and women, ranging in age from 20 to 58, were now struggling with two very diverse cultures spread over five locations, in five states of Australia.

This story may be the hallmark of business in the nineteen-nineties. The answer to everything is to merge, take over, and acquire. Big is better. Funny how rarely the promised economies of scale materialise… but that's another chapter. For now, imagine a group of people in relative shock. There had been a few retrenchments but not enough to justify the anxiety that permeated the business. Five months after the merger, I was invited in to do my Honesty Audit in order to find out what the people of the business thought were its strengths and weaknesses. I had to see if I could identify a path through to the future that would make sense to the majority.

Over several weeks, I interviewed everyone. The picture that emerged was not pretty. There was abundant evidence of poor management, inadequate planning, appalling communication, lack of clarity over the purpose of the merger, and substantial 'values clashes' between the cultures of the two merged businesses (one was inclined to bureaucratic lethargy, the other to entrepreneurial, shooting star excesses). People were confused, uncertain about their job roles and, lacking themselves any surety about the future, were unsure how to manage their customer base.

One thing, however, stood out above all the other problems. People were absolutely sure that if the leadership team got it right, the merger was the right thing to do for all concerned. The problem was that the majority of people doubted if the leadership team could get it right. The team was seen to be argumentative and divisive, publicly so. They were described as a bunch of self-seeking power brokers more interested in the isolated success of their various departments than they were in the overall success of the business.

I took the findings of my research and wrote them up into a comprehensive 60-page report, to be presented to the leadership team. I included a range of recommendations, based on the feedback from people, to be implemented over the next twelve to twenty-four months.

I guess it takes a lot of courage for a leader to sit quietly while some outsider delivers a fairly hefty broadside, but the whole leadership team of eight people sat as quiet as church mice throughout my two hour presentation. For the better part you could have heard a pin drop, the silence punctuated periodically as someone scribbled a note on a particular point in question. When I had finished the presentation, I turned and looked at each individual. With one exception, they were shaking their heads in disbelief and, beyond a shadow of doubt, with a certain degree of shame.

In turn, the Managing Director looked at each member of the team and then looked at me. "I can't imagine anyone disagreeing with you. I am glad it is out in the open. When can we begin on your recommendations."

That attitude set the tone for a year of activities which brought this diverse, fractionated, irritable, ambitious group of people together as a visionary, synergistic business with an excited and exciting sense of the future. The leadership gracefully acknowledged its weaknesses, and with a commitment to see the process through to a conclusion, copies of the report were given to every member of the company.

Whatever else this leadership team may have been accused of, their behaviour during the (re)building process was characterised by an extraordinary willingness to honourably and honestly take on each challenge to the full extent of their ability. (All this was done in a business environment which could, at best, be described as frantic.)

They looked at their style of communication with each other and with the people of the business. They stopped their public brawling. They carefully considered the impact their actions were having on the people of the business. They invited and then listened to constant feedback. They went into retreat on the future of the business but then carefully invited extensive feedback from the people of the business — and then they acted on that feedback.

There were internal creative projects focusing teams on communication improvements to assist breaking down the barriers between the two cultures, there were external projects to assuage the fears of confused clients unsure of future servicing. There were team activities to bring various departments together, to improve the sharing of ideas and to elevate the standard of customer service. Individual skill and career audits were conducted to establish what dreams and aspirations individuals had, what education they were seeking and where in the business they would like to move.

On the outer of all this not uncommon level of activity sat the illusive Board, a collection of seemingly powerful individuals. With the passage of time, a slight schism between the Board's sense of where the business should be heading and where the people of the business, and in particular the Managing Director, felt the organisation should be heading, turned into a Grand Canyon over which few were able to pass. With hindsight, this problem could have been resolved with dialogue and an increased understanding of the motivations of the relevant parties. Instead, the Managing Director of the business chose to resign "due to irreconcilable differences of opinion".

In essence, his resignation shouldn't have been so precipitous. After all, we had just spent twelve months working on building a solid organisation whose strength reflected the wisdom of many. Most people felt confident that a new Managing Director would see the value of the work that had been done and, while changes no doubt would flow from a new appointment, there was only marginal anxiety about the pending change.

Eventually a new Managing Director was in place. Within a fortnight of the appointment I started to receive anxious phone calls from the leadership team. They were saying that the new guy was the wrong person; he was an old-world leader who operated from a 'right way' model in which his way was the right way. They said that he made overtures of listening but proceeded to ignore everyone and do what he thought was the right thing. His ego was walking in front of him and he wasn't much interested in what other people thought.

I met with the new managing director. I was expecting a grilling: what had I been doing for the company? Why? What had it achieved? What yet remained to be done? What were the expected outcomes? At the least, I expected to be asked these things — after all, I had been working in a senior capacity with the business for nearly twelve months.

The 'interview' was as far removed from this as it is possible to get. What actually happened was that the new Managing Director talked at me (with rare exception), telling me how bad things were, how much was wrong, what fools the leadership team were, how removed they were from the Board's perceptions of what the business should be doing, and so on. I listened in stunned silence. The man's opinions were already clearly formed after just three weeks in the job. He was not interested in getting information from me, nor listening to any thoughts I had on what might be the best way to handle the transition from old MD to new.

When I left the meeting the hairs on the back of my neck were standing on end. I wondered if it was my ego: I was disappointed that he had been so little interested in the work we had been engaged in. However, with the passage of time, I realised my anger was for the people of the business. I felt as each of them must have felt: valueless. All the effort, thought, imagination, commitment, passion, vision and innovation I had bought to my work on behalf of the business amounted to nothing. As it was true for me, it was to become clearly evident for many individuals in the business and, in particular, for the leadership team.

Over the following eight weeks, the new Managing Director cast his cloak over the business. He undid in this short time all that we had achieved in the preceding twelve months. He re-instilled fear and anxiety into the organisation. By his seemingly ruthless lack of consultation, his intimidating interviewing strategies and by his apparent disregard for the endeavours of many staff, he managed to rob people of their commitment and their sense of place.

Within twelve weeks of the appointment, most of the senior leadership team and sixty percent of the research and development team (the 'brains trust' of the organisation) had left. Many more were actively looking for jobs. My work terminated at the end of the next assignment. There was no handover — I was simply asked to box up the material I was preparing and send it to the company by courier.

Some months after my last contact with the people of the company I received a heartbreaking letter from one member of the leadership team who had moved onto another job. "We were so close to getting it right. It is amazing to see how much damage one man can do and in such an extraordinarily short period of time. It's not that I ever disagreed with what he wanted to do, it's the way he went about doing it that was so hard."

For me, this last comment sunk deeply home. Yes, the truth was there was much wisdom in the actions of the new MD. They could have added so much to what had already been done, but the truth is that there was never a chance to give support, never a chance to think it through and integrate it, never a chance to thoughtfully move forward.

Attila the Hun had taken over the country and he was too busy beheading the enemy to realise they were actually his own soldiers.

CAN THERE BE A SIMPLE DEFINITION FOR "LEADER"?

There are leaders I have met, responsible for thousands of people and millions of dollars worth of resources, who seem anything but leaders. They vacillate between a Board's demands, commercial reality and the genuine needs of the work force. Given their indecision, their lack of personal fortitude, their political and often selfish motivation, are they leaders still?

There are managers who are seen by all as great coaches, mentors, friends; they are genuinely respected and valued by their team. Are they then leaders? I have met employees — forklift drivers, pizza cooks, insurance sales people, computer software engineers — who accept personal respon-sibility on behalf of the company that employs them such that their every action elevates the business at every turn. They lead by example. Are they leaders?

The water is murky, but of one thing I am certain: in this changeable, chaotic, technologically rampant, information laden world, the whole concept of leadership in business has fundamentally changed. The question is, however, have the leaders? As you read this chapter, hold in the forefront of your mind the following definition:

A leader is like the conductor of an orchestra — someone who deeply and profoundly appreciates what the whole is trying to achieve, but who recognises at their core that each and every member of the orchestra is critically important to the whole, and needs to be valued, supported, educated, elevated. Such a leader knows that their greatest achievements will only ever arise from the result of synergy — where each and every player brings their own level of excellence into perfect harmony with every other player. It is this ideal for which they continuously aim.

Yet a 'leader' is also each and every member of the orchestra: the success of the whole is determined by the individual effort, commitment and personal responsibility of the individual.

THE ABSENCE OF QUALITY LEADERSHIP

There is no rule about how to lead, no certificate of leadership and, most importantly of all, no natural genetic encoding that makes for a great or even just a good leader. Consider this: sometime in 1889, in Braunau-am-Inn, Austria, no urgent bulletin went out to the world's media announcing the birth of a future megalomaniac who could be expected to put to death many millions of people in the pursuit of a super race. There was a similar absence of publicity surrounding an equally important birth on 30

November 1874 at Blenheim Palace, England. None of us knew that the chubby boy with a silver spoon in his mouth was to become one of the greatest leaders of all time and certainly one of the key protagonists in the drama that was to affect the world from 1939 to 1945.

Ah, no. Leaders do not leap from the womb, biologically programmed for leadership and some for greatness. Rather, they evolve over time and through circumstance, with a mixture of grit and determination, education and opportunity. They learn, by trial and error, what works and what doesn't. Initially, their power is exercised in small domains, but over time, with more successes than failures, more learning and greater opportunity, their influence expands. Eventually, leaders *may* reach their ultimate goal — for some it will be as head of a country, an army, an organisation. For others it will be a level of management or some degree of responsibility for people or resources. For others still it will be the quiet moment of real-isation when they understand absolutely that they are in charge of their own lives and that neither fortune nor misfortune will occur without them having a hand in managing the outcomes.

Whatever their rite of passage, I have met and interviewed few leaders who have fallen accidentally into leadership positions. They may not be overtly ambitious, but somewhere in their story there is a piece of the jigsaw puzzle which clearly shows that in one form or another they have chosen their path.

Unfortunately, in business, the majority of people move into management positions or senior leadership by virtue of their technical knowledge or expertise in a given industry, or because they have demonstrated excellent financial skills or an ability in difficult situations to deal strongly with people. In my experience, they are not often appointed because they have shown a genuine understanding of and rapport with people, outstanding communication skills or (with the possible exception of athletic coaches and musical conductors) exceptional mentoring and coaching abilities.

Instead, they are chosen because they excel in their field and have produced, in prior positions, excellent financial results on behalf of previous employers.

Superficially, this would seem a reasonable criteria for selection. I, for one, would want to know that a potential leader I was selecting to run my business (a) had an easy familiarity with my industry and (b) came with a track record of financial success. After all, I am going to put my capital investments into his or her hands. Perhaps I might decide that it isn't important how they have achieved (a) and (b). Perhaps it is enough for me to have proof of their results alone.

Unfortunately, dig a little deeper and what might superficially seem appropriate criteria for selection is no longer an appropriate or adequate method for the selection of leadership positions. More and more, it would seem that there is a glaring mismatch between the selection of many leaders and the real needs of the workplace. No matter how we might argue that leaders and managers are increasingly recognising the changing requirements of the workplace, leaders still do not fully understand the needs of their people or, if they do understand them intellectually, the majority certainly don't own them emotionally.

CALLING FROM ON HIGH FOR CHANGE...

In 1991 Cabinet commissioned a report on leadership and management skills in Australia. An industry Task Force was formed in 1992 and headed by David Karpin (at the time, Group Executive in charge of Economic Resources, Financial & Strategic Planning and Legal & Group Business Services on behalf of CRA Ltd). The results of the Task Force's extensive national research was presented to Government and, shortly after, to the rest of the country, in a report entitled *Enterprising Nation* (April, 1995).

There is absolutely nothing in this research that disagrees with my experience. (Or, less presumptuously, nothing that I have found that is in disagreement with the Karpin report!) There is a problem with Australian leadership: actual leadership skills are wanting, leaders themselves need education urgently, they need to be able to manage diversity, they need to value the education and training of their people, they need to learn about what is happening in the rest of the world.

The Task Force made a series of recommendations on how to address the problem. They advocate a further education (by upgrading TAFE's capacity to deliver management development courses), the establishment of formal and informal networks, and the setting up of a national strategy for women (to encourage both their participation in the management of private sector businesses and placement on Corporate Boards, etc). The Task Force recommends formalising "Best Practice Management" — identifying what, exactly, makes for a good manager — a benchmark for the requirements, if you will. They also recommend industry tours — a "let's go out and see what good managers do/are" approach. Finally, they recommend investment in and the upgrading of Management Schools. Under each of their various recommendations there are cascading sub-recommendations. The report (which incidentally, is worth reading, even if it is only the executive summary) is extensive, highly academic, comprehensive, involved a lot of people and, no doubt, cost a lot of money.

Here's my prediction: we might get some level of improved TAFE education and more money going into Management Schools. We might even get a few 'Women In Business' organisations established, to consult with Government on issues raised by various 'Glass Ceiling' research initiatives. But when push comes to shove, neither the Karpin Report, Government mandates or more money will change Australian leadership.

In the end, only leaders will change how leaders behave. It is they who have to accept responsibility for doing 'leadership' differently. If we really want to fast-track change, it is time to start listening to what people have to say about the people who would lead them and, having listened, we need to act.

There is a bag of issues that cascade under leadership in Australia that are not covered in reports such as the Karpin Report and are rarely talked about in business — but the issues are raised by employees everywhere. The question is whether or not we can come up with a solution that will fast-track the results we are after or whether or not change is actually the result of a slower process of evolution and, as with all things subject to the exigencies of evolution, we must wait for our brains and bodies to catch up with our heart's desires.

WHAT LEADERSHIP ISSUES DO EMPLOYEES RAISE AND WHY?

Hold in your mind's eye the world view outlined in Chapter 1 — a world moving faster and faster, where information is no longer in the hands of an elite few. The 'information superhighway' (the term we've coined for the world information marketplace) is here and is accessible to anyone with a PC and a modem. Technological change is rapid; invention and innovation are the stock-in-trade of all businesses. People are better educated, more able, have access to and make use of quality information. Despite this, the future is still anyone's guess. Paradigms — and therefore the rules for your success, my success and everybody's outlook — are changing daily.

In this world it seems glaringly apparent to me that no one person can possibly have an absolute solution that will guide us from pitch-black winter into sun-filled spring. In fact, 'success' is a notion which at worst is mythological or, at best, is fleeting. Despite the obsession in the late nineteen-eighties and early nineteen-nineties with self-help books of every kind — for the individual and the organisation — I think most of us are beginning to realise it is entirely in our own pragmatic, thoughtful hands that our own prosperity resides. There are no absolute answers — just a continuously compounding series of learnings, one experience adding to another, one learning adding to another, that reflect a continuously changing world.

What we need, in all walks of life and never more so than in business, are people thinking and acting towards a common purpose, thoughtfully contributing in whatever way they can to the whole and being willing to learn, continuously, how to do things differently.

Here then are what people believe are the leadership-driven roadblocks to achieving this ideal...

TOO MANY BLOODY RESTRUCTURES, MERGERS, CHANGE PROCESSES...

On Monday, 11 September 1995, I was the keynote speaker on behalf of the Australian Quality Council at their annual conference, held in South Australia. My topic was the Myth of Quality (more on this later). In the course of setting up my key proposition, I asked the audience (some 500 people, comprising senior managers or managers in charge of quality processes in small, medium and large organisations from around Australia) the following series of questions (the percentage responses are my guesstimates):

How many of you have been through a restructure in the last 12 months?
85% of the hands were raised.

How many of you have been through two or more restructures in the last 24 to 36 months?
80% of the hands were raised.

How many of you felt the restructures you have been through were well managed (that is, the business was tangibly improved and employees felt involved)?
5% show of hands.

How many of you felt the restructure was poorly handled (that is, business did not improve measurably)?
80% of the hands went up.

How many of you were consulted during the restructure as to how best to effect it?
5% show of hands.

How many of you felt that either you or your work was devalued as a result of the restructure?
80% show of hands.

Speaker and audience alike were appropriately surprised by these results. Senator Chris Schacht, then Federal Minister for Small Business, Customs and Construction, was also present, as was the then Chairman of the Australian Quality Council, Barry Murphy. Both men talked to me after my session about the responses to the questions.

Two weeks later I spoke at the annual conference for the Australian Industry Training & Development Council (AITD). Wanting to cross-check the Australian Quality Council's results against a very different audience (but also intrinsically involved with people), I asked the same set of questions. If anything, the results were worse.

What madness was this? I could excuse the results, saying they were taken in a biased manner; I could excuse them because of the composition of the two audiences (perhaps, for instance, the results might have been different if the groups had been cross-representational of a variety of industries or a range of different positions within those businesses). But truthfully, these audiences validated, en masse, what I have found in the many one-on-one interviews I have conducted.

Leaders have lost immense credibility through the process of change. There have simply been too many changes, too poorly thought through, with far too little consultation. They've produced too few results and rarely have the promised efficiencies and scales of economy been achieved. Repeatedly I have listened to employees cite 'leadership idiocies' — decisions which have produced crazy results — *results that were predicted by the people they affected* but about which they had no say.

People are tired of restructures being used as an excuse to improve business when the result is questionable. They are tired of decisions being taken in isolation during restructures by leaders who, for some unfathomable reason, feel obliged to lead by 'right way' models (that is, "my way's the right way; do it and all will be well"). Cynicism is now commonplace — particularly in large organisations or publicly listed businesses where leadership is not constant. The result is a rise in the nine-to-five mentality; people start to wonder why they should bother putting in more when their efforts are likely to be thrown out the door during the next restructure.

I remember learning about the 'right way' tree some time ago. I can't remember the source but I suspect, as with all these things, that no one person can really lay claim to the idea. The 'right way' tree describes a style of decision making that is typical of restructures or major change processes, especially in larger organisations. I have seen this occur many times. It goes something like this…

The organisation or business is perceived to be in trouble — for argument's sake, let's say serious trouble. Owners, Board and shareholders determine that the problem is the management. So it's out with the old and in with the new. New management are appointed. They do the obvious (well, obvious to some): they slash and burn. Retrench and reorganise. They take a metaphorical gun, pointing it at everyone in the business and, as if shooting at unwanted birds on ripe fruit, take aim and fire. The birds rise into the air as one. Some, so astonished by the noise, smoke and activity, fall to the ground dead (post-retrenchment heart attacks, psoriasis, cancer, depression); others have seen it all before and take off into the distance, holding onto their satchel of goodies (that is, their retrenchment packages), never to be seen again (voluntary retrenchment packages tend to be taken by the very people the business needs to hold onto; those who fear being able to get another job rarely take voluntary redundancy offers). The rest of the birds settle back on new branches, designated by the new management.

The process takes an average of two years, at the end of which there is an organisation perfectly suited to the circumstances of two years ago. At this point, not infrequently, the management team or key members of it are head hunted. They leave.

It is the birds just settled on the new branches who are left to manage the inefficiencies generated by the change processes. As they try to settle down, a new management team are appointed and the cycle threatens to start all over again.

Is it any wonder that there is a high degree of cynicism in the workplace?

BARRIERS TO PARTICIPATION — THE PSYCHOLOGICAL BARRIERS BETWEEN MANAGERS AND EMPLOYEES

Have you ever met a famous person or watched someone else meet a famous person? I have — done both, that is — and it is fascinating to observe what happens. I remember re-meeting Olivia Newton John in the late nineteen-seventies, at the height of her singing fame. I say 're-met' because Olivia used to live next door to us as children. I remember her well. She loved horses but didn't have any of her own. We did — my brother Simon, most memorably! Simon actually didn't particularly enjoy riding or, more to the point, all the responsibilities that went with it, especially mucking out the stables in winter. Unlike Simon, Olivia loved horses, everything about them, with considerable passion. She was thrilled when Simon let her muck out the stables, groom Tiger (Simon's remarkably bright pony) and, with luck, actually go riding.

I thought little of Olivia. I liked her. She was then (as now) friendly, warm, kind, natural. I talked to her without inhibition (or ignored her completely, as children are wont to do if the occasion requires it). She and her family ebbed in and out of our lives, as we did in theirs.

As Olivia carved herself a place in the world music scene, she became, in no uncertain terms, famous. On the other hand, we remained in Australia, carving ourselves a place of fame in the figment of our own imaginations!

At the height of Olivia's fame, I had the opportunity to meet her after a concert at the Dallas Brooks Hall, Melbourne. My mother and I were invited back stage (together with about another hundred or so people hungry to touch the hem of fame). We had a small gift for Olivia, lovingly wrapped in tissue paper.

Under normal circumstances I was an articulate and intelligent young woman; my mother even more so, just a little older. Unfortunately, as soon as we managed to find Olivia and speak to her, our anxiety about doing the right thing, making a lasting impression, basking momentarily in the sunshine of her success put paid to even the slightest vestiges of intelligence in either of us (my mother and I, that is).

We mumbled and stumbled our way through our 'hellos', managed inelegantly to remind Olivia who we were, were so overwhelmed when she remembered us all (Simon and Tiger included) that we were lost for words. We thrust our present clumsily into her hand, explaining like a couple of hillbillies that "it was Tiger's tail and he was dead so she could have it." I seem to remember that Olivia went visibly pale, softly and politely said she had to move on, and then bolted into the crowd with the speed of a cat being pursued by rabid dogs.

I laugh about it now (and I hope Olivia does too), but at the time, it was a nightmare. Among horse-loving people, it is not uncommon to take the hair from the tail of a horse you have loved. It is washed, silver bound and is often a prized item. Giving it to Olivia was a genuine sign of respectful friendship and understanding from people who loved horses.

"But did you have to say he was dead and he wouldn't be needing it any more," I groaned in the car, "just like that, out of the blue." My mother was mortified. "I don't know where that came from. I was so dumbstruck when we finally got to talk to her I couldn't think what to say."

This, of course, is the 'star-struck' syndrome. It happens with most of us when we meet famous people.

The 'star-struck' syndrome can also affect employees when they meet senior management. Imagine spending your working days in a yard, operating a forklift. You mix with other men and women who work in the yard — drivers, dock hands, administrative staff. You wear rough-and-ready clothing, overalls, jeans, t-shirts, company battle jackets for the cold weather. Nothing fancy. People call a spade a spade. Jokes abound, sometimes pretty crude. No one is too fussed if you swear. It's a down-to-earth, friendly atmosphere that suits everyone.

Then, one day, after working in the business for quite a long time, you get a message that the new CEO is coming to visit your site. Initially, you are nonchalant, but as the anticipation of the visit hots up, local management send out instructions to 'tidy things up' and make sure the yard is ship-shape. Everyone is told to look their best and be on best behaviour.

Eventually, the CEO arrives. You see him arrive, in a Mercedes. Someone else is driving. When he gets out, you wipe your now-sweaty hands on your pants, already feeling inadequate, even from this distance. He is tall, and wears the sort of suit you see people on television wear. He disappears into the local manager's office. Everyone in the yard is waiting for him to reappear; two hours pass. Eventually he emerges and, wearing a broad smile, he approaches your area. He appears confident, relaxed, very much at ease. He is flanked by the local manager and another senior executive from Head Office. Your local manager introduces you but the CEO appears to already know your name. You shake hands. His hand is cool, your is sticky. The man speaks to you, asks you some key questions, but you are so overwhelmed by the person's proximity and the very real difference in dress and presence that you can't think of anything to say — despite the fact that yesterday you could have filled three books with comments on what was happening to the business and how things could be done differently. You are star-struck. You don't want to be, but you are.

The CEO goes around and meets a few other people. He spends five, ten, maybe fifteen minutes here at the coalface, then disappears. The moment he leaves there is a universal sigh, and then everyone starts talking at once. Some say what a great bloke he is and how things might be different now he is in the top seat — after all, he's started on the right footing by coming out to meet the troops. But something in your gut doesn't feel right and over the next couple of days, conversations around the yard tell you that a lot of people don't feel right about the visit. You start asking questions: What was actually achieved by the visit? Did he *really* meet anyone, see anything of importance? Why couldn't it all have been done informally? Why did you have to meet the CEO in the presence of the local manager? Why was the CEO dressed the way he was? What would it have been like if he had spent two hours with the troops and fifteen minutes with the manager?

A week after the CEO's flying visit, the rumble of concern has turned into an articulate message of frustration — a sentiment at odds with the CEO's picture of reality. The people at the coalface still cry "We don't see senior management enough" yet the CEO says "but I was just there, talking to everyone and they seemed more than happy."

Crazy really. And do you know what it boils down to? A barrier. A barrier artificially set up by distance, the clothing we wear and the way we speak. The tragedy is that mis-communication abounds as a result of the barrier. One group of people think one thing is happening, and another, something entirely different. The barrier is exaggerated by distance and lack of genuine interpersonal familiarity.

Is addressing the problem really the stuff of MBAs and further education for leaders? Or is it the stuff of logic and common sense? Do we just have to think about what we need to do differently in order to have more productive contact and be less intimidating or intimidated when we meet people?

If so many employees feel that business could be improved substantially if contact with their business leaders was more frequent and less fraught with anxiety, then surely that should provide adequate motivation for new strategies.

POLITICS — THE POWER OF KNOWING THE RIGHT PEOPLE AT THE RIGHT TIME AND IN THE RIGHT PLACE

I once was involved with a company holding a series of national meetings designed to roll out the vision of the organisation and to get everyone thinking about what exactly they were going to do, state by state, to turn this vision into a reality.

I had visited three states so far and the process had been enormously successful. People were excited and motivated. The General Manager was making sure everyone had the opportunity to contribute to the design of the strategic plan to support the vision.

At the last meeting, twenty or so people were present, representing all levels of the particular state's business. The day was proceeding better than most people had anticipated and everyone was enjoying themselves. We interrupted proceedings for lunch. People were animated and, even during the break, were continuing discussions over sandwiches. Unbeknownst to me, the most senior manager in the meeting took a call during lunch. Apparently, he and two other members of the team had been recalled to head office to answer "critically urgent queries from the CEO of the organisation." There was no question of debating the demand. The request was from the most senior person in the business; if people valued their jobs, they would jump to it. The atmosphere in the room plummeted. The people didn't want to leave. No one wanted them to leave. Though we felt it was the wrong thing to do, no one felt able to challenge the request.

I was irritated. The capacity of senior management to intimidate or emasculate people without even knowing they are doing it appalls me. (It also appalls senior management when they find out what has happened — something that happens all too rarely.)

I dug my heals in. I made it clear that I thought that the departure of the people in question would make the day untenable. I was told there was nothing that could be done. I disagreed. I was sure that the leader in question had no idea of the repercussions of the request. I also was sure that if the leader was made aware of the effect of the request, an alternative plan would happily be agreed to.

My resolve prompted a flurry of phone calls, whispered conversations and eventually, with grins all round, the return to the meeting of the people in question. It was a salutary lesson for all of us.

When I mentioned the episode, in private, to the General Manager he was astonished at the reaction in the meeting. His frustration was that no matter how often (in his mind) he had told his people to stand up for something if they believed in it, they were still being intimidated.

We talked for a long time about the impact of politics and the fear that a political hierarchy causes in an organisation. We ignore the generation of fear at our own peril. It is one of the few things that will move me to anger. Political hierarchies are not about good business practices. They are about people protecting power bases; they are about what people look like, how they talk, what they get paid and what cars they drive. They are about isolation and disassociation. They are not about working together, valuing people, synergy.

I have spent my life growing up with, and now working with, so-called famous people, high achievers — leaders in many quarters, political, social and business. Overall, one thing stands out: truly great leaders are not motivated by politics and they do not instil fear in the people around them. There is a degree of humility. They always leave you feeling valued, as if they have listened carefully to what you said. They are curious and genuinely interested in learning.

Ultimately, if we genuinely want participation, then in large organisations especially, the first step is to get rid of the politics of rank and title, and replace the fear factor with the power of respect. In the words of Corelli Barnett, an American historian (writing in *The Power Of Leadership — The Definitive Masterclass*, the scripts, Vols 1 & 2, page 6):

> *One has to say that if you in fact draw your officers from one very distinct social class and the rank and file from another, and especially if the education system gives the upper class the monopoly of higher education, then they have an in built advantage in terms of telling other people what to do and how to do it. Now, when that evens up and everybody has been pretty well educated there is a very broad spread of developed intelligence. Then the officer, or in industry for that matter the manager, can't count on the sort of in built advantages as a leader, and therefore people have got to be able to lead on their own merits and not simply count on rank badges or social badges.*

DO LEADERS OWN THE PROCESS OF PARTICIPATION OR DO THEY MERELY GIVE LIP SERVICE TO IT?

Although some leaders genuinely own the process of participation and value its outcomes, there are many who still don't really understand what the implications are of the simple statement "Our people are our most important asset." I have heard countless managers and senior leaders make unequivocal statements about the importance of staff. They declare that "without our people we have no business" yet in the next breath talk about education, resources, wage negotiations, restructures, terminations, redundancies, consultation as if they were involved in a numbers game. These people glide from heart to head with ease — and along the way they lose something vital. That they've lost something is sadly apparent when cynicism prevails in the workplace.

An extraordinary number of Australian organisations have, in the last decade, undergone restructures, mergers, change processes, takeovers or downsizing, many several times over. In each instance several or all of the following have occurred:

– redundancies without consultation with the staff (albeit extensively with influential unions, to avoid possible industrial action);

– management of redundancies 'by the book', with little regard for the emotional impact of the process, either for those retrenched or those left behind;

– systems changes without consultation with or adequate explanation to employees;

– halting quality processes dead — in a merger one party has quality accreditation, the other doesn't;

– importation of external management, in the belief that there are inadequately skilled people in the business but without adequate internal research or appropriate support education of existing staff;

– secretive management meetings, the broad content of which everyone knows, the substantive content of which no one will share; or

– cost cutting, especially of education and human resource needs, without reference to those affected.

At some stage in the business cycle, the very people who have had to weather some or all of the above are asked to take a new leadership team seriously. They are expected to respond positively when these leaders propose a new order, a new future which (in theory, at least) places the people of the organisation at the top of the business stakes.

Why should management be believed? Why should they be supported? Until leaders demonstrate with action the rhetoric they have become fond of espousing in recent years, support from employees is going to be slow in coming.

Many Australian employees feel that the processes which support empowerment and broadly based participation are not fully understood by senior management. Management may have heard about the processes, read about them, had the theory explained, but implementation is delegated. Although delegation sometimes may be appropriate, tasks all too frequently end up in the hands of those without the appropriate leverage or authority. The process of change is then easily sabotaged, perhaps inadvertently, by senior management who place their needs over those of the person delegated to support the process of participation.

It happens all too frequently. It's corrosive effect is subtle, but damaging. Harm can come from deliberate decisions. Take the decision by the head office to put all accounts on minimum 30 day payment schedules from date of receipt of final invoice. The decision makes sense in terms of head office administrative efficiencies, it will save time and money at head office, but there is no reference to those in the field, the people actually affected, who day by day deal with suppliers. Unfortunately and typically, the repercussions of this sort of action can be disproportionate in relation to the apparent simplicity of the decision. In our current scenario, out in the field, supplies are cut from a local stationer that the business has been using for fifteen years because their 7 day invoice has not been paid. The first the local employees hear of the head office decision is when they find they cannot get A4 paper to produce their monthly report on for Head Office administration!

Harm can also come from indirect neglect. People might not fully consider the repercussions of a decision they are taking. There might be a discussion between the marketing and sales department about increasing the price on a particular product the company is selling. They decide to increase the price by ten percent. Customers are advised, but the service department (who have had nothing to do with the decision) are not informed. The first they hear about the change is when they notice an increase in service calls and a shift in the relationship with customers who are feeling unhappy about the price increase and are compensating for it by making greater use of the service facility included as part of the purchase price.

Many people, isolated in head offices, away from where business actually takes place, forget that they are in a servicing role. They begin to see much of what happens at the coalface of the business (where, incidentally, the customer often lives) as an inconvenience, an irritant. Decisions that flow from the top erode the principal of participation and make the work of coalface management doubly difficult. People begin to ask why they should bother; they begin to doubt that decisions taken locally will be supported by head office.

Whatever the seeming cause — geographic spread of locations, or staff — the problems really reflect a lack of quality thinking. Repercussions are ill-considered and feedback — after the decision is taken — is poorly assessed.

HUMAN RESOURCES — PART OF THE POWER GAME OR BACK-ROOM BROKER?

I have pondered at length this particular paradox: most leaders acknowledge the importance of people in the overall scheme of things, yet many fail to support adequately or even identify the tools which will help people achieve their personal and united best. I think there are two parts to the equation: the first is that majority of leaders are poorly skilled in managing people; the second is that a majority of experts in human resource management are poorly skilled leaders. The leader doesn't understand the Human Resource paradigm, and the human resource expert lacks the tools of leadership, the power of persuasion and the management of a position of authority. In the usual order of business, this mismatch sees the interests of the senior manager win through, at the expense of the interests of the human resource expert.

So it is that in many companies, employees struggle with the position held by Human Resources. Few believe that their leaders take HR seriously — certainly not as seriously as finance or production — despite repeatedly saying how important people are.

Most HR people I have worked with can readily identify problems they face:

– inadequate funding to achieve the ambitions of leadership;

– inadequate funding to address the needs of the business;

– policies determined by leadership which adversely affect the execution of HR plans (for instance, the dictum "we will not use any external providers for the delivery of this or that training" might seem alright — until it is discovered that the organisation has neither the expertise nor the time to deliver the perceived much-needed programs);

– relegation of HR requests to the bottom of the list in senior management meetings (with sales, production, finance problems being debated ahead of HR issues);

– inadequate (sometimes non-existent) senior leadership support for, understanding of or interest in HR plans.

These problems are not true of all businesses but they are true of many. Those organisations in which they are not an issue are often businesses that have elevated the importance of HR. The CEO or Managing Director may have this expertise or, more commonly, recognises its importance and the 2IC to the MD will be an HR director. (How do you like my TLAs? Two-and three-letter acronyms!)

STAYING POWER — WILL THIS MANAGEMENT TEAM STICK AROUND?

In my experience, businesses that have constancy of leadership are more stable and more united. High leadership turnover leads to instability, cynicism, lack of business continuity and a decline in commitment at all levels.

Without consultation, without decision makers drawing upon the combined intelligence of all the people affected by the decision, the departure of key leaders will impact on not only every aspect of the business but also on the levels of motivation of the people in the business.

As solutions become more complex in business, the environment more frenetic, we have, in the changeable and some would say chaotic end of the twentieth century, been inclined to clutch at straws to save ourselves. For instance, some have turned to the 'whiz kid' leaders — purportedly very clever, exceptional young dynamic leaders — whose track record appears to be so astonishing that all are invited to bow down in the wake of their genius.

Of course, as with much that we desire, their attractiveness not infrequently turns out to be marketing hype more than anything else. The whiz kids are head hunted — and paid extraordinarily well — to help turn a sick company into a well company. But this is what frequently occurs in these 'turn-around' processes:

- 'diagnostics' are conducted which involve predominantly senior management, to confirm that the business is in a serious mess (for instance, it may be found that the business is, weekly, losing a substantial sum of money);

- within a short time, members of the management team are replaced, the CEO or MD preferring people he has selected himself, and a 'them versus us' attitude develops between old management and new;

- internal mergers of certain departments take place (instead, say, of having administration functions in five states, administration is consolidated into head office), providing impetus for planned redundancies (retrenchment payouts being balanced against anticipated future savings);

- twenty percent of the workforce are deemed expendable — the finance department demonstrating that this alone will bring the company to a break-even point within twelve months;

- all 'extraneous expenditures' are stopped immediately, affecting advertising and human resources (training) first.

Even if little else is done, such actions will very quickly yield (or can be made to show) bottom line results. The MD is seen to be doing the job remarkably well and the head hunters, who have never really lost contact with the whiz kid they helped place, start the corrosive process of suggesting to the MD they have an even better job opportunity waiting around the corner.

Two to three years after taking up the appointment (and frequently sooner) the MD has departed. In isolation this would not be as frustrating to the business as it actually is — if it only affected the MD and his staff. However, with each new senior appointment comes a plethora of associated management changes. It also frequently becomes apparent that the changes initiated have not produced the anticipated savings but have actually produced more harm than good.

The whiz kid cycle occurs often in business; staff find the strategy objectionable. Firstly staff resent the suggestion that all solutions lie in the hands of senior managers. Then they rightly ask, if these managers are such solution-providers, why are they constantly changed?

No one minds, necessarily, change. Indeed, many see value in restructuring (or, to use a more recent buzz word, 'organisational reinvention'). What they are frustrated by is the extent of change, the frequency, the absence of consultation and the isolated yet frequently changing management structure.

What leadership issues do leaders raise and why?

While many of the comments made so far relate to managers as well as employees, there are a few issues which reflect the exclusive frustrations of leaders. So, what follows is the leadership perspective on the challenges of leadership in business today.

CHANGING RESPONSIBILITIES OF LEADERSHIP

Once upon a time, the parameters defining good leadership were fairly clear. As Corelli Barnett observes, when education was the exclusive domain of upper social class and rank, the function of leadership was clear. Leaders had skills that the rank and file lacked, so they were respected — regardless of their interpersonal skills. Today, education is more broadly applied and we have a resulting "spread of developed intelligence". So what are leaders required to do, if it not to give us instructions? Let's face it, we resent being told what to do; after all, we have our own ideas based on our own experience. We want different things from leaders; some of those new skills involve the following:

MENTORING: Supporting our education and learning cycle, mentors are interested in our welfare and development. If we are satisfied and continuously developing, we see that this has an immediate and long term benefit for the business; increasingly we see the responsibility of mentoring in the hands of leaders.

COACHING: If a leader knows more than an employee, there is an expectation that the leader will be able to teach, motivate and enthuse. The coach looks at the performance of the whole and ensures that all team members are pulling in the same direction; the coach also supports individuals who may be having difficulties. We expect a leader to be a coach.

BEING A FRIEND: No one wants a standover person in a senior position; no one wants a bad tempered, arrogant, bullish, narrow minded, bigoted manager. We perform far better when our manager is our friend, someone we can talk to easily, confide in, admit our mistakes to, discuss what to do next with — and all without fear of reprisal.

BEING A FUTURIST: As discussed in the previous chapter, employees are looking for guidance on the future. If employees are responsible for the day-to-day management of a business, they want to know that their managers are looking to the future. They want managers to be strategic futurists, envisioning an otherwise murky future. They want managers to harness the potential views of all employees and to focus endeavour on a common sense of the future.

Given these new demands, and considering where we have come from and the usual criteria of selection for many managers, it is not hard to see where some management anxiety comes from. Many leaders want to be able to fulfil these new needs, but they lack the skills. Coaching and mentoring doesn't come naturally to everyone. As for envisioning the future — we've already identified the considerable challenges in doing this.

Many leaders recognise they need additional education, but frequently, they don't know how to arrange it, let alone find the time, given their business and family commitments. The know their responsibilities have changed but they, like all of us facing the need to re-educate ourselves, are genuinely uncertain about their ability to succeed playing a familiar game with very unfamiliar tools.

FEAR OF FAILURE — RAPIDITY OF REPLACEMENT

Many managers are also genuinely afraid of retrenchment. They feel watched over and think that as a result of changing work practices, they are no longer needed. Some feel intimidated by politics and feel that decisions are made with undue reference to more senior management.

Despite the increasingly common rhetoric among senior managers about the value of generating learning environments in which mistakes are seen as 'learning opportunities', most people — who are not at the very top of the business ladder — don't believe the rhetoric. In fact, a large number of managers believe that mistakes are frowned upon and are used as evidence of incompetence, rather than as an indicator of learning. In a politically motivated hierarchy mistakes can be hoarded, publicised, manipulated — at a range of levels in the business — and rarely to the benefit of the person who made the mistake. Managers then learn to either cover their mistakes or, perhaps far more commonly, avoid taking risky decisions.

I am reminded of a meeting I had some time ago with senior management of a bank. They were discussing training for 'relationship managers' with me. Relationship managers were really commercial lending managers, responsible for working with reasonably large accounts. These managers were thought to be timid with their lending initiatives, insofar as they tended only to respond to requests for money from clients within the constraints of the specific request.

If the client's financial status didn't fit the 'rules' of the bank, then they would say "sorry — no go on the loan application." Senior management were frustrated. They said they wanted their relationship managers to think more laterally — to look for solutions and not to be so hidebound by the so-called rule book. I asked a question: "What would be your response to a relationship manager who botched up a loan?" "Well," came the answer, "we wouldn't expect that to happen. But if it did, we would have to look seriously at whether or not the person was well suited to being a relationship manager."

That response, of course, revealed to me why relationship managers were timid. In such an environment, I would be too. We closed our discussions shortly thereafter.

I recognise that the anxiety over making mistakes can go all the way to the top. No one likes mistakes, especially costly ones. But mistakes should be expected: we should allow latitude in the learning cycle. Rather than being punitive, we should reinforce the learning opportunities that mistakes generate. Rather than being blamed for engendering a politically motivated environment, they should be the backbone of the learning organisation.

FEAR OF THE COALFACE

Many leaders feel uncomfortable at the coalface of their own businesses. If some employees feel star-struck (albeit momentarily) when meeting very senior management, many leaders really don't like or don't feel comfortable meeting their own employees (although they will rarely own up to it). A CEO will meet the 'workers' flanked by the local manager and another head office executive *because he doesn't feel comfortable doing it alone.*

Many senior managers have little contact with the hands-on side of their businesses. They are imported into the business because of their prior work history (in many cases, because they have been consistently in management for a considerable number of years), perhaps because of their academic record and, of course, because of their senior management track record. To such people, the coalface can become (or always has been) alien territory: clothing, language, faces, forms, style and culture are totally different. They are not sure how to behave or speak.

Looked at this way, we begin to see how two-way communication becomes vexed when both parties are anxious and unsure of the rules!

COMPLEXITY OF A POLITICALLY MOTIVATED ENVIRONMENT

Although many leaders and managers are very good at playing politics, very few like it. Most believe life and business would be better without it. The trouble is, once entrenched, few people know how to break the cycle.

The irony of a strongly political environment is that everyone knows about it and it is frequently the topic of conversation after hours over a drink — how to beat it, win it, defeat it, manage it. People know who sits in which political camp and why; who to deal with to produce what outcome and by when; who to avoid and why. It's as if we are part of a game, chess perhaps. We are the pieces on the board, each moving according to certain rules that guide or restrict our movement, unsure, however, of the overall game plan and rarely confident that the people who sit in the Grand Masters chairs are, indeed, the Grand Masters they claim themselves to be. Few of us want to be part of the game, and yet we play on, not knowing how to escape. It is the Abilene Paradox at its worst. Speak up and you might lose your head; be silent in the wrong context and you might be demoted. People watch their backs and are wary of other hungrier, better qualified, more politically adept up-and-comings. The political environment can be manifestly overt, present on a daily basis, or covert, subtly permeating decisions at all levels (and never more so than in the hallowed corridors of the Executive team or the Board).

There are particular business outcomes that result from a politically motivated leadership:

– middle management decisions reflect less the perceived best course of action and more the 'right' course of action according to the prevailing political power base;

– information is hoarded as a tool for exercising power; dissemination is selective — to give it away liberally is to undermine the power base;

– bully tactics are used by those who've got political clout over those who haven't; people can be manipulated into doing things that their better instincts suggest they shouldn't do;

– consultative processes don't work, or work inadequately: it isn't possible to consult effectively when the results of consultation will be overridden by the prevailing political power base;

– change initiatives become obtuse; people take indirect paths to achieve results because they need to be seen to be doing the right thing (and, to get an outcome, they might first need to gain the support of a key political figure).

In real time, where things are happening rapidly, any and all of these outcomes slow business down and diminish individual responsibility and innovation.

SECRECY — PLAYING THE GAME CLOSE TO YOUR CHEST

There is a not uncommon notion among senior management that the rank and file — including all management not at senior executive level —

should not be informed of certain business decisions. The fear is that if the rank and file were to know the truth, they might (a) leave in their dozens or hundreds or (b) might run to the opposition and reveal all.

Many senior managers are uncomfortable with secrecy but still have a concern about whether or not (a) or (b) will occur. I am convinced the concern is based on a lack of real understanding of how information travels. Firstly, the grapevine between you and your opposition is the fastest form of communication known to man. Short of turning your business into a Fort Knox and at night locking up all employees, you can be sure that information will travel — people talk. The extraordinary thing is that information on critical issues gets out into the public domain at about the same time that management talk about it. How this occurs is anyone's guess. I suspect it happens because senior management themselves talk — to secretaries, friends, spouses, close business associates — before they discuss it with senior management teams! How's that for a paradigm shift?

Whatever the source, information about most things travels swiftly. Unfortunately, gossip is unconfirmed and is subject to embellishment. More frequently than seems reasonable, competitors hear the unembellished truth before the people who work in the organisation. That does wonders for commitment and motivation!

Secrecy undermines values and challenges the integrity of many leaders. Those closer to the coalface understand that people won't leave in their droves if they hear the truth about plans for retrenchments, mergers, takeovers and so on. In fact, if people are informed they respect the fact that they have been trusted with information. If the information signals a possible change in their own circumstances, they then assume that they will also have the opportunity to discuss the changes and put their penny-worth in. (More on this in the next chapter.)

SOMETHING ELSE TO PONDER...

We've just finished talking about the major leadership issues raised by the majority of people I have encountered in the course of my work, but I want to highlight another factor before closing the discussion.

A large part of the leadership problem is to do with the acute shortage of women in senior management positions. I will give free reign to a variety of thoughts I have on women in business in the chapter that deals with this exclusively, but it warrants a mention here because it is very possible that many of the problems we are experiencing in the mismanagement of people reflect the paucity of relationship skills among leaders *and they may have more to do with gender than education.*

Perhaps nature is wise in that 'she' seeks a balance in the order of the universe and whenever that order is undermined, something goes wrong. I am not suggesting that women are the answer — far from it. I am rather suggesting that when one group of people make a decision for all of us without adequate representation of the opinions of the people they will affect, then the probability of their decision making being inadequate is fairly high.

I would further suggest that women generally (though not in all cases) are very good at managing relationships and broadly-based communication. That is not to say that men can't manage these as well; it is simply that women may find it easier. Unfortunately, while the majority of senior positions of power and authority are held by men, women are not going to surface at the most senior levels in anything like the quantity we need simply because the process of selection is predicated upon a biased paradigm. Will women ever be able to fulfil the requirements set by male MDs and CEOs? If they do, will we see them bringing into the decision making process those very skills that are currently missing from so many leadership circles? Or will the process of selection already have screened out those women who would be able to do this in preference to those women who fit the existing paradigm?

At the beginning of *An Anthropologist On Mars* (Oliver Sacks, Picador, 1995), Sacks (of *Awakenings* fame), a gentle and compassionate man, makes the following observation:

For me, as a physician, nature's richness is to be studied in the phenomena of health and disease, in the endless forms of individual adaptation by which human organisms, people, adapt and reconstruct themselves, faced with the challenges and vicissitudes of life.

I would like to suggest that it is in the capacity of humans — faced with the challenges and vicissitudes of life — to adapt and reconstruct themselves that our greatest opportunities lie. Who better to harness our greatness than the leaders — those who would be coaches, mentors, friends and visionaries. Leadership is a privilege that people bestow on individuals who they feel can best serve them. Don't be mistaken into thinking leadership is something bestowed by other leaders or Boards. It may appear so, but nothing is more powerless than a leader with a title who the troops do not respect.

Practical help

LEADERSHIP APPRAISAL

I HAVE INCLUDED HERE GENERIC APPRAISAL FORMS FOR LEADERSHIP. ONE IS FOR EMPLOYEES TO FILL OUT, THE OTHER IS FOR MANAGERS. THEY PROVIDE THE OPPORTUNITY TO DETERMINE WHERE YOUR LEADER'S FOCUS OF ATTENTION COULD BE PLACED, IF THEY WANT TO IMPROVE THEIR ABILITIES AS A LEADER. IF THIS IS THE FIRST TIME YOU AS A MANAGER OR EMPLOYEE HAVE APPRAISED OR BEEN APPRAISED IN THIS MANNER, DON'T BE AFRAID! I DID IT A COUPLE OF YEARS AGO AND IT HAS BEEN ONE OF THE MOST VALUABLE FEEDBACK TOOLS I HAVE EVER HAD.

CERTAINLY, LEADERSHIP APPRAISAL CAN CAUSE ANXIETY. EMPLOYEES FEEL THAT THEY MIGHT GET INTO TROUBLE IF THEY APPRAISE A LEADER HONESTLY; LEADERS CAN FEEL INTIMIDATED BY THE RESULTS. IF YOU WANT TO DO THIS YOURSELF INSTEAD OF USING A FACILITATOR, HERE IS MY RECOMMENDATION. TO BEGIN WITH, DO THE APPRAISALS ANONYMOUSLY. TAKE A LEADERSHIP TEAM LIST AND PUT AGAINST EACH PERSON A QUANTITY OF RESPONDENTS ONLY. FOR INSTANCE, "JIM BLOGGS, SEVEN PEOPLE" REFERS TO THE NUMBER OF APPRAISALS YOU CAN EXPECT TO RECEIVE FOR JIM. THE APPRAISAL FORMS ARE SENT OUT TO RESPONDENTS TOGETHER WITH A STAMPED, SELF-ADDRESSED ENVELOPE. NOMINATE AN OUTSIDE PERSON WHO CAN COLLATE RESPONSES ON BEHALF OF EMPLOYEES AND LEADERS. THIS PERSON TAKES THE RESPONSES FOR, SAY, JIM AND COLLATES THEM INTO AN AVERAGE ON ONE SHEET.

THIS SHEET IS THEN SENT TO JIM DIRECTLY. (IF YOU'RE USING A FACILITATOR, IT FORMS PART OF A MANAGEMENT RETREAT. AT THE RETREAT, LEADERS ARE TAKEN THROUGH THEIR FORMS AND GIVEN THE OPPORTUNITY TO DISCUSS RESULTS AND DEVELOP PERSONAL PLANS FOR IMPROVING THEIR PERFORMANCE.)

IT IS IMPORTANT TO LOOK AFTER LEADERS IN THIS PROCESS. I AM VERY RESPECTFUL OF THE COURAGE IT TAKES TO RECEIVE FEEDBACK OF THIS KIND, SO ANONYMITY ON BOTH SIDES SHOULD BE PRESERVED. BY THE SAME TOKEN, MUCH AS IT IS EASIER TO LOSE WEIGHT OR TAKE UP EXERCISE WHEN YOU SHARE YOUR AMBITIONS WITH OTHERS, LEADERS WHO SHARE THEIR PLANS FOR IMPROVEMENT WITH THEIR TEAMS AND WHO INVITE FEEDBACK WILL ACTUALLY ACHIEVE TWO THINGS: THEY WILL ACCELERATE THEIR LEARNING, AND THEY WILL GO UP IN THE

LEADERSHIP STAKES. IT HAS BEEN MY EXPERIENCE THAT PEOPLE GREATLY RESPECT A LEADER WHO DEMONSTRATES AN HONEST WILLINGNESS TO LEARN FROM FEEDBACK.

IT IS USEFUL IN THIS TYPE OF APPRAISAL PROCESS IF THE LEADER DOES THEIR APPRAISAL SEPARATELY. HOW THEY THINK THEY WOULD BE RATED BY THEIR PEOPLE CAN THEN BE MATCHED AGAINST ACTUAL RESULTS. SOMETIMES THIS PRODUCES MORE INTERESTING RESULTS THAN THE STAFF APPRAISAL ALONE!

THE APPRAISAL IS IN THREE SECTIONS: THE FIRST ASSESSES THE INDIVIDUAL IN TERMS OF LEADERSHIP SKILLS AND BEHAVIOURS, THE SECOND LOOKS AT THEIR ABILITY TO WORK IN A TEAM ENVIRONMENT AND THE THIRD FOCUSES ON THEIR BUSINESS ACUMEN. IN THIS LAST CATEGORY YOU WILL NOTICE THAT I HAVE A SECTION FOR ASSESSING MERCHANDISING SKILLS. FOR ANYONE IN RETAILING, THIS WILL MAKE SENSE; HOWEVER, IF YOU ARE IN A SERVICE INDUSTRY, OR SOME OTHER SECTOR, SIMPLY REPLACE MERCHANDISING WITH THE APPROPRIATE PRODUCT CATEGORY.

God is in his heaven but does anyone trust him anymore?

LEADERSHIP APPRAISAL (FOR EMPLOYEES)

RATE YOUR LEADER FROM 1 (BEING POOR) TO 5 (BEING EXCELLENT) ON THE CATEGORIES
LISTED BELOW.

LEADER'S NAME: ....

LOCATION: ....

HOW WELL DOES YOUR LEADER DEMONSTRATE THE FOLLOWING:

LEADERSHIP   DO THEY HAVE THE ABILITY TO LEAD THE
                    TEAM BY SETTING AN EXAMPLE?   [   ]

RESPONSIBILITY   DO THEY ACCEPT THE CONSEQUENCES OF
                    THEIR ACTIONS AND ARE THEY WILLING TO
                    MAKE DAY-TO-DAY DECISIONS?   [   ]

FLEXIBILITY   DO THEY ACCEPT OR CREATE NEW IDEAS
                    AND CHANGES EASILY?   [   ]

COMMITMENT   DO THEY MAINTAIN MOTIVATION, ENTHUSIASM
                    AND DO WHATEVER IT TAKES TO GET THE JOB DONE?   [   ]

TRUSTWORTHINESS   DO THEY ACT IN WAYS THAT ENCOURAGE
                    PEOPLE TO TRUST THEM — DO THEY KEEP
                    THEIR AGREEMENTS?   [   ]

HOW WOULD YOU RATE YOUR LEADER IN TERMS OF WORKING WITH YOU:

TEAM BUILDING   DO THEY ENCOURAGE TEAMWORK AND WORK
                    AS PART OF THE TEAM?   [   ]

DELEGATING   DO THEY DELEGATE EFFECTIVELY, GIVE YOU
                    RESPONSIBILITY?   [   ]

FEEDBACK   DO THEY ENCOURAGE OPEN FEEDBACK, BOTH
                    FOR THEMSELVES AND TO YOU INDIVIDUALLY?   [   ]

111

LISTENING SKILLS   DO THEY LISTEN WELL TO STAFF AND TO
CUSTOMERS AND ACT ACCORDINGLY?   [   ]

INFORMATION   DO THEY SHARE INFORMATION (REPORTS, MEMOS,
CIRCULARS) WITH YOU?   [   ]

DECISION MAKING   DO THEY MAKE GOOD QUALITY DECISIONS
WITHOUT PROCRASTINATING?   [   ]

ORGANISATION   ARE THEY INDIVIDUALLY WELL ORGANISED; DO
THEY ORGANISE THE BUSINESS EFFECTIVELY?   [   ]

COACHING   DO THEY SPEND TIME HELPING OTHERS TO DEVELOP
THEIR SKILLS — DO THEY INVEST IN/VALUE YOUR
EDUCATION?   [   ]

DOES YOUR LEADER HAVE A GOOD KNOWLEDGE OF THE FOLLOWING:

PLANNING   DO THEY HAVE A PLAN AND A SENSE OF THE
FUTURE; IS IT SHARED WITH AND OWNED BY THE
PEOPLE OF THE BUSINESS?   [   ]

PROCEDURES   DO THEY MANAGE CLEAR AND EFFECTIVE SYSTEMS
THAT REFLECT THE INTERESTS OF THE OVERALL GROUP? [   ]

MERCHANDISING   DO THEY INVOLVE THEMSELVES IN MERCHANDISING,
DO THEY ENCOURAGE OTHER PEOPLE TO IMPLEMENT
NEW MERCHANDISING IDEAS?   [   ]

FINANCES   DO THEY HAVE A CLEAR GRASP ON MANAGING
SALES, GROSS MARGIN AND EXPENSES AND RETURN
ON INVESTMENT?   [   ]

RESPONSIBILITIES   DO THEY UNDERSTAND WHAT PEOPLE DO AND WHY?   [   ]

IF YOU WOULD LIKE TO MAKE FURTHER COMMENTS, FEEL FREE TO DO SO.

God is in his heaven but does anyone trust him anymore?

LEADERSHIP APPRAISAL (FOR THE MANAGER)

RATE YOUR LEADER FROM 1 (BEING POOR) TO 5 (BEING EXCELLENT) ON THE CATEGORIES LISTED BELOW.

LEADER'S NAME: ....

LOCATION: ....

HOW WELL DO YOU BELIEVE YOU DEMONSTRATE THE FOLLOWING:

LEADERSHIP DO YOU HAVE THE ABILITY TO LEAD THE TEAM BY
SETTING AN EXAMPLE? [ ]

RESPONSIBILITY DO YOU ACCEPT THE CONSEQUENCES OF YOUR
ACTIONS AND ARE YOU WILLING TO MAKE DAY-TO-DAY
DECISIONS? [ ]

FLEXIBILITY DO YOU ACCEPT OR CREATE NEW IDEAS AND
CHANGES EASILY? [ ]

COMMITMENT DO YOU MAINTAIN MOTIVATION, ENTHUSIASM AND
DO WHATEVER IT TAKES TO GET THE JOB DONE? [ ]

TRUSTWORTHINESS DO YOU ACT IN WAYS THAT ENCOURAGE PEOPLE
TO TRUST YOU — DO YOU KEEP YOUR AGREEMENTS? [ ]

HOW WOULD YOU RATE YOURSELF IN TERMS OF WORKING WITH YOUR TEAM:

TEAM BUILDING DO YOU ENCOURAGE TEAMWORK AND WORK AS
PART OF THE TEAM? [ ]

DELEGATING DO YOU DELEGATE EFFECTIVELY, GIVE YOUR TEAM
RESPONSIBILITY? [ ]

FEEDBACK DO YOU ENCOURAGE OPEN FEEDBACK, BOTH FOR
YOURSELF AND TO INDIVIDUAL MEMBERS OF YOUR TEAM? [ ]

LISTENING SKILLS	DO YOU LISTEN WELL TO STAFF AND TO CUSTOMERS AND ACT ACCORDINGLY?	[ ]
INFORMATION	DO YOU SHARE INFORMATION (REPORTS, MEMOS, CIRCULARS) WITH STAFF?	[ ]
DECISION MAKING	DO YOU MAKE GOOD QUALITY DECISIONS WITHOUT PROCRASTINATING?	[ ]
ORGANISATION	ARE YOU INDIVIDUALLY WELL ORGANISED; DO YOU ORGANISE THE BUSINESS EFFECTIVELY?	[ ]
COACHING	DO YOU SPEND TIME HELPING OTHERS TO DEVELOP THEIR SKILLS — DO YOU INVEST IN/VALUE THEIR EDUCATION?	[ ]

DO YOU HAVE A GOOD KNOWLEDGE OF THE FOLLOWING:

PLANNING	DO YOU HAVE A PLAN AND A SENSE OF THE FUTURE; IS IT SHARED WITH AND OWNED BY THE PEOPLE OF THE BUSINESS?	[ ]
PROCEDURES	DO YOU MANAGE CLEAR AND EFFECTIVE SYSTEMS THAT REFLECT THE INTERESTS OF THE OVERALL GROUP?	[ ]
MERCHANDISING	DO YOU INVOLVE YOURSELF IN MERCHANDISING, DO YOU ENCOURAGE OTHER PEOPLE TO IMPLEMENT NEW MERCHANDISING IDEAS?	[ ]
FINANCES	DO YOU HAVE A CLEAR GRASP ON MANAGING SALES, GROSS MARGIN AND EXPENSES AND RETURN ON INVESTMENT?	[ ]
RESPONSIBILITIES	DO YOU UNDERSTAND WHAT PEOPLE DO AND WHY?	[ ]

IF YOU WOULD LIKE TO MAKE FURTHER OBSERVATIONS ABOUT YOURSELF, RECORD THEM ON A SEPARATE PAGE.

God is in his heaven but does anyone trust him anymore?

ACTION FOR EMPLOYEES

EMPLOYEES CAN DO SOMETHING ABOUT PROBLEMS WITH LEADERS. HERE ARE SOME IDEAS AND SUGGESTIONS:

1. DO THE DUMMY-SPIT

WHEN CHANGE COMES YOUR WAY THAT YOU THINK IS WRONG, ILL CONSIDERED OR LACKS ADEQUATE CONSULTATION, DO EVERYTHING YOU KNOW HOW NOT TO ACCEPT IT. WRITE TO THE SOURCE OF THE DIRECTIVE, SPEAK UP AT MEETINGS, ARRANGE AN APPOINTMENT WITH A SENIOR LEADER.

WHY?

BECAUSE TOO FEW LEADERS GET FEEDBACK FROM THE PEOPLE WHO ARE AFFECTED BY THEIR DECISIONS. DON'T BE AFRAID; YOU'LL BE SURPRISED HOW MANY MANAGERS ARE ACTUALLY SURPRISED AND DELIGHTED BY YOUR FEEDBACK.

2. SUPPORT THE LEARNING CYCLE OF YOUR MANAGER

— ASK YOUR MANAGER TO READ THIS CHAPTER AND ASK FOR THEIR FEEDBACK.

— SUGGEST THE IDEA OF A LEADERSHIP APPRAISAL, PARTICIPATE AND ENCOURAGE THE PARTICIPATION OF OTHER PEOPLE.

WHY?

BECAUSE IT IS EASIER TO LEARN WHEN YOU ARE SUPPORTED. MANY MANAGERS WANT TO LEARN BUT DON'T KNOW WHERE TO TURN FOR HELP. YOU, THIS BOOK, YOUR IDEAS MAY BE THE FIRST SOURCE. REMEMBER, THEY MAY BE AS ANXIOUS ABOUT COMING TO YOU AS YOU ARE ABOUT GOING TO THEM. WHO'S GOING TO MAKE THE FIRST MOVE?

3. DRESS TO KILL

— IF YOU ARE GOING TO MEET WITH SENIOR MANAGEMENT AND YOU DON'T HAVE A SUIT, BEG, BORROW OR 'STEAL' ONE, AND MAKE SURE THE MANAGER KNOWS YOU'VE DRESSED TO SET THEM AT EASE.

— WHEN A SENIOR MANAGER VISITS YOUR SITE, HAVE FUN AND DRESS THEM IN THE GEAR THAT IS APPROPRIATE - OVERALLS, SAFETY HAT, BOOTS, GLASSES, BATTLE JACKET. TAKE THEIR SUIT JACKET AND HANG IT UP; GET THEIR TIE OFF.

– IF A SENIOR MANAGER VISITS, HAVE MORNING TEA WITH THEM: FOOD AND GOOD HUMOUR DO MUCH TO BREAK DOWN THE BARRIERS IN MOST ENVIRONMENTS.

WHY?

YOU MIGHT NEED TO MAKE THE FIRST MOVE. BEING FIRM AND GOOD-NATURED IS THE BEST WAY I KNOW TO AFFECT CHANGE. INDEED, MOST SENIOR LEADERS WOULD BE DELIGHTED WITH AN INITIATIVE OF THIS KIND. WHEN MANAGEMENT COMES TO VISIT, BY MAKING SURE THEY LOOK LIKE EVERYONE ELSE YOU IMPROVE THEIR LISTENING SKILLS - AFTER ALL, IT'S HARD TO PAY ATTENTION WHEN YOU'RE THE LAST PENGUIN ON THE ICE FLOW AND YOU ARE SURROUNDED BY HUNGRY SEALS!

4. ACKNOWLEDGE THE POWER OF POLITICS

– IDENTIFY POLITICS IN YOUR BUSINESS.

– CREATE AN INFORMAL PROCESS TO DISCUSS ITS INFLUENCE - NEGATIVE AND POSITIVE.

– DRAW ATTENTION TO POLITICS AND SUGGEST WAYS TO AVOID IT.

– FIND OUT WHETHER THE POLITICS THAT YOU IMAGINE IS IN PLACE, IS, IN FACT, IN PLACE: SPEAK TO MANAGEMENT WHO YOU FEEL COMFORTABLE WITH; SEE IF THEY PERCEIVE THE SAME LEVEL OF POLITICS AS YOU.

– CHALLENGE OLD WAYS OF RESPONDING TO POWERFUL PEOPLE; ASK YOURSELF WHETHER THE SENIOR LEADERS IN YOUR BUSINESS REALLY UNDERSTAND THE REPERCUSSIONS OF WHAT THEY DO - DO THEY REALLY CARE?

WHY?

IF WE NEVER CHALLENGE THE WAY THINGS ARE, THEN THEY WON'T CHANGE - OR IF THEY DO CHANGE, IT WILL BE BY ACCIDENT RATHER THAN DESIGN. ONCE A POLITICAL FRAMEWORK IS EXPOSED, IT IS HARDER TO SUSTAIN. SOMEHOW, IT SEEMS A LITTLE SILLY IN THE BRIGHT LIGHT OF DAY.

5. CONSIDER HUMAN RESOURCES AND THE PROCESS OF PARTICIPATION

— Make sure you are an advocate of both.

— Watch for cynicism in your own dialogue: irrespective of how many things have gone wrong today, with the right attitude, things may be better tomorrow. The human resource function will guide the development of the business through the support and education of the people (that is, you).

— Take part in designing a process that will ensure all senior managers understand how the process of participation has changed the work you do.

— If new leaders move into your business, don't wait for them to decide when they'll visit you: extend your own invitation.

WHY?

How people talk about the world has a way of turning their vision into a reality. If you believe that people really are critical to the business, act accordingly. It might mean thinking about how you relate to other employees, how committed you are to your own education and how willing you are to accept responsibility for educating leaders, present and future.

ACTION FOR LEADERS

LEADERS WOULD DO WELL TO THINK ABOUT THE FOLLOWING IDEAS ON ADDRESSING PROBLEMS RELATED TO LEADERSHIP.

1. COMMIT TO THE APPRAISAL PROCESS

— DO IT! AND ACT ON THE FEEDBACK.

— CALIBRATE YOUR PERFORMANCE EVERY SIX MONTHS.

— INVITE INFORMAL FEEDBACK FROM PEOPLE WITH WHOM YOU ARE COMFORTABLE.

WHY?

IT IS THE ONLY TOOL YOU HAVE ON YOUR PERFORMANCE. YOU CAN GET FEEDBACK FROM PEERS OR SUPERIORS, BUT ULTIMATELY THE REAL MEASURE OF LEADERSHIP IS THE FEEDBACK YOU GET FROM YOUR OWN PEOPLE.

2. THINK ABOUT EDUCATION

— COMMIT TO YOUR OWN EDUCATION AS A CONTINUOUS PART OF YOUR LEADERSHIP RESPON-SIBILITIES.

— MAKE THE MOST OF THE EDUCATIONAL OPPORTUNITIES WITHIN YOUR BUSINESS: THE PROGRAMS BEING RUN, LEADERS THAT YOU AND STAFF ADMIRE.

— FIND OUT ABOUT EDUCATIONAL OPPORTUNITIES AT TAFEs, MANAGEMENT COLLEGES AND THROUGH PRIVATE PROVIDERS.

— MAKE TIME FOR EDUCATION, NOT BY SACRIFICING FAMILY TIME BUT BY (A) RECOGNISING THAT AN INVESTMENT IN YOUR EDUCATION IS PART OF YOUR JOB AND (B) BY PLANNING TO TAKE TIME OFF FOR EDUCATION.

WHY?

BECAUSE THE LACK OF MANAGEMENT EDUCATION REMAINS THE SINGLE BIGGEST PROBLEM WE CURRENTLY FACE IN AUSTRALIA. TOO FEW LEADERS HAVE WELL DEVELOPED COMMUNICATION AND PEOPLE SKILLS - YET EMPLOYEES ARE CRYING OUT FOR THEM.

3. BREAK THE POLITICAL PARADIGM

- CONDUCT AN INFORMAL WORKSHOP WITH ALL POLITICAL PLAYERS TO DISCUSS THE INFLU-ENCE OF POLITICS IN THE BUSINESS. COMMIT TO BEING HONEST IN THIS PROCESS.

- LOOK AT THE INFLUENCE OF POLITICS ON YOUR OWN PERFORMANCE: IN A 'PROS AND CONS' LIST, LOOK AT WHAT IS WORKING FOR AND AGAINST YOU; CONSIDER HOW TO RESPOND TO YOUR OWN ASSESSMENT.

- LOOK FOR SUPPORT IN BREAKING DOWN POLITICS: FIND OUT WHO ELSE IS FINDING IT UNHELPFUL.

- WHEN POLITICS SURFACES IN PUBLIC (IN A MEETING, FOR INSTANCE), YELL OUT "POLITICS IS IN THE ROOM, CAN WE KICK IT OUT!"

WHY?

POLITICAL MANAGEMENT IS ITS OWN CATCH 22 - IT LEADS NOWHERE AND, IN THE END, HURTS BOTH THE BUSINESS AND THE PEOPLE EMBROILED IN THE POLITICAL FURORE. ALL IT TAKES TO RID OURSELVES OF THE POLITICS WHICH SHADOWS US IS FOR A FEW PEOPLE TO DECIDE TO CHANGE, TO HAVE AN ENVIRONMENT IN WHICH IT IS SAFE TO EXPOSE PROBLEMS AND SEEK A CREATIVE COMMITMENT TO THEIR RESOLUTION.

4. CROSS THE FEAR BARRIER

- ARE YOU SCARED OF BEING SEEN TO MAKE MISTAKES? IF SO, WORK OUT WHY. CONSIDER MISTAKES THAT HAVE ACTUALLY WORKED FOR YOU, HELPED YOU LEARN SOMETHING, IN THE PAST: WALKING, TALKING, DANCING, WRITING, MANAGING. WORK OUT WHERE MAKING MISTAKES HAS HINDERED YOU, AND COMPARE YOUR LISTS.

WHY?

YOU REMIND YOURSELF THAT MAKING MISTAKES IS ACTUALLY HOW HUMAN BEINGS LEARN. YOU MIGHT, OF COURSE, NOT WANT TO LEARN ANYTHING MORE. THAT'S OKAY, BUT YOU WILL SOON FIND THAT YOU ARE NOT WELL PLACED IN A MANAGEMENT POSITION.

5. BREAK DOWN THE BARRIERS BETWEEN YOU AND THE COALFACE

— Visit the coalface more frequently. Expose the excuses you are using for not visiting people. Prioritise your time: if you say people are important, then act that way.

— Dress appropriately for your visit. You wouldn't turn up at a friend's barbeque wearing a tuxedo - you'd feel a dork and everyone else would feel awkward - so don't turn up at the factory wearing a Zegna suit.

— Invite employees to spend time in your office, working with you. A day a month, rotated among employees, will do a great deal to improve the coalface's understanding of what, exactly, management are doing.

WHY?

Anything you do to break down the barriers between managers and employees will improve business performance. Managers consistently underestimate the impact their every action has on the people around them. If you are seen to be committed to your people, your people will commit to the business.

Communication – challenging the mushroom syndrome

We don't share information well. Not only do we not think through the repercussions of the decisions we take, we also don't share enough information with the people who need or want it.

No one would suggest that communication between people is necessarily easy. However, if only a small portion of our professional attention were directed at learning to communicate better, the majority of people who work would be enjoying their working days a whole lot better!

A FRAME OF REFERENCE

Paddy walked into the pub. He was tired. It had been a long day. He walked up to the bartender and ordered a pint of Guinness. The bartender was polishing the counter. The pub was relatively quiet. He pulled Paddy's beer and pushed it across the counter. He then picked up his cloth and resumed his polishing.

Paddy took a good strong pull and let out a sigh of satisfaction. The bartender looked at Paddy and then a little surreptitiously to his left and right. Then, leaning close into Paddy, he whispered, "Hey, Paddy lad, do you want to see something absolutely amazin'?" "Sure," said

Paddy. The bartender then reached down below the counter and placed in front of Paddy a perfect baby grand piano, its diminutive ivory and ebony keys perfect in every degree. The bartender propped open the lid. It was a sight to behold.

"Well, I'll be damned," said Paddy. "That's truly amazin'. Where did you get it?" "Well," said the bartender, grinning, "if you think that's amazin', have a look at this!" He then carefully reached into his pocket and to Paddy's astonishment, he placed next to the piano a little six inch man wearing a tuxedo and carrying a small piano stool. The little man winked at Paddy. Paddy's jaw fell down to his knees.

The little man drew his stool up by the piano, placed himself in front of it, flicked back his coat tails and sat down. He adjusted his miniature sleeves, closed his eyes in sublime concentration and then began to play. Oh, and how he played; Rachmaninov, Shostakovitch, Beethoven, Bach. It was extraordinary.

Paddy was dumbfounded, lost for words (a rare occasion for an Irishman). "Well, I'll be stuffed up a chimney! Where did you get 'im?" The bartender smiled, putting away the piano and the little man. "Well, now Paddy lad, that's a story and a half. I was on me way home one night after lockin' up the pub and I'll be damned if I didn't find this wee rusty little lamp on the pavement. Well, I picked it up and gave it a wee rub and this bloody great big Genie appeared. He gave me one wish and," said the bartender, patting his pocket gently, "this is what I got."

Dollar signs flickered in front of Paddy's eyes. "You don't suppose I could have a look at the wee little lamp do you?" "Sure, Paddy lad," said the bartender, reaching once more below the counter. Paddy took the small rusty old oil lamp in his right hand and scratched his stubble with his left. He eventually gave the lamp a vigorous rub and low and behold a huge Genie appeared before him. "You have one wish," boomed the decidedly Russian sounding Genie. "Well, I'll be damned," said Paddy, "I don't want no wee silly little piano and no wee little piano player. I know what I'll have, I'll have a million bloody bucks, that's what I'll have, a million bloody bucks."

The words were hardly out of his mouth when the Genie disappeared in a cloud of smoke and the room began to fill — every nook and cranny, in through the doors, under the tables and chairs, behind the bar, up the walls, under the other patrons — as far as the eye could see — with ducks!

Paddy was horrified. He looked around him with disbelief. "I didn't order a million bloody ducks, I ordered a million bloody bucks." He looked angrily at the bartender who had resumed his polishing with just a touch of a smile playing across his lips. "Well now, Paddy lad," he said, looking into Paddy's eyes without blinking, "You don't really think I ordered a six inch pianist now do you?"

(If you don't get this, try saying it out loud!)

TALL TALES AND TRUE FROM THE COALFACE
It was once a beautiful piece of equipment to look at, bright red, big, very expensive. Standing at the back of the yard, its complete uselessness stood as lasting testament to failed communication.

The main shed was, unarguably, an old shed. In fact, its layout, facilities, docks looked Dickensian in their poverty. People had been griping about conditions and the inefficiency of the layout for a long time. The purpose the shed served was simple enough — goods came in one end, received from a diversity of locations, passed through a series of conveyor belts and handling stations for resorting and then despatched out the other end.

Most of the people working in the yard had been in the job for a long time. The company was relatively big and geographically spread. By Australian standards it was an old business, well known to the customer base. For quite some time, staff had been complaining that the facilities in the yard were jeopardising customers' goods and that the conveyor setup was in urgent need of upgrading.

It appeared that their concerns were falling on deaf ears. Staff heard, now and then, that "Head Office had the matter in hand." The message had been heard from different sources over quite a long period of time, so staff stopped paying any attention — they just did the best they could with what they had.

Then one delightful day in late February, the local state manager came into the yard wearing a smile from ear to ear. He called everyone together: "You're not going to believe this but guess what's going to be installed over the Easter break?" There was silence from the gathering of thirty. "No idea?" They had none. "A new conveyor system for the yard!" The silence continued. Then someone let out a whoop of excitement and someone else said "About bloody time." One-liners abounded as people expressed their excitement and their astonishment that Head Office had finally decided to do something to help them do their job better.

When the initial excitement died down, someone piped up; "When will we see the design?" The manager looked blank. "Well, we won't be seeing the design — its already being made." "Have *you* seen the design?" said someone else. "No... first I heard about it was last night... but it will be great... apparently."

The meeting broke up a little while later on a fairly high note. At least something was being done, and even if no one had bothered to speak to the local people, a conveyor system wasn't that complicated. It would work.

When the Easter break came, people were full of jokes as they tidied up the yard, moving goods and old equipment to make room for the new conveyor. They were excited. In the preceding weeks, executives, architects, logistics experts from Head Office had visited the site, measuring this, looking at that, scratching their heads, scribbling things down, working out layout, writing up instructions for the local people — what to move, when and where.

In all this, there were no details given to staff. Nothing was explained in any meaningful detail. Still, people remained positive. The equipment had been a long time coming so no one was going to grizzle about a little misplaced communication at this time.

On the Tuesday morning following Easter, staff turned up unusually early, animated and excited. For once, walking into the yard was a pleasure. In the early morning light, their new conveyor system shone like a child's toy train under the tree on Christmas morning. They walked around it, patted it, looked at the joinery, the construction of the conveyor system. They went to the control panel — it all looked simple enough.

No one was too sure how the process was to work, so they waited for Head Office staff to turn up and explain the new receipt and dispatch process they would have to work to. Clearly, the configuration had changed — goods coming in from location X were not going to come in on the left hand side of the loading dock, which now housed the control mechanism. And the trucks coming in from the eastern part of the state would not have access through the north door of the yard, because that was now blocked with part of the conveyor assembly. But no one was overly concerned. No doubt this had all been carefully considered by Head Office.

At 7.30 am the key designers and Head Office executives arrived. Outside, trucks were beginning to queue up to unload their goods. Everyone was being patient — delays were expected. Coffee and take-away breakfasts were on hand to help maintain patience.

With some pride and no small amount of authority, the key designer and Head Office executive began the process of walking staff through the assembly, explaining how the configuration was to work. About fifteen minutes into the briefing, local staff were beginning to look a little anxious. Thirty minutes into the briefing there were audible mumbles and people were looking at the local manager. He looked decidedly uncomfortable, as if he were hoping a large hole would appear in the floor in front of him and swallow him up.

Eventually the mumbles had turned into a rumbling of discontent that could not go unnoticed. The Head Office executive stopped the briefing and turned to the state manager: "What's the matter?" The manager took a deep breath and looked at his people; they nodded their encouragement, many of them urging him to speak up.

"Ok guys, we need to go back to the beginning. I think we might have some problems here." The Head Office people looked bemused and assumed that somewhere in the briefing they had been unclear. Everyone then returned to the start of the conveyor system and the manager began to speak, quietly at first but, with the support of his people, with increasing certainty.

The Head Office people tried, initially to offer explanations to each of the obstacles raised by the manager and his team. However, as the problems became apparent, their silence became leaden. "And just to finish," he said, "McDougall's goods are received here and they represent 40% of the traffic being distributed on Mondays, Wednesdays and Fridays and as far as I can see, the goods won't fit on the conveyor at all!" You could have heard a pin fall when he'd finished.

Now, remembering that this is a true story (changed in part only to protect the innocent!), resolution of the problem was not straightforward — there was no admission that the whole thing was a complete and total cock-up. What actually happened was that for the next three months, engineers, architects and designers endeavoured to make modifications to the system. Local staff tried to use the system.

However, time and tide wait for nobody and, as is the way in many businesses, the company underwent another restructure. The people responsible for the design of the conveyor system were, surprisingly, retrenched in the restructure. With their disappearance, investigations into the conveyor system ceased. The yard staff quietly moved the conveyor system to the back of the property and there, to this day, going quietly rusty, its paint now tarnished, the belt now perishing, lies the conveyor system — testimony to the cost of communication at its very worst.

TALL TALES AND TRUE FROM THE TOP

Even to this day I find the following story hard to believe. I understand it, I value it, but it still has me shaking my head in amazement. The story is 100% dinky die true — no embellishments, no storyteller's dressings. So here it is, as it happened.

The General Manager had been in the job for about two days — enough time to meet senior management and to find his way around the Head Office, learning where critical support systems were such as the coffee machine and the toilet. The company he had decided to join was a large business specialising in providing low profile mining equipment to the mining industry. It was a large organisation with many hundreds of employees spread over thirty sites across five states. The business was in trouble: there were diminishing returns, discontent in the field, inadequate internal systems and customer dissatisfaction, especially with the service backup on the equipment. The GM's appointment was part of the new leadership setup being initiated by the Board. There was also a new Managing Director.

The GM was a fairly down-to-earth character, not particularly ambitious, surprised though not phased at his own good fortune. He was a relatively big man who could appear imposing, but who preferred not to be. He was known for his ability to produce results; he had been selected on the basis on what he had achieved in New Zealand in a similar turn-around process.

His secretary approached him on the morning of his third day and suggested that he might like to meet some of the staff. He was sitting at his desk. "Yes, that would be an excellent idea." He started getting out of his chair. The secretary assumed he was going somewhere. She lifted her pen and paper and said "When would you like me to organise the function and who would you like to attend?" The GM looked puzzled. "I've missed something — what's this for?" The secretary frowned, and ventured, "To meet the staff?" The GM sat down again. "I thought I could just go and say 'hello' now. I don't want any fancy do. I just want to meet people."

The secretary was secretly pleased. She said little, only that she couldn't see any reason why that wouldn't be okay, and that she was more than happy to introduce him to people in the Head Office building (which housed 120 staff). The rest of the day was spent meeting administration, sales, purchasing and general support staff. The GM shook everyone's hands, asked about what they did, whether they enjoyed their work, what improvements they would like to see in place. He let everyone know he was looking forward to working with them and he thanked them for their support.

At the end of the day, he sat down with his secretary and mapped out site visits to be conducted over the next two weeks.

At the time all this was occurring, I was in one of the states doing work with the staff. At about the time the GM would have been halfway through meeting staff in Head Office, we were breaking for lunch. Over sandwiches, someone mentioned that the new GM had just started and that apparently he was going to break the mould, do things differently. "What makes you think that," I asked, with no small amount of interest. "Well, we've just heard from one of the girls in administration in Head Office that he just spent half an hour sitting on the edge of her desk talking to her. To my knowledge, and I've been with this company for twenty-five years, he's the first senior manager to meet his staff!"

By the end of the day staff were exchanging the story over coffee, during smokos, at the photocopier, by their cars, in the toilets.

Next day, I flew to another location, in another state. The story was whipping around the corridors with equal speed and thoroughness. I was astonished. What seemed a simple, natural act of courtesy and respect was regarded by staff as evidence that this general manager was going to run the business differently. People were talking about his consultative skills, his style of leadership, his humanity, even his sense of humour — and all this within 48 hours of it occurring in another state.

I rang the GM (who I had met previously) and relayed the story. He was amazed and embarrassed. All either of us could say was "It says a lot about the previous management!"

And it did.

COMMUNICATION — THE ART OF GROOMING AND GROWING PEOPLE

Communication, how we do it, why we do it and whether we are effective, is an issue for everyone. Many say that dealing with communication issues is like considering the nature of the universe — an endless process fuelled by the 'And what's next?' approach. In the range of issues identified in this overview, you will see certain common theories appearing. This leads me to believe that if we got the basics right, much else may follow.

Communication, or the poor handling of communication, is an issue in — dare I say it — all organisations. It boils down to degrees and expectations. It is to do with how bad the problem is perceived to be, what actually are the business and personal repercussions of communication being done badly and what improvements would occur both individually and for the business if it was done well.

GETTING A HANDLE ON THE TERM

Communication is not what we say, write or do, it is the response we get. If communication is poor, the response we get doesn't match our need. If it is good, the response we get matches our expectations.

Communication doesn't go wrong when the other person is stupid or slow to comprehend or bloody minded. It more often than not goes wrong when the communicator doesn't accept responsibility for the process of communication.

Effective communication can only be confirmed through feedback. In the absence of successful communication and quality feedback, people 'hallucinate' the communicator's need. They may or may not hallucinate the need successfully. Nevertheless, they will act on their hallucination irrespective of their accuracy.

No one knowingly, in the immediacy of the moment, does the wrong thing. We only think they do, when their actions do not serve our expectations. The real question is, did they ever understand our expectations in the first place?

IS ANYONE REALLY GETTING THROUGH?

I made a decision, some ten years ago, not to lose my temper. I made the decision because I didn't enjoy getting angry, saying things that I regretted later and always being left with the feeling that I could have handled myself better. I have had many close calls since, even lost the plot a couple of times. However, over the years I have learnt to manage my communication just a little better. In the process, I have observed, countless times, the harm we do ourselves by not taking responsibility for all that we say and do in life. I have come to the conclusion that by not taking responsibility for communication you *make* yourself the victim (with rare exceptions — deaf Genies do exist). I have never been big on being a victim, preferring instead to have a sense of control over my life. This has proven valuable in dealing with change and adversity, learning and moving forward. No doubt there are many strategies that are as useful. However, it might be worth your while reading the following with a view to diagnosing not only the ills around you but also, and perhaps more importantly, the ills you are responsible for generating.

Consider how human beings learn to communicate, where and with what outcomes in mind. We learn how to speak at home, somewhere between the age of 0 and 5, we learn how to read and write at school somewhere between the age of 5 and 9. We learn at school to collect our thoughts, sometimes for debating purposes, sometimes for the purpose of criticism, sometimes by rote to pass an exam, between the ages of 9 and 17. A small percentage of us go on as adults to refine those skills at universities and TAFEs.

But where in all this education are we really taught to communicate, to understand the purpose of communication in the management of our relationships with other people? Where are we supported in the learning cycle to take feedback from other people without being defensive? Who explained to you that many of the challenges of communication lie in understanding someone else's world view, their cultural upbringing, family influences, education, age, sex, values, beliefs and so on? Who in your life suggested that you needed to understand as much about your own world view and how it prejudices your level of perception, your way of understanding the world? And God help us, who on the planet gave us time to develop flexibility, practice different ways of behaving, so that when we did run into someone whose world view was totally different from ours, we didn't either deck them or back away in disbelief?

The answer is no one. Perhaps that, in part, explains why the human race continues to struggle with war, violence and racial and religious hatred.

We frequently don't know how to understand one another and, fearing what we don't understand, we dismiss another's view as incompetent, stupid or simply alien.

I believe that everyone is really trying their best, in every passing moment. I therefore do what I can to support people, uplift them in their efforts. I was never given licence to hurt or diminish the worth of another human being. There will always be people faster than me and there will always be people slower than me. The journey between birth and death is brief and, in the end, we will measure the worth of our journey not by what we acquire (which must, after all, be left behind) but by the richness of the relationships we have enjoyed with people.

In business, the benefits arising from quality communication are significant; the consequences of poor communication can be momentous in a different way. To withhold information, to fail to explain the purpose behind an action, to assume fault on the part of the other party if they fail to comprehend our purpose or act according to our demands makes life difficult (and less profitable) for everyone concerned.

The process of improving business communication is not as hard as you might think. Much depends on your level of motivation: Does your current situation bother you? Is change important? Can you sense the possible outcomes from getting it right — and do those outcomes attract you?

If you want to continuously improve your skills as a communicator then look for the 'pattern that connects' the comments that you are about to read. Look for simplicity, not complexity. Look to identify patterns of behaviour that are typical in your business or in your performance individually. It may be that the first step towards getting communication right is to admit where we are getting it wrong.

Much has been written about communication and how to improve it — whether it be at home, with families and adolescents, in the community at large or in business. If you go into any decent book shop you will discover hundreds of books on the topic, by people who have dedicated much of their lives to doing it better.

Although I respect this and recognise the immense value of all this writing, I have to own up to finding the reading of much of the material tedious. I either don't understand the language (it's too academic) or feel that I have to be in a human resource or training role to make use of it. It is not my intention (nor do I have the qualifications to compete) to repeat this material. Instead, I am offering a 'diagnostic' perspective. I look at what people believe are the driving issues and provide a simple range of recommendations on how to effect change. Some of those recommendations will flow from the comments, some will appear in the *Practical help* at the end of the chapter.

WHAT COMMUNICATION ISSUES DO PEOPLE RAISE AND WHY?

When it comes to communication, people talk about all sorts of issues. Dip into the following grab bag and ponder a few for yourself.

THERE'S NO CONSULTATION

Decisions are made without first (a) explaining their purpose, (b) inviting comment or (c) even bothering to tell the people affected that decisions have been made. This is a doozey — a big one, a barrel load of venomous spiders, a tank of tarantulas. This gets blood boiling, fists bunched, this is the territory of the almighty dummy spit, the breeding ground of cynicism and discontent. You know what I mean?

Not to consult with or inform an adult when you are about to effect a change that will certainly affect them is not only insulting but short-sighted. Doing this is definitely not good communication. It's also arrogant, selfish, stupid, destructive, disrespectful, thoughtless and down-right bloody awful business practice! Phew!

Notwithstanding the stories I've already shared, I have many hundreds more stored up. But no doubt you can come up with your own list — things that have happened to you as a result of poor or non-existent consultation. Think for a moment about why it occurs. Here are my best guesses as to why people don't consult:

- They don't think things through adequately — they become embroiled in the process of problem solving, change, improving performance. Having generated a solution that excites them and appears to resolve all concerns, they go straight to implementation.

- They think the responsibility of solving a problem lies with them. Leaders believe that their job is to solve a problem and the employees' job is to implement the solution — with no explanation required.

- Even with best intentions and despite thinking through the repercussions of a decision, they simply fail to consider all aspects.

- They have become disassociated from the coalface. Leaders making decisions have forgotten what it is like to be on the receiving end of a decision that comes with no explanation — they no longer think it is such a problem. After all (they figure), there are so many other things to worry about; we can't consult on everything with everybody.

Whatever the reason, the result is the same: demotivation of the people affected. The neurological response is basically to turn off the thinking process. If I tell you what to do without explaining the purpose or the expected outcome, you are forced to perform your tasks in a rote fashion. To think about what you are doing is frustrating and dysfunctional: you will generate questions that you cannot answer or are not empowered to answer.

However, if I pose a problem to you and — despite having a solution myself — ask you to make recommendations, you are forced to think about the problem. Perhaps you might not make what I think is the best suggestion, but I can still put my solution to you: I might ask "Have you considered doing *X*?" or state that "I am curious to know whether *X* will resolve our problem." By doing this, I engage your thinking and, more importantly, assess a level of innovation based on *your* information base rather than just mine. Conversely, if I simply make a decision and ask you to implement it, I neither access your thinking nor your information base nor your capacity for innovation. It makes no sense.

The repercussions in business from this one communication weakness are often long term. Not only does it fail to maximise the opportunities represented by harnessing a diversity of opinions on a problem, it actually turns the listener 'off'. Next time round, turning them 'on' will be that much harder.

I had an experience quite some time ago that brought home to me how horrible it is to be on the receiving end of change when there is no explanation or an opportunity for input. I was working with a company which had an unexpected change of leadership. I had been doing a lot of work in the business identifying the heroes (the company experts), helping them to capture their expertise into trainable, transferable 'packages' or teaching units. The heroes had the expertise, I had the teaching skills. We had had a lot of fun over the preceding three months combining our skills to produce a twelve month training program for the company.

We were very close to finishing our work and were confident that we had something that would really be of value to the people of the business. Unfortunately, with the change of leadership came a clampdown on (predictably) the Human Resource budget. Without consultation with our team, the new Managing Director put a stop to our work.

When I first heard about this I was angry. I felt like a champagne bottle that had been shaken violently. There was a lot I wanted to say and wanted the opportunity to discuss this decision. I made an appointment with the MD. Coming from a finance background, his understanding of education and the management of people was limited. He said the decision was final.

How did I feel? Valueless, as if all the work I had put in had been a complete waste of time. Worse, I felt like everything else I was doing might be equally valueless. The rest of the team were the same. I lost respect for the leader in question. I didn't trust his decision making ability. His inability to consult told me much about what he really thought about his people. This in turn put into doubt the company's vision, which was all about achieving success through the committed efforts of all staff. How could we all commit if we could so easily be overridden?

If only I had know then what I know now, I would have handled things very differently. I would have brought a level of creativity to the situation which the leader in question failed to access; I would have suggested explaining, in detail, the current business predicament to the people of the business. I would then have challenged the leader to *consult us* in order to find a way to cut expenditure without jeopardising everyone's work or the contribution made by that leader. Our team's conclusions might well have been to put our work on hold for twelve months, but the decision would have been considered, thoughtful and *ours*. We would have owned the conclusion and not felt as if all our efforts had been ignored or simply not even recognised.

The worst part of not being consulted in the decision making process is that it makes us feel futile, unimportant. And if we don't have a value, why should we bother continuing to contribute?

Now, there are degrees of decision making, the repercussions of which should vary. There is a big difference between suddenly switching company accounts to 30 day payment terms and putting a complete halt to a group's endeavours without adequate explanation or the opportunity for consultation. However, the impact on people is often the same: those affected by the actions of the decision maker start to feel that the leader doesn't particularly care about them, their customers, or their work.

To our detriment we ignore this seemingly unique human ability — namely, that events can happen in one part of our life and the learning generated can be then extrapolated into all subsequent events with similar parameters. For instance, a baby might burn its finger on a heater at the age of eight months; from that point, that human's brain can, in a variety of situations, calibrate the danger factor of heat — whether it be from an open fire, a cooker, a gas burner or the sun.

So, when we are *not* told of a decision that affects us at work, or are *not* given an adequate explanation for why this decision was taken, if we are *not* given the chance to provide input into the decision, we learn, appropriately or not, that we are obviously not worthy of involvement in this situation. Unfortunately our brains then leap to a range of conclusions about our apparent worth in the overall scheme of things.

"STRATEGIC PLANS EXIST, BUT WE HAVE NEVER SEEN THEM"

This is another pet hate of mine. Let me tell you a story before I discuss the feedback I've had. I was working in a large multinational that had an extensive franchisee network. My job was to help divisional management design a learning environment for franchisees to encourage the improvement of leadership skills. The idea was to help the franchisees recognise where they could actually execute innovative leadership skills, outside the rules of their basic franchise agreements. We were trying to encourage a visionary, future-oriented perspective.

In designing the programs I was to run, I felt it was important to get a sense of the strategic processes at work in the company responsible for the franchisees — in other words, the multinational. I started by asking the divisional managers for copies of any company based strategic plans they had. They didn't have any. I then asked the regional head for plans. No luck. I then decided it would be simpler just to get the company's vision — I couldn't find even that. It never even occurred to me that it hadn't actually been done! I just assumed I wasn't looking in the right place.

Eventually, I decided to go to the CEO of the company in Australia — surely *he* would be able to help me locate the material. Now, before I tell you the conclusion to the story, let me remind you of my motivation. I was responsible for designing a learning environment for 120 of the company's franchisees. That was a reasonably large chunk of the company's Australian franchisee network. I believed it was important for me to understand the company's ambitions before training 120 leaders (albeit franchisees). I have always believed that planning should cascade and that every action should be tied to a clear understanding of the overall ambitions of the organisation. In this way, we each add value, sometimes in small ways, often in substantial ways.

I left a message with the CEO's secretary, explaining in a friendly way what I was after and why. She understood and said she would get back to me, or ask the CEO to give me a ring. What actually happened was that the regional managers working with me were finally tracked down by the CEO and were given the message "Who is this nosy woman — get rid of her!"

Well, you could have knocked me down with a feather. In the end, we all ended up laughing about the situation, which may be summarised as follows: I was being asked to teach the external franchisees something which it appeared the company itself had failed to do — envision, plan the future and then cascade it down to the employees. Fortunately, the regional head was not a lie-down-and-die character. He saw the silliness of the situation, made a point of talking to the CEO and, in support of my original intent, eventually tracked the necessary material down. It had actually been done, though few people were using it to support their decision making!

From my point of view at least, all was saved and I was able to design a program which had every chance of adding value to the whole. However, I was left wondering how many other people in the organisation (which employed, in Australia alone, many thousands) were going about their daily work guessing at the ultimate ambitions of the business rather than working towards them cohesively and synergistically.

It is interesting talking to employees about this. Despite a popular belief to the contrary, most employees want to know more about where the businesses they work for are heading and why. None of us like to think that what we do is futile, no matter how minor it may seem in the broader context.

Employees express great frustration over the absence of a clearly communicated plan. Although we covered some of this in Chapter 2, it is worth making a couple of additional distinctions on the process of developing a vision and a plan to implement it.

If we communicate a plan clearly to every one, then we allow them to think about what they are doing and how it adds to the over all picture. We are giving people a 'tool of distinction', a yardstick for measuring activity and determining its appropriateness. If I know what you want to achieve, if I agree with you and see worth in the ambition, then I can really watch what I do and look for improvements to the big picture.

I can also think about what Joe is doing in production, or Jill in distribution, or Samantha in design. Our discussions become focused and united rather than fractionated. Generally, actions become fractionated when people are not working to a common purpose, or with a common understanding. If we are guessing the purpose of the business, chances are we are guessing differently. If we guess differently, then the so-called big picture that guides our actions, varies from individual to individual or department to department. Whether we make the right decision will have more to do with luck than good design. Further, decisions can be right for one department but at odds with another which, because their actions are based on their own unique perceptions, may be working to a different version of the company's overall ambitions.

Let me give you an example of how corrosive this can be. Take two companies, Company A and (imaginatively) Company B. Both produce fine-calibration instruments for testing electronic equipment. In the products they manufacture there is a small but critical component. The component can be purchased from a variety of manufacturers around the world and the price varies from $5 to $20. With the change in price comes a change in reliability and durability.

In Company A, there is a vision which goes something like this:

"We have a commitment to quality in all we do; we will produce the best calibration equipment that money can buy, we will never be the cheapest but we will always be the best."

In Company B, the vision is as follows:

"Simply the cheapest — no one will beat us on price."

Imagine both companies are multi-million dollar organisations, employing many hundreds of people. Let's look at the purchasing department, where responsibility for the purchase of the component lies and consider the following two scenarios.

Company A: The formulation of the company vision was a long, thought-out process. Executives had gone on retreat to consider their market position and to come up with a plan that would enable them to capture it. They returned from their retreat excited by their decisions and willing to fight hard to make their ideas turn into a reality. Over time, as is often the way of the world, they became embroiled in the incredible 'busyness' of their rapidly expanding organisation and, although their hearts supported their ambitions, time just simply didn't materialise to ensure all the people of the business understood the implications of the words on the well publicised vision statement.

Now, some eight months after the visionary work, the person in charge of purchasing is looking at the purchasing budget for the year and is figuring out how to come in under the budgeted figures. He is a good manager and is aware that if he can save money, it will be good for the business — and he might just get the promotion he is after. Part of his strategy can be fulfilled by making the right purchase for the critical component that runs the calibration equipment the company sells. He has had a couple of external salespeople in and he now knows the price range is $5 to $20. He realises that he can save $220,000 in purchase costs alone if he purchases the $5 component, to say nothing of helping to reduce the cost of the finished unit and so increase overall profitability. He proceeds.

Four months later, the financial results are through and management are astonished at the savings in purchases this year. They ask the manager in question to visit the Boardroom. He is given a good bonus and is offered an important promotion. He is thrilled and so are senior management.

Unfortunately, eight months after this happy meeting, customers start to complain about the calibration equipment the company is selling: faults are commonplace. The company resolves the problem by upgrading their customer service department and by providing replacements or refunds, a costly but necessary response to the problem.

Two years down the track, the company is in serious financial difficulties. Retrenchments have occurred, restructuring is imminent, the customer base is seriously under threat. The new leadership team are investigating the problems of the business. After a great deal of searching, they uncover a range of problems, not least of which is the mistake made with the purchasing of the critical component. The manager in question, now head of production, is fired for his incompetency.

Ask yourself: Was there a mistake in purchasing or a mistake in the process of sharing information? Was the person who made the purchasing decision incompetent, or was the leadership team incompetent?

Company B: You can probably guess the scenario. The leadership team made sure the vision was cascaded into the business. Everyone understood it, thought about it, considered what, in their actions, contributed towards achieving it. In Company B's purchasing department, a manager faces a choice similar to the one in Company A: should she buy the $5 item, the $20 or any of the ones in between?

She thinks at length and eventually settles on a $7 component. It's cheap, but not the cheapest. It offers some degree of reliability without being excessive. She doesn't want to buy poor quality — she knows that this will bump up the company's operating costs in terms of managing returns. She's discussed her decision with production, sales and marketing. They agree with her decision. They still believe their vision "simply the cheapest — no one will beat us on price" will be achievable despite a slight increase in the cost of goods. They, together, calculate the greater reliability will reduce potential costly comebacks to the business from dissatisfied customers.

Our purchasing manager doesn't save a lot on her purchasing budget that year. She is not a star performer — she is not a company hero. Instead, she is part of a team of heroes, informed and empowered to act, who together think about what they are doing and how their actions add value to the total business.

The company shows a steady growth in profit. Staff are rewarded for their efforts by a continuously growing share in company profits.

Seems pretty obvious, doesn't it? It isn't even so complex. No matter how sophisticated our systems may be, sharing plans is about ensuring people know where they are going and why. They are then empowered to make wise and informed decisions.

SECRECY — THE CHALLENGE OF FORBIDDEN FRUIT

Have you ever noticed that the minute you say to someone "I really shouldn't tell you this, but…" the information becomes massively more attractive? I've often thought that if you genuinely have something you don't want other people to know, the best way to keep it secret is to treat it as though it were publicly available!

All jests aside, people genuinely hate secrecy. It is seen as a power game, and the people who have the information become power brokers. This fuels a political environment where people trade information as part of the management of power. I transfer some power to you by sharing some highly confidential information; I demonstrate my trust in you by asking you not to discuss it with anyone else.

I don't advocate sharing all information with all people, but I don't think that in business information should be withheld because it is too sensitive, it will cause an adverse reaction, or will have people leaving in droves. The truth is that people in business know more than they are given credit for knowing. Instead of being secretive and thereby encouraging the swift and remarkably effective gossip system, the originating source of information could be open about it, explaining the importance of keeping the information 'in house' (that is, in the business).

Recently, I had an experience with a company which, as part of a merger process, had to rationalise senior management positions. Even a halfwit would have realised that the newly merged business was not going to need all the senior managers that were working in the two old businesses. I sat in on a strategic meeting of senior management discussing this. The issue of what to tell people and why was raised by a couple of the managers. The agreement was to wait until a decision on who should stay and who would go had been made before discussing the matter publicly. I disagreed with this, arguing that during the eight weeks preceding the release of such details, speculation would be rife and it would erode everyone's confidence. I suggested we tell people the truth (and, in fact, support them by explaining how retrenchments would be handled) and give a guarantee that no one would be seriously disadvantaged. Senior management agreed with my reasoning. The feedback from staff when we 'went public' was spontaneous and unanimous. They understood what management were doing and why, and in response they volunteered suggestions on how to manage the process.

Sometimes in business tough decisions have to be taken. Tough or otherwise, fact is rarely more alarming than fiction — and it is more honourable and certainly more decent to be up-front and honest with people. That is how I like and expect to be treated. I can't imagine anyone else is much different.

As for the need for secrecy, which is founded on 'the opposition mustn't find out' myth, who are we kidding? Industrial espionage has been continuously refined throughout this century. Anyone who is sufficiently determined can find out just about anything; we can be very confident that if we make information highly secretive then we will also make it highly desirable. Truthfully, if we are really anxious about keeping information from competitors, then one of the most powerful ways to keep it in house is to bring people into the fold. Then the secret belongs to staff, as one team. The chances of slippage are high anyway — but at least this way we value the people who count.

POLITICS AND PLAYERS

As I have noted in Chapter 3, people hate politics. People don't trust political players. Leaders who feed a political environment will pay the ultimate price: they will lose the trust and respect of their people.

Most people I have encountered have been very astute in summarising the role of politics in their organisations — large or small. These perceptive individuals see that a highly political environment is fine providing you are among the powerful people, but if you are not, it is demotivating and frustrating. Political factions hoard information and use it as a tool of trade. People do what they think is the right thing, which is just a reflection of currently-prevailing opinion, rather than what they believe is the best thing, which would be a reflection of their own well considered opinions.

There is a delightful piece of humour about the way politics transforms information, in a recent publication, *The Penguin Book of Jokes From Cyberspace* (Phillip Adams & Patrice Newell, Penguin, 1995, p 146):

In the beginning was the Plan

And then came the Assumptions.

And the Assumptions were without form.

And the Plan was without substance.

And darkness was upon the face of the Workers.

And they spoke amongst themselves, saying, "It is a crock of shit, and it stinketh."

And the Workers went unto their Supervisors and said, "It is a pail of dung, and none may abide the odour thereof."

And the Supervisors went unto their Managers, saying, "It is a container of excrement, and it is very strong, such that none may abide by it."

And the Managers went unto their Directors, saying, "It is a vessel of fertiliser, and none may abide its strength."

And the Directors spoke amongst themselves, saying to one another, "It contains that which aids plant growth, and it is very powerful."

And the Vice President went unto the President, saying unto him, "This new plan will actively promote the growth and vigour of the company, with powerful effects."

And the President looked upon the Plan, and saw that it was good.

And the Plan became Policy.

This is how Shit happens.

I don't know about you but I have seen this so-called joke actually happen on more occasions than I like to admit. Crazy, isn't it!

DISTRIBUTION OF INFORMATION — AD HOC OR SELECTIVE, WHO GETS IT AND WHY?

What actually is the purpose of sharing information? I would have thought it was pretty straightforward. Giving people information helps them do something — better. Information solves problems, answers worries, explains actions. Although some two hundred years ago it may have been possible to know most of the things human beings had invented, were thinking about or had discovered, it is certainly not the case now. In an epoch in which it is impossible to know more than a fraction of all that is known, sharing knowledge helps us make better use of information — as it interacts with, affects or adds value to your information. In business, access to useful information may be the only competitive advantage we have.

At the moment, it would seem that we don't share information well. Not only do we not think through the repercussions of the decisions we take, we also don't share enough information with the people who need or want it.

In business, there appear to be two distinct categories of information that people want — namely, *specific information* that affects what they do or adds value to what they do, and *general information* about current and predicted business performance.

The sharing of specific information is obvious. If I am doing a job for you, then any and all information you can give me about the job will empower me to do the job better. The problem we run into with the sharing of specific information is that we appear to only partially address the need.

For instance, if I am responsible for site audits for a company that is responsible for monitoring air quality in a mining site, there are a range of immediate things I might want to know (for instance, information about the company, the site, problems they have had, issues that concern them at this time). I want to know how to operate the equipment I am going to use, what can go wrong with it, what's involved in fixing it and so on. That's the obvious stuff.

Now, maybe the Managing Director of my business has just gone to a European show and has seen new equipment. No purchases are being made yet, but the show was interesting because it indicated the direction air monitoring is heading. One of our salespeople picks up some gossip about a leadership change in the mining company. Our accounts department notices that our invoices are being paid slowly. All these various pieces of information don't directly affect my job — namely going out to the site and actually doing the air testing, so do I actually need to know this information?

I would say "yes." It is the broad spectrum of (albeit specific) business information that enables me to think about my work. If I know of new equipment being developed, I can keep my ear to the ground about competitors, what they are investing in and why. I might hear of field trials before senior management. But if I don't know new equipment has been shown at the European shows, I won't even be looking for competitor activity until, possibly, it is too late. Do I need to know about a change in leadership in the company I am testing? Of course I do. I can watch for coalface changes which might either jeopardise the work we are doing or which might actually represent new opportunities for us. And do I need to know about slow payments? Yes, because I am the closest to the business. I visit the site for air testing each week. Maybe I will pick up other bits and pieces of information that will tell me this business is in trouble.

Overall, information that affects what we do can be drawn from a broad field. If we assume the 'spread of intelligence' is occurring as a result of the education most of us are receiving, then the spread of information will only enhance what we do. Despite its seeming breadth, this is what I refer to as *specific information*.

General information, by contrast, may seem on the face of it, less important. For instance, if you work in production, do you really need to know how the sales department are performing? Again, I would say "yes." General information in a business helps us all feel like we belong, that it is our company. We can all become watchdogs for the overall business. The more general information we have, the more able we are to share quality information with others.

General information can refer to the company's progressive financial performance, proposed marketing plans and their rationale, sales figures, source and performance against budget, new appointments. We might learn about competitors, new ideas being developed, information about our industry within Australia, information about our industry from abroad. All this information helps us to become educated in our field, and the more educated we are, the greater the intelligence we can bring to our jobs.

Information which is held selectively by departments generates barriers — them-versus-us attitudes — between departments or geographically separated locations. If they are not tackled, such barriers turn into steel-plated partitions which keep ideas out and information in. This, in turn, leads to decisions being taken by departments (remember the Head Office that thought it was okay to arbitrarily change company accounts to 30 days without consultation with the field?) with little thought as to who will be affected. And so on. A great, unwieldy catch 22. The barriers feed on misinformation or inadequate information. The more that comes in, the thicker the barriers; the thicker the barriers, the more demotivating the working environment; the more demotivating the environment, the less information we share because, hey, who gives a damn anyway?

SOCIAL INTERACTION — ARE OUR BARBEQUES MISSING SOMETHING?

I am always impressed with how willingly people commit to the social side of a business. People want to like (or, more importantly, trust) the people they work with. If we can trust people, we feel safe. What better way to build up trust that to take time out, away from the pressures of day-to-day work, and just talk, or eat and drink, or play a friendly game?

Many companies have some sort of social activity. In many instances, people like what is happening, particularly as it affects employees. However, there are two categories of feedback that I have received which invite further thought. The first relates to management's recognition that social activity improves business performance, the second asks why management doesn't participate.

In the first instance, many people feel that management don't take seriously the social activities that staff organise. They're regarded as nice, but not essential. Staff often disagree. They see social interaction as a way of sharing information in an informal environment, getting to know one another, relaxing, having fun, building a sense of community, of commonly shared interests and values — all of which add value to the business.

Management signifies its lack of support by interrupting social activities, calling people away to attend meetings or cancelling social activities altogether because something of greater importance has occurred. They also fail to provide either physical or financial resources.

People are also frustrated by the demarcation that often occurs at social functions — management either don't turn up at all or, if they do show, they interact with a select group of staff. Staff find it hard to accept that senior managers might be uncomfortable or might not know how to mingle. Their lack of participation is interpreted as being a function of the hierarchy — they are 'above' such unimportant activities.

You may have noticed that I made no distinction in this chapter between concerns raised by employees and concerns raised by leaders. That's because, apart from the question of leadership communication skills, they actually don't appear to be any different; it is only a matter of degree. Most feel that communication is important and few are satisfied with how we are managing it at the moment.

As for education, for leaders or anyone else, it has to happen. We have to learn to communicate more effectively. The price we pay for poor communication is far too high. In our world today, too much is going wrong for people. Stress related disorders are escalating, more people are seeing councillors, psychologists, psychiatrists, doctors, witch doctors, alternative medicine specialists. We are taking more sick leave, need more compensation, and take more drugs to alleviate our woes. Why?

I believe that because we communicate so poorly, trust — the consequence of good communication — is dying in the workplace. We are uncertain about our futures and suspicious of people's motivations when they seek our support or participation in a project. We don't trust our leaders and, to an extent, we don't really trust other employees. We don't trust that what is meant to happen tomorrow will actually happen, or if it does happen, we doubt it will benefit us.

Being trusted and trusting others is critical in life generally, let alone in business. Trust is what makes us feel safe and warm, valued and respected. Trust honours us and the contribution we make. Trust in us causes us to trust in turn. It brings out our best characteristics. People who are trusted accept personal responsibility with dignity and commitment, and there is no better way to build business than to have responsible people, trusting one another enough to share information, to communicate effectively and to do so with respect for the whole and not only to the part over which they hold dominion.

Practical help

ACTION FOR EMPLOYEES

HERE ARE SOME IDEAS ON HOW YOU MIGHT ADDRESS COMMUNICATION PROBLEMS.

1. BREAK DOWN BARRIERS WITH MANAGERS

— HOW LONG SINCE YOU TALKED TO A MANAGER ABOUT THEIR PERSONAL LIFE OR YOURS?

— VISIT THE MANAGERS OFFICE! DON'T THINK YOU WON'T BE WELCOME, YOU WILL BE.

— INVITE A MANAGER WHO DOESN'T UNDERSTAND YOUR WORK TO VISIT THE FACTORY, WARE-HOUSE OR OFFICE; SHOW THEM AROUND, AND EXPLAIN WHAT YOU DO OR ARE TRYING TO DO.

— ORGANISE A BREAKFAST, A LUNCH OR AFTER-WORK DRINKS AND INVITE A GROUP OF SENIOR LEADERS TO ATTEND; DON'T EARBASH THEM ABOUT PROBLEMS, BUT DO GIVE THEM A 'SHOW AND TELL' SESSION — THINGS THAT YOU AND YOUR AREA ARE DOING AND WHY.

— MAKE SURE THAT YOU GREET ANY AND ALL MANAGERS WHEN THEY PASS THROUGH YOUR AREA; DON'T WAIT FOR THEM TO COME TO YOU, MOVE TOWARDS THEM, SHAKE THEIR HANDS AND SAY "HELLO."

WHY?

THESE ACTIONS WILL PRODUCE RESULTS. IF THE 'BOSSES' WON'T COME TO YOU, GO TO THEM. IF THEY DON'T INVITE YOU INTO THE 'CORRIDORS OF POWER' ASK THEM INTO THE 'BOWELS' OF THE ORGANISATION WHERE 'THINGS REALLY HAPPEN'. DON'T BE INSULTED WHEN A MANAGER WALKS STRAIGHT PAST YOU IN THE MORNING WITHOUT BOTHERING TO SAY 'GOOD MORNING', BUT YELL THE GREETING TO THEM. SOMEONE, SOMEWHERE, HAS TO BEGIN THE PROCESS OF DIALOGUE AND IF IT ISN'T COMING FROM THE LEADERS OF AN ORGANISATION, IT CAN COME FROM YOU.

2. KNOW YOURSELF AND YOUR VALUE TO THE BUSINESS

— WRITE DOWN ON A PIECE OF PAPER EVERYTHING THAT WOULDN'T HAPPEN IF YOU DIDN'T DO YOUR JOB.

— NEXT TO THIS LIST, WRITE DOWN EVERYTHING THAT WOULD HAPPEN IF YOU DID YOUR JOB BADLY.

— LIST THE MANAGERS IN THE BUSINESS WHO COULD DO THE JOB AS WELL AS YOU — THEN LIST THE MANAGERS WHO COULDN'T.

WHY?

TOO MANY PEOPLE DON'T REALISE THEIR REAL VALUE IN THE WORKPLACE. I OFTEN HEAR PEOPLE SAY THINGS LIKE "OH, I'M JUST A FORKIE," OR "I'M JUST A RECEPTIONIST." TO WHICH I RESPOND, "JUST WHAT WOULD HAPPEN TO THE BUSINESS IF YOUR JOB WAS NOT DONE AT ALL OR DONE POORLY?" MOST PEOPLE THEN SEE THAT THEIR JOBS HAVE A CLEAR AND IMPORTANT FUNCTION WITHIN THE CONTEXT OF THE OVERALL BUSINESS. WE MISTAKENLY VALUE OURSELVES ON THE APPARENT SIMPLICITY OF A JOB OR THE EASE WITH WHICH WE CAN BE REPLACED. REMEMBER, REPLACING ANYONE, NO MATTER WHAT THE JOB, IS A COSTLY EXERCISE.

3. THE WAY YOU TALK IS YOUR REALITY

— LISTEN TO HOW YOU TALK TO YOURSELF ABOUT THE POWER YOU HAVE AT WORK.

— IF YOU SAY "YOU CAN," YOU CAN; IF YOU SAY "YOU CAN'T" YOU CAN'T — EITHER WAY YOU WILL BE RIGHT. HOW DO YOU SPEAK TO YOURSELF ABOUT YOUR CONTRIBUTION TO YOUR COMPANY? WHAT CONTRIBUTION ARE YOU REALLY MAKING?

— HOW DO YOU TALK ABOUT WORK AT HOME? HOW DO YOU TALK ABOUT WORK AT WORK?

— WHAT WOULD YOU LIKE TO ACHIEVE AT WORK AND WHY? WRITE IT DOWN.

— WHAT ARE THE STEPS YOU NEED TO TAKE AND WHY? WRITE THEM DOWN.

— SIT DOWN WITH YOUR MANAGER AND DISCUSS THIS AS PART OF YOUR COMMUNICATION STRATEGY. SEE WHAT DIFFERENCES IT WILL GENERATE.

WHY?

HOW WE THINK ABOUT THE WORLD AROUND US CAN BE EXTRAORDINARILY INFLUENTIAL. IF WE REALLY WANT TO CHANGE THE WAY WE COMMUNICATE, WE HAVE TO BEGIN BY UNDER-STANDING OUR REAL WORTH AND TALKING AND THINKING TO OURSELVES ABOUT IT. AN IDLE CONVERSATION AROUND THE COFFEE MACHINE ABOUT WHAT IS WRONG IN THE UNIVERSE (THE BUSINESS) AND HOW LITTLE WE CAN DO TO AFFECT IT WEAKENS EVERYONE CONCERNED.

FINDING A PLACE OF INFLUENCE AND BEGINNING THE PROCESS OF CHANGE IS HOW SMALL AMBITIONS TURN INTO LARGE ONES.

4. DECISION MAKING — ARE YOU HAPPY WITH IT?

— IF A DECISION IS MADE WITHOUT ADEQUATE CONSULTATION IN YOUR AREA, MAKE SURE THE MANAGER OR EMPLOYEE IN QUESTION UNDERSTANDS THE REPERCUSSIONS FROM YOUR POINT OF VIEW. IF YOU CAN'T REDRESS THE IMMEDIATE SITUATION, YOUR COMMENTS AND ACTION MAY STOP IT OCCURRING NEXT TIME AROUND.

— IF A DECISION IS TAKEN BY A SENIOR MANAGER WITH WHOM YOU HAVE NO DIRECT CONTACT, WRITE TO THEM. TOO OFTEN THEY ASSUME ALL IS OKAY BECAUSE THEY NEVER GET DIRECT FEEDBACK.

WHY?

GRUMBLES FROM MANY PEOPLE ABOUT A RANGE OF SMALL AND RELATIVELY UNIMPORTANT DECISIONS WILL OFTEN TRANSLATE INTO QUALITY CONSULTATIVE PROCESSES ON THE MAJOR ISSUES. YOU HAVE TO START SOME TIME, SO START NOW! START WITH THE FIRST AVAILABLE OPPORTUNITY YOU GET; YOU WILL FIND THAT CHANGE WILL FLOW RAPIDLY.

5. DISTRIBUTION OF INFORMATION — WHO GETS IT AND WHY?

— WHAT INFORMATION DO YOU NEED? MAKE A CAREFUL LIST — ADD TO IT OVER TIME. MAKE SURE KEY MANAGERS HAVE A COPY OF THIS LIST. DISCUSS IT WITH THEM. MAKE SURE THEY UNDERSTAND WHY IT IS IMPORTANT TO YOU IN THE CONTEXT OF HOW IT AFFECTS YOUR WORK.

— WHAT INFORMATION DO YOU WANT? MAKE ANOTHER CAREFUL LIST — ADD TO IT OVER TIME. THINK TO YOURSELF WHY YOU WANT THIS INFORMATION, HOW IT ADDS VALUE TO YOU. MAKE NOTES. SIT DOWN WITH YOUR MANAGER AND GO THROUGH THIS LIST. EXPLAIN THE BROADER PICTURE AND HOW IT IS IMPROVED WITH GENERAL INFORMATION.

— LOOK AT THE WAY INFORMATION IS CURRENTLY DISTRIBUTED: MEETINGS, MEMOS, E-MAILS, AD HOC DISCUSSIONS. CONSIDER WHICH IS CURRENTLY MOST USEFUL AND WHY. CONSIDER WHAT CHANGES YOU WOULD LIKE TO MAKE AND WHY. IF YOUR COMPANY HAS REGULAR STAFF MEETINGS, ARE THEY INTERESTING, USEFUL, INFORMATIVE, PARTICIPATIVE? IF NOT,

CHANGE THE PROCESS. WRITE DOWN THE CHANGES YOU WOULD LIKE TO TEST AND EXPLAIN WHY YOU THINK THEY'RE WORTHWHILE. DISCUSS YOUR IDEAS WITH YOUR MANAGER.

WHY?

OFTEN, SENIOR MANAGEMENT THINK THEY ARE DOING THE RIGHT THING IN THE WAY THEY DISTRIBUTE INFORMATION. NO ONE SPEAKS DIRECTLY TO THEM IF IT ISN'T ANY GOOD. STAFF SIMPLY TELL EACH OTHER THE INFORMATION ISN'T ANY GOOD OR THEY BIN IT. IF PEOPLE DON'T KNOW THEY ARE DOING SOMETHING WRONG, HOW CAN THEY CHANGE?

6. SOCIAL ACTIVITIES — ARE WE HAVING FUN YET?

— DO YOU HAVE A SOCIAL CLUB? IS IT ANY GOOD? IF IT IS, THEN WHY? IF IT ISN'T, WHY NOT? WHAT CHANGES NEED TO BE MADE? DO OTHER STAFF AGREE WITH YOU? HOW WILL YOU CREATE AN ENVIRONMENT FOR EXPERIMENTING AND LEARNING HOW TO RUN THE CLUB BETTER? IF YOU DON'T WANT A CLUB, WHAT SOCIAL ACTIVITIES DO YOU WANT? WHAT BENEFITS FLOW FROM THESE ACTIVITIES?

— ARE MANAGERS PARTICIPATING IN SOCIAL ACTIVITIES WITH STAFF? DO STAFF WANT THEM TO PARTICIPATE? IF THEY WANT THEM TO PARTICIPATE, WHAT DO YOU ALL NEED TO DO DIFFERENTLY?

WHY?

SOCIAL CLUBS FALL BY THE WAYSIDE BECAUSE STAFF OR MANAGEMENT STOP EXPERIMENTING. ONE OR TWO ACTIVITIES ARE TRIED, PARTICIPATION IS MEDIOCRE, SO WE USE THIS AS EVIDENCE OF DISINTEREST IN BUSINESS SOCIAL ACTIVITIES. BUT IT MAY BE THAT WE HAVE CHOSEN THE WRONG ACTIVITY: BUNGY JUMPING IS NO GOOD IF HALF THE STAFF HAVE BACK PROBLEMS; BOWLS IS ILL-ADVISED WHEN THE STAFF ARE ALL UNDER 25 AND ARE LOOKING FOR AN ADRENALINE HIT!

ACTION FOR LEADERS

LEADERS, TOO, CAN ADDRESS COMMUNICATION PROBLEMS.

1. KNOW YOUR PEOPLE

— HOW LONG IS IT SINCE YOU SPENT QUALITY TIME WITH YOUR PEOPLE?

— HOW WELL DO YOU REALLY KNOW THEIR JOBS, THE CONTRIBUTION THEY MAKE, THE THINGS THEY ARE PROUD OF, WORRIED ABOUT, EXCITED BY?

— HOW LONG IS IT SINCE YOU SAT DOWN WITH INDIVIDUAL STAFF WHO ARE DIRECT REPORTS TO YOU AND LISTENED TO WHAT IS FRUSTRATING THEM ABOUT THE WAY THE BUSINESS IS RUN? WHEN DID YOU LAST LISTEN SIMILARLY TO A SELECTION OF THE BROADER COMMUNITY?

— HOW DO YOU RATE YOUR TRACK RECORD IN RESPONDING TO THEIR REQUESTS?

— IF YOU'VE DONE A LEADERSHIP APPRAISAL, CAN STAFF SEE IMPROVEMENTS?

WHY?

LISTENING IS THE FIRST AND MOST CRITICAL PART OF COMMUNICATION. GENERALLY, EMPLOYEES FEEL THAT MANAGERS AND LEADERS LISTEN INADEQUATELY. QUALITY LISTENING WILL BUILD COMMITMENT AND TRUST.

2. DECISION MAKING — WHO DO YOU AFFECT AND WHY?

— ARE YOU RESPONSIBLE FOR DECISION MAKING? IF YES, WHAT KIND OF DECISIONS ARE THEY, AND WHO IN YOUR BUSINESS DO THEY AFFECT? MAKE A LIST. SPEAK TO THE PEOPLE AFFECTED AND SEE WHETHER OR NOT THEY FEEL THEY HAVE BEEN GETTING ADEQUATE OPPORTUNITY TO CONSULT.

— DO YOU LET PEOPLE KNOW WHEN A DECISION IS BEING MADE THAT MIGHT BE OUTSIDE YOUR CONTROL? IF YOU DON'T, WHY NOT? IF YOU DO, DO YOU DO SO IN A TIMELY MANNER?

— OBSERVE THE NATURE OF FEEDBACK TO OTHER DECISION MAKERS: DO YOU SEE OTHER MANAGERS MAKING DECISIONS WITHOUT THINKING ABOUT THE REPERCUSSIONS THAT FLOW FROM THESE DECISIONS? IF SO, WHAT CAN YOU DO ABOUT IT?

WHY?

THIS IS A VERY BIG BUGBEAR FOR EMPLOYEES. REMEMBER, IT MAKES THEM FEEL DEVALUED, UNIMPORTANT. HOW DO YOU FEEL WHEN A DECISION IS TAKEN THAT AFFECTS YOUR WORK OR YOUR PERSONAL LIFE? TOO MANY MANAGERS CITE LACK OF TIME AS AN EXCUSE FOR NOT CREATING A QUALITY CONSULTATIVE PROCESS. REMEMBER THAT THE LACK OF CONSULTATION GENERATES FAR MORE PROBLEMS THAT REQUIRE MORE TIME TO SOLVE.

3. SHARING THE RIGHT INFORMATION WITH THE RIGHT PEOPLE

— ARE YOU RESPONSIBLE FOR THE DISSEMINATION OF INFORMATION? IF YOU ARE, DO YOU REALLY UNDERSTAND WHO NEEDS TO HEAR IT AND WHY? HOW DO YOU KNOW YOU ARE RIGHT? INVITE FEEDBACK FROM STAFF.

— DO YOU PROVIDE GENERAL OR SPECIFIC INFORMATION? WHAT ADDITIONAL INFORMATION WOULD PEOPLE LIKE OR NEED?

— HOW IS INFORMATION DISSEMINATED? IS IT INTERESTING AND USEFUL? FOR INSTANCE, IF YOU HAVE A NEWSLETTER, DOES ANYONE READ IT? IF THEY DON'T, WHAT CHANGES COULD BE MADE?

— ARE STAFF MEETINGS WELL ATTENDED? DO STAFF PARTICIPATE? DO THEY ENJOY THEM? ARE STAFF FREE TO TALK OPENLY? HOW DO YOU KNOW THEY WILL TALK OPENLY?

— DO YOU HOARD INFORMATION AS PART OF A POWER BASE? IF YOUR HONEST ANSWER TO THIS QUESTION IS "YES," ASK YOURSELF WHY YOU THINK YOU DO IT. HOW WOULD YOU GO ABOUT CHANGING THIS? MAKE A LIST OF THE BENEFITS AND COSTS OF DOING THIS.

WHY?

INFORMATION IS THE FERTILISER TO PEOPLE'S THINKING AND INNOVATION. IF PEOPLE ARE A CRITICAL COMPONENT IN THE SUCCESS OF YOUR BUSINESS OR DIVISION, THERE IS NO BETTER WAY TO IMPROVE PERFORMANCE THAN TO ENSURE THEY RECEIVE WHAT THEY NEED AND, REASONABLY, WHAT THEY WANT. MAKING TIME TO DO THIS IS A CRITICAL RESPONSIBILITY OF MANAGEMENT.

Education — a lifetime of learning

Education will be the Holy Grail of business in the twenty-first century.

Education today is least of all what happens to us only between the ages 18 to 40 and most of all about the lifetime of learning that we can choose to commit ourselves to. This chapter looks at what people in business are asking for and looks at some of the roadblocks that stop people getting what they want or need.

As you read on, keep this proposition in mind: you are the 'customer', the educator is the 'seller'. It's a wonderful paradigm to work from because it measures the quality of the teacher, not the intellectual aptitude of the student.

A FRAME OF REFERENCE

My faithful, dog-eared Webster defines education as follows:

n. **1.** The act or process of educating; the imparting or acquisition of knowledge, skill, etc.; the systematic instruction or training. **2.** The result produced by instruction, training or study. **3.** The science or art of teaching; pedagogics.

Not bad, but not quite enough. I would like to add in the following:

– it should be totally engaging and stimulating

– it produces a useful result based on a clear outcome

– its success is measured by feedback from the 'student', which clearly demonstrates comprehension, and not on the apparent completion of course material by the 'educator'.

Here's what it *isn't*: something that puts you to sleep!

I remember a geography lesson at school. I must have been 15 at the time. I always sat at the back of the class (an advantageous place to be in geography). The teacher was a small, round, plain woman who permanently smelt of chalk. I didn't like her and I don't think she liked me. This one afternoon I had managed successfully to prop myself up behind our main geography text and, for all intents and purposes, was hoping to appear to be clearly deep in thought. In this position I had gone blissfully to sleep. I am not sure how long I had been dreaming before a nudge from a close mate alerted me to my pending execution. The dreaded geography teacher was standing next to my desk, impatiently tapping the edge of her black gown with a tough looking ruler.

I pronged to full alert hoping, to bluff my way to safety. It didn't work. I was told to go and splash cold water over my face and, considering I was not interested in learning anything, to wait outside and see her at the end of the lesson. (Oh, I should mention she was the Assistant Head Mistress as well as the geography teacher.)

My heart in my mouth, I waited outside. Eventually, the bell went and the class exploded from the room and ran past me without a backward glance. The teacher marched out and, gathering me in her wake, headed straight to the Head Mistress's office. Once an audience was granted with God Herself, I was subjected to a thorough verbal beating (by both women) — about my attitude, my selfishness, my lack of commitment to my own education, my slothfulness and my general decline into wantonness!

Naturally, I had no response to the demand, "Well, have you anything to say for yourself?" — except in the privacy of my own head. As I remained mute on the outside, World War Three erupted on the inside:

"Who in God's name gave you the right to stand on a stage and bore your listeners witless? How blind are your eyes, deaf your ears, dead your skin that you cannot see, hear or feel that the entire class detests your teaching style, finds you excruciatingly boring and, to top it off, can't stand your dress sense!"

On this exact day I declared war on education that bored the pants off the would-be educated. The injustice of the accusation, the inability of two apparently successful educators to identify the real culprit and the wanton squandering of real learning time burnt into my skin and left an indelible mark which I carry to this day.

TALL TALES AND TRUE FROM THE COALFACE

He was a big man. He entered my office shyly, clearly wishing he was elsewhere. He carried his hat in his hands, turning it slowly, even as he entered. He did not look at me but I could see how red his eyes were and rheumy, like old man's eyes, but he wasn't old. His face was deeply lined, his complexion ruddy. He had an unkempt quality about him.

I motioned for him to sit down and, as I sat next to him, I introduced myself and explained the purpose of our interview. I talked about what I did in the process of developing an Honesty Audit. I said my job was carefully to listen to the people of the business, in the course of a range of one-on-one interviews, to record what I heard and to try to look for common threads of concern. From this process I would build a composite picture of the business, its strengths and weaknesses. This information would be presented — as an accurate, concise report on what the people in the business really had to say — to the management in a no-holds-barred session in which I would hold nothing back.

I have always prided myself in my ability to set people at ease and to quickly build quality rapport with them, making sure, particularly in a business environment, that they recognise I am very serious about understanding their perspective of the universe. When I am engaged in research for a business I will usually talk to someone for ten to fifteen minutes before I get down to the serious 'nitty gritty' of the interview.

We might talk about anything — what they do, how long they have been with the company, what they are interested in, what their ambitions are, have they got children, how old the children are and so on. In this way we build bridges, become more human in the process and so feel comfortable being honest about what works and what doesn't work for them in the context of the work they do.

In this particular interview, my skills were found wanting, to put it mildly. It was one of those occasions where I knew I'd got it wrong from the start but couldn't quite pick the point at which I started to go astray. I talked, he nodded. I asked questions, he gave monosyllabic, one word replies. I could hear time passing, second by second, slowly and agonisingly. He sat hunched over his hat, turning it slowly and methodically and I sat next to him, moving from eloquence to stilted statements to silence.

Outside, I could hear the sound of heavy transport passing our window. We were perched on the edge of one of Sydney's major transport arteries. It had a mesmerising quality — the steady thrum of traffic. In the room, the silence lengthened and I began to wonder if, in fact, the person before me had a serious problem. Maybe he couldn't speak, maybe he had brain damage, maybe he didn't work in the business after all but had slipped through the door — a phantasm from another planet! Such thoughts do slip through the professional screen — even of someone as experienced as myself!

Eventually, the big man before me took a huge sigh, as if the effort of bringing his spirit into the room was almost unbearable. He fixed me with his bloodshot and rheumy eyes for the first time. He scrutinised my face in slow detail, he shook his head and then, as if going against his better judgment, he said these words:

> *For want of a nail, the shoe is lost;*
> *For want of a shoe, the horse is lost;*
> *For want of a horse, the battle is lost;*
...I'm the guy without the nail.

I sat in stunned silence and then managed to say one of the most regrettable and certainly one of the most stupid things I have said in a long time. "I didn't expect to have a proverb quoted to me..." and before I compounded the problem by saying "from a labourer," I managed to shut my mouth. Unfortunately, he understood perfectly well what I had thoughtlessly been about to say so he finished the sentence for me. He then proceeded to launch into one of the most humbling and fiercely-delivered lectures I have had in a long time.

"I can't believe the arrogance. There is this blind assumption that just because we are involved in a labouring job we have left our brains somewhere else or that we are not educated or don't read. I read, every day of my life. I just don't happen ever to have been invited to share my knowledge or to use my brains in this bloody business. The assumption is that only halfwits do labouring work, drive forks, load or unload, but it's not true, and if management were half as good as they like to think they are, they would be down on the shop floor talking to people, finding out what support they need, making use of what we know and developing our skills. I've been here for a decade and I haven't met a manager and I have never had any so-called education. Is it any wonder we stop caring!"

I was horrified. I had just had a serious attack of 'foot and mouth' disease. In fact, I was doubly horrified because it did not reflect how I really felt, it was just one of those moments where, despite the very best of intentions, things had gone the wrong way. In shock and feeling seriously chastised, I proceeded to apologise and to make my way back to this man, as honestly as I knew how.

Some twenty minutes later we started to talk, without rancour, as equals, and it was one of the most useful interviews I have ever done. We talked about the role of education in business, we talked about who would be responsible for it and why, we talked about management's involvement in education. We talked about the future of the business, its strengths and weaknesses, its ambitions and opportunities.

As the shadows started to lengthen in the room and I realised we had long since exceeded our allocated hour together, I reluctantly had to close our dialogue. The man stood, extended his enormous hand, and shook mine slowly and thoughtfully. He turned to leave and just as he was about to pass out of my life and I from his, he turned around and quoted me this parting piece of wisdom:

> *We are faced with the paradoxical fact that education*
> *has become one of the chief obstacles to intelligence*
> *and freedom of thought.*

He continued, "Bertrand Russell said that and I've often thought that there is a barrier developing between employees and managers that is measured by education or what they think they know. It's almost like we are forgetting how to talk to one another... maybe *that* should be the focus of everyone's education — not just a case of training Pavlov's dog to do a few more tricks. It's a thought anyway."

With that, he left and I had much to think on.

Now, some years later, I am still left with the echoes of that interview.

It makes for a good lesson, I believe.

TALL TALES AND TRUE FROM THE TOP

Participative work practices and quality education increase the performance of business measurably. Here is an Australian success story that adds weight to this proposition.

The company was a small Western Australian firm specialising in asbestos reclamation and survey work predominantly in the mining industry, to determine the level of air, water and soil contaminants. It had, since the discovery of the harmful side effects of asbestos and the passing of legislation that required asbestos audits be done in all buildings, not surprisingly, done very well.

However, nothing stays the same. Management, who also owned the business, were concerned that the asbestos market was close to being fully covered, and they were unsure as to how the business should refocus. I remember our first meeting vividly. There were four key players (all of whom owned major shares in the business) plus a fifth, non-shareholder, who was the eccentric 'brains' of the business.

We stood in their main laboratory, leaning in various ways against temporarily dormant lab benches (the lab staff had already gone home). They were a marvellous bunch — one had a hairdo that would have done Einstein proud; another looked like a Sumo wrestler; another had the smooth, polished look of a practiced insurance salesperson; another could easily have graced the boardroom of any large corporation and the last, and most incongruous, was a young woman, quiet, withdrawn, pleasing, who looked more like a hippie than a shareholder in a highly technical business.

I stood and listened to them argue back and forth about what they wanted their business to be and do; what they believed it had to do to survive. It was wonderfully animated; no one agreed with anyone else. We talked for a long time and it was finally the young hippie who focused the familiar debate by asking the only outsider — me — some pertinent questions like, "Why are you here?" "What can you offer us?" "Where have you been successful and why?" "Who can we speak to who you have worked with?"

Some hours later we surfaced from an intensive interrogation of my qualifications and experience to sign an agreement to work together. My job was to first establish how staff saw the business and what it thought were its strengths and weaknesses; secondly, I had then to facilitate a retreat with the owners and a selection of staff to determine once and for all where the business was to go.

Weeks passed, fascinating for me and insightful for the management. My recommendation for the 'Future's Retreat' was to invite all staff along. My theory was that it was a small business (25 staff in all) and that we could only benefit from the combined intelligence of these people in our deliberations.

I remember our first retreat (many more than were originally anticipated followed). It was conducted one weekend in the house of one of the shareholders. His wife did all the catering and we were cramped into a room that would have comfortably accommodated ten people. Twenty-five of us were intimately connected before the day began!

In two days, thanks in no small part to the courage of the Managing Director, we travelled light-years together. All the staff had read my report following the preliminary research and, at the outset of the weekend, the MD had made a point of stressing how important our journey was and how much it represented a learning cycle for everyone. This became the catchcry for the work I did with this group of people over the next two years. Repeatedly I would hear the MD, and then, increasingly, other managers, repeat the importance of learning, of trying and learning, continuously.

So much was changed in the process. A fractionated, visionless business was turned into a focused enterprise. Staff, a little tired and uncertain about the future, became passionate and determined. Education, something that many had done at university but not subsequently, resurfaced as a daily part of how the business ran. Teamwork and individual participation became the norm and in the process the business became a star performer.

In 1995 this small undirected business was so transformed it won a national award for quality management and best practice. Some time after the business had received the award, I remember travelling to the airport with the MD and asking him what he thought had been the single biggest contributor to the company's undisputed success. He laughed, a big and infectious laugh. "There can be no arguing on that score... it is how much we have all learnt — and no one more than me.

It's been an education, from beginning to end... and do you know what, I realise we are just at the beginning of the journey!"

Although I provided some of the learning environments as part of a more formal training agenda, the truth was that by far the more valued education he referred to was generated by the process of trial and error. It was supported by a leadership team who were open to scrutiny, who actively encouraged fearless feedback and who were themselves willing and able to do things differently. It was fuelled by a curious and hungry staff who took the opportunity provided and used it to the best of their ability, for their own benefit and for the benefit of the business.

Ultimately this should be the purpose of all business education.

A BIT OF POTTED HISTORY

In what follows, I am not endeavouring to be historically pedantic; rather, I am trying to provide an insight into how our broader perceptions of education might have evolved. So come on a journey for a moment as I compress perhaps three hundred years of history into a little story...

There was a nobleman. Before he was a nobleman he was a pubescent teenager and before that a snotty-nosed child. He lived some two hundred years ago, in the late eighteenth century. Money was no problem to his successful family of traders. Not only were they profitably trading spices (being principle shareholders in the East India Company), they could also trace their lineage back to Henry VIII. Good noble blood, if not a tad inclined to multiple marriages!

Now, let's speculate a moment or two on our young noble gent's education: let's consider what he would have been learning around the age of three to twelve: hmm... probably English, Latin, French, history (and his part in it), etiquette, geography, science, physics, mathematics, the arts and, of course, how to behave like a gentleman. Travel on in time and let's look at his education from twelve to seventeen: probably more of the same, but let's add in some if not all of the following: deportment, dancing, chivalry, warmaking (his role as a leader therein), swordsmanship, penmanship, philosophy, politics, horse riding, estate management. All good stuff. Now let's consider our young noble gent from the age of eighteen into his early twenties: perhaps, relieved from the tedium of private tutelage at home, he has embarked on the travails of a university education. He studies philosophy. He sails through university and, on graduation, enters his father's firm.

At the age of twenty-four, he begins to learn the spice trade — how to lead it and profit from it. He is introduced to the who's who of business, is provided with secure tenures in a variety of distant locations and is, by all accounts, turning into an outstanding leader, feared and admired by all.

Meanwhile, back at the farm, let's check on some of *our* forebears — good peasant stock all! My folks worked for a feudal lord, tilling tough land, turning turbulent sod and cursing the weather. I was about seven when the Industrial Revolution turned everything upside down. After dad died of the pox and the feudal lord kicked us out, my mother took me and my brother to the town to see if we could make our fortune. Mother, bless her soul, cooked for us and sewed for a living (by a dim light for twelve to fourteen hours a day); my brother (a fourteen-year-old) was employed in a warehouse moving bales of spice; I went to school.

Some people believed that scruffy young troublemakers like me needed a good education: together with the abiding principle, 'spare the rod and spoil the child'. The Industrial Revolution demanded obedient factory fodder, and that meant people who could read and write and do basic maths. Why? So they could follow basic instructions and perform basic tasks.

NOW, TRAVEL FORWARD IN TIME...

Initially, many noble families prospered during the Industrial Revolution. After all, they had the education to make things happen: they were not born to lead; they were educated to lead. Everyone else wasn't born to follow, we were educated to follow.

However, as is often the case, no one quite foresaw the way things would turn out. Intelligence, freedom of thought and innovation belonged to anyone, and so the Industrial Revolution fed the fortunes of many people whose heritage dictated a quite different life's course from the one they were enterprising enough to generate for themselves.

These first few entrepreneurs broke the stranglehold the educated nobility and gentry had over the ownership of enterprise. They became the dreaded, tasteless and, in many cases hopelessly successful 'nouveau riche' (see the lady daintily place a sweet smelling hanky to her nose for fear of contamination).

LET'S MOVE ON AGAIN...

Over time, education for the masses improved. Instead of being a luxury for the few, it became compulsory for everyone. Subjects included many that had traditionally been the privilege of the 'upper class'. Over time, working conditions were challenged and unions blossomed to protect the rights of people trapped in factories and mines, dingy offices and sweat-shops, working twelve to fourteen hours a day, six days a week from the age of fourteen or younger.

Our world evolved and the world of education evolved with it. In the nine-teen-fifties, education supported a conservative Western world desperately trying to accommodate the explosion of work that followed World War Two. We were taught to think in a linear, sequential fashion. Business wanted well planned, literate, numerate employees, who would still do what they were told to do, albeit in a reforming environment. There was so much for everyone to do and we were all having a lot of fun doing it.

Managers in a diversity of businesses were employed to tell people what to do. Their positions were won through education and experience. They were *men* (women were at home wearing aprons, cooking scones, sewing skirts and preparing the evening meal). They were authoritarian. They worked from the 'right way' principle — that is, "my way's the right way." Employees hung up their brains at the factory gate, worked an eight hour shift and then collected their brains on the way out. They were employed, a fair day's pay for a fair day's work, to do not to think.

It all worked gloriously well until the information revolution came and turned it all upside down!

We hit the late twentieth century and the universe turned upside down. The whole notion of learning, of education, was tumbled into the dishwasher and it hasn't been retrieved yet! Information explodes around us every minute of our lives like a perpetual fireworks display. No one, no matter how clever, can understand in their lifetime, even a fraction of what has been explored, uncovered, invented, developed, changed, written about, thought on, postulated, theorised over. It just isn't possible.

TODAY

Everyone has to be on the ball. Managers can't insist on a 'right way' to do something because though it may be right today, it could be horribly wrong tomorrow. Certainty is the one cannon shot that can send our fragile boat to the bottom of the bright cold briny sea. Certainty that there is only one way to do something, one answer to a problem, one way to take advantage of an opportunity, one way to deal with adversity. Today, with so much changing, we need to learn to harness a multiplicity of possibilities. In this scenario, education should be our Holy Grail. Everyone, to the full extent of their will and ability, must contribute.

Innovation and creativity are every bit as valuable in business as a capacity to think sequentially, plan strategically, manage systems and so on. We have discovered much about how the brain learns. We understand more about 'right-brained', spatial, lateral learning as opposed to 'left-brained' sequential learning. We appreciate why star performers at school are not necessarily successful in business, and why poor scholars often become clever entrepreneurs. (How often is it remarked that "formal education isn't worth the paper it is written on"?) Both positions having more to do with learning styles than the act of learning.

Education feeds us all. Educators today accept high levels of personal accountability for the results they produce. It is possible to ask (among other things) the following questions and not be shouted out of the assembly hall:

– How can you grade a child when their performance may be a function of the way they are taught? For instance, if they learn by physically doing something yet all they are presented with is theory, how successfully will their interest and capacity to think be engaged?

– Why would you give someone a frame of reference that tells them they are hopeless? For instance, in spelling tasks, wouldn't it be more useful to say, "It was an eight letter word and you got one letter wrong; seven out of eight ain't half bad?" Wouldn't that encourage the person to give it another shot?

– If education is about producing results, shouldn't we find out from those who want to be educated how they prefer to learn? We should provide a diversity of learning environments, assess what works, for whom, and why.

– Shouldn't we stop doing student assessments and start doing teacher assessments? How can a teacher know what to do differently unless they get quality feedback from students?

– Why is it more important to assess students from "F" to "A" than to ask how we would ensure the majority of students become A-graders?

About twenty years ago, for the majority of us, education was something we suffered from the age of five to the age of, say, twenty-four (if you went onto tertiary studies). Today, more and more people are embracing the idea that education or learning is a lifetime thing. No matter what your age, no matter what your current skill level or training, everything and anything is possible tomorrow. Agreement on when education is meant to occur has definitely undergone a quantum shift.

What do you want to be? Where do you want to go? What do you want to do when you retire? What do you want to do right now? What would you need to learn to do to achieve your ambitions? Where will you go to satisfy your learning requirements?

Courses are being created left, right and centre to accommodate new demands for learning by a broader demographic range. TAFEs are moving rapidly to accommodate the learning requirements of adult learners. Thirty percent of postgraduate placements in universities are being taken up by people over the age of thirty; people in their sixties are returning to do first degrees. The age barriers are down, learning opportunities are everywhere. It's a bonanza!

With this explosion in learning, the demands on educators have skyrocketed. Although I may have stood as quiet as a church mouse in the Head Mistress's office to receive my dressing-down for going to sleep in Geography, now, as an adult learner, I will walk out of the class, refuse to pay and then proceed to give the educational institution a lambasting for the poor quality of its educators!

As all people are being asked to consider the power of personal responsibility and accountability, none are having expectations of performance placed on them as solidly as today's educators, and particularly in business. But good news! They are embracing it better than a lot of other people. And bad news, too — they have a long way to go.

The learning process is said to involve the following stages:

1. *Unconscious incompetence:* We don't know what it is we don't know (assume, for instance, that you have never sat behind the wheel of a car: you are unconsciously incompetent; you don't know what it is you need to know to drive effectively).

2. *Conscious incompetence*: We know what it is we don't yet know (you have your first driving lesson and, as you deal with the instruction to turn right into oncoming traffic, you realise that you are terrified, haven't the vaguest idea what to do and now value the instructor's knowledge).

3. *Conscious competence*: We know what we are good at but only if we concentrate (you go for your test to get your driving licence; throughout the ordeal, you talk to yourself, reminding yourself of all the things you have just spent the last several months learning).

4. *Unconscious competence*: We don't know any more what it is we know (a decade after getting your licence, you quickly avoid a potential head-on accident by deft and brilliant handling of the car; once your heartbeat has resumed its normal rate you have a moment to bask in the glory of your own skill, before hurling abuse out your window at the halfwit who 'won their licence in a lottery').

Business education is, I believe, at stage two; we know what we need, but we just can't do it yet or do it consistently. At least the journey has commenced!

WHAT ISSUES DO PEOPLE RAISE WITH REGARD TO EDUCATION AND WHY?

Given that many of us have somewhat less than useful memories of child-hood education, over the years I have been astonished at how committed many adults are to improving themselves through further education. There seems to be few people in business, irrespective of level, who can't see the value of ongoing learning and aren't willing to put in the necessary effort. However, frustrations with quality, process and availability of education abound. Here are the most commonly raised concerns.

SPOT FIRE EDUCATION VERSUS A PLANNED APPROACH TO DEVELOPMENT

This is a very big area, and there are many people who have a greater level of expertise than I. Though they can address the problems it reflects more thoroughly, I will try to give an overview and touch on issues which I think are raised either poorly, infrequently or not at all.

Given that people see the need for ongoing education, I believe that what frustrates them most is that there is, in a large number of businesses, no formal educational strategy connected to either the long term ambitions of the business or their individual development. There are, of course, some organisations in Australia that have very good training strategies, but they tend to be found in very large businesses in which education has been longstanding, although predominantly capability-based. Mostly, education is still poorly tackled by many businesses. We should explore some of the reasons why this should be so; in doing so, we might discover some useful strategies.

THE RELATIONSHIP OF EDUCATION TO THE VISION OF THE BUSINESS: We need to be clear on where we are going and ensure that the educational strategy supports not only what we do now but what we will be doing in the short to medium term. Many people are frus-trated by the panic attacks that come when a long-foreseen business development suddenly causes a shortage of resources. This sort of educational crisis is particularly true of high-tech businesses whose continued development relies on the skills of employees to set the right pace for the introduction of new, bigger, brighter technologies.

People believe that the sales and marketing of new technologies are managed more effectively than the education of staff to support the services driven by these technologies. It reflects both the skill and focus of attention of leadership. It also may reflect the lack of quality strategic thinking in education.

THE RELATIONSHIP OF PLANNED EDUCATION TO PERSONAL DEVELOPMENT — APPRAISALS AND MENTORING: I believe that there will be major developments in this area in the next decade. Appraisal systems as we know them today will disappear; in their place, mentor programs will rise, and rise.

Appraisal systems, in many instances, exemplify the Abilene Paradox at its most horrible. Many, if not all of us can recall a negative experience of formal appraisal processes. The smack of 'big brother' peering over our shoulders. We are squeezed into a process that no one likes, which produces questionable results, for obscure and often unfulfilled business outcomes — all because someone, somewhere, decided it was the right thing to do. Sometimes (although, in my experience, rarely) team input is used in individual appraisals. Even less frequently, the appraisal process is two-way (that is, leaders are appraised at the same time). And almost non-existent is the concept of 360° appraisal — from below, from peers and from superiors. However, notwithstanding more enlightened practices, appraisals generally are done poorly.

Problems with the appraisal process include the following:

– Appraisals of performance are often done to quota, with bonus distributions determining how many people are graded as excellent. Managers and employees alike hate this.

– There can be confusion over the purpose of appraisals. Though they may be claimed to be done to support individual goals in terms of work ambitions, the process is more tightly tied to salary increases rather than to achievement of stated objectives.

– The worker's relationship with their manager can determine the outcome of an appraisal.

– Appraisals are done sporadically and are then not used for anything, the individual who has been appraised receiving little or no feedback.

– Appraisals may be used as tools for fast-tracking 'high achievers' (that is, those who 'fit the mould' and who will move rapidly up the organisation's hierarchy).

– Despite requests for support education to achieve agreed goals, the education isn't received; despite this the individual in question is still judged against the original goals and a judgment is entered into based on not achieving those goals.

– Despite the not infrequent opportunity during appraisals for employees to state why certain things have been achieved and others haven't, a manager's point of view carries more weight.

– Appraisals frequently don't allow for feedback on poor leadership.

– Appraisals are rarely done in an environment of complete trust and honesty.

– Appraisals are generally done once a year, so they lose their immediacy. (Quarterly appraisals would allow regular feedback to the individual being appraised.)

In some companies, people claim to prefer an ad hoc feedback process. However these, too, appear to have substantial liabilities. For instance they:

– may or may not actually take place;

– have a tendency (but not always) to happen when someone has done something wrong;

– sometimes reflect a given leader's current 'favourite' (that is, they are not done for all staff);

– contain 'mood-of-the-moment promises' which may never actually materialise;

– have a way of not being communicated laterally and vertically in the organisation, to other team members or to leaders who might need to know of certain issues;

– end up not being connected to an agreed long term plan (whether it be for the business or the individual).

There are, of course, very considerable advantages to any sort of appraisal process over no process at all. At an informal level, we all value the quality of our relationship with a respected leader. Their intimate knowledge of our work and our daily endeavours helps us to feel valued, acknowledged, important. In a trusting relationship, we are open to constructive feedback on how to do things better and we are more receptive to suggestions about doing further education or training.

In the formal process we also recognise that we are addressing some of the shortfalls of the ad hoc appraisal process: we are adding an objective dimension to our appraisal which can be viewed by a variety of people. We are setting agreed criteria, agreed time frames and agreed outcomes.

The challenge, then, is to harness the quality of an *informal* process with a trusted leader and the *formal* process where we set down with our manager agreed, measurable criteria for our development over a sustained period of time.

Mentor programs are done in a tiny percentage of organisations, but I will take this opportunity to present their case so you can consider their value in the light of the need for a quality tool for supporting individual development against a clear vision in the business. In this chapter's Practical help I have included an outline of how I would run a mentor program. Although it can be a complex exercise and most certainly requires training, it is, in principle, similar in nature to how parents teach children.

Essentially, an ideal mentor program ensures that every individual in the business has someone they respect supporting their development. A mentor is someone we trust, whose knowledge embraces an area we are interested in or whose position and skill enables them to provide access to other helpful people or training. A mentor is someone we select and who agrees to the mentor process. They may or may not be a manager or direct boss. They understand our personal ambitions and help us to plan achieving them. They help us to identify what education we need, what the company provides and what outside education might be appropriate. A good mentor also clearly understands what the business and our department is trying to achieve, and helps us tie our personal plans into overall business objectives.

A mentor is someone who isn't shy of telling us where to get off, shutting us up when we need to listen or offering constructive criticism when we need to learn something — perhaps in a hurry. Most important of all, however, a mentor is a friend, who we genuinely believe has our best interests at heart.

Geared to a well considered educational strategy, a mentor program is one of the most powerful tools I can think of to support individual and organisational learning.

STRATEGIC PLANNING OF EDUCATION: Apart from large organisations, this is something few businesses do well. In companies that don't plan their education, training tends to be 'spot fire' related or specifically skill based. Skill based education refers to the acquisition of specific skills to perform a specific task: someone employed as data processor requires basic computer literacy and a good operational understanding of a particular word processing program. Skill based education is usually done on the job, learn-as-you-go. Sometimes larger organisations run courses, as part of an induction process or on an ongoing basis, to ensure the development and maintenance of certain basic competencies.

When I refer to 'spot fire' education, I mean the type of education which is fired off in response to a new appointment or an apparent weakness. For instance, if a salesperson sells brilliantly and is promoted to sales manager, management might decide that that individual needs strategic planning skills. Someone rings some institute of management, and bingo! The person is sent off for a one day course to do strategic planning. Their education isn't planned; indeed, there may be other things they need to do before tackling strategic planning (developing, perhaps, communication or leadership skills). The selection of a course is rarely matched with any care to the individual's learning style or picked with the long term outcomes of the business in mind.

Spot fire education also commonly rears its ugly head around issues such as the supposed management of time (time management courses being, in my opinion, in large part one of the great hoaxes of the nineteen-eighties and nineteen-nineties). In response to an increasingly frantic work environment, executives who are finding it almost impossible to manage their workload assume the problem is related to their inability to manage their time. They go off to a course to improve their time management skills! Surprise, surprise, the time management course produces tremendous results in the first week, interesting results in the second and third weeks, some results in the fourth, fifth and six weeks, and thereafter, nothing!

The long term ineffectiveness of a time management course may reflect the lack of application of the learnt skills on the part of the manager (or employee), but chances are they reflect the fact that time management was not the real problem. The manager in question might not have a vision, might not know what strategic planning is, might find it hard to say "I've got too much bloody work to do!", might never have entertained the thought of delegation, and concluded that "hey, it's just a case of learning to prioritise, isn't it?"

An enormous amount of business education is being wasted because there is no educational plan tied to a clear business plan (short, medium and long term) and there is no individual plan for development.

Key components to a planned approach to education include:

– clear business vision;

– clear short, medium, long term strategies for getting there;

– clear HR vision, cascading from the business vision;

– clear HR short, medium, long term strategies for achieving the HR
  vision, including identification of:

– where are we going;

– current staff levels;

– skills that staff currently have;

– levels of competency;

– additional education needs and wants;

– sources for additional education;

– internal knowledge centres;

– external sources;

– costs to achieve outcomes;

– alternative educational fund allocations if funding is limited;

– accountabilities and tools for measuring achievement of outcomes.

On this last point it is worth noting that even in organisations with quite sophisticated educational strategies, quality measurement processes — which determine relevance of education to the business plans, and needs content actually learnt by participants (in the short, medium or long term) and measurable job performance improvement — are rarely implemented effectively.

ABSENCE OF ANY EDUCATION

I still find it hard to believe, but a very large number of businesses fail to provide their employees with any education whatsoever — despite the fact that employees may ask for it, despite the fact that it is needed and despite the fact that the business will benefit. The absence of education may result from one of the following four scenarios:

– Current management are not in touch with the developments that have occurred in business education. They may cling to this sort of declaration: "I employ Joe to do a job. Joe does the job. Joe does not need any further education." Such a manager fails to take advantage of the informed and creative input each and every one of their staff are able to provide — especially when they receive ongoing education.

– People in a position to make a decision about education strategy don't allocate adequate time to think about it. They may be in a fast-growing business in which everyone is having such trouble managing existing commitments they cannot even consider additional learning.

– The people who would make a decision about education have a personal fear of it. Such people may relate business education to what they experienced at school; they hold to a belief that the best learning is done on the job and so discount all but the immediately available learning opportunities.

– The business in question is experiencing constant 'peaks and valleys' in cash flow (because it is erratic or strongly seasonal). Education in these circumstances is seen as non-essential; it tends to be the first expense to be cut. Sometimes this is appropriate emergency action; often, however, a questionable short term gain is made (a money saving) at the expense of individual motivation, long term development and quality human resource planning. Such a cycle tends to be self-perpetuating.

In all four scenarios both individuals and eventually the business pays a hefty price for a limited world view. People learn nothing new or learn only from company experts. Over time, the learning can become insular, making both the business and the individual vulnerable to competitors — competitors who may have been taking into their learning cycle the offerings of the globe rather than just their own backyard.

EDUCATION IS AN INTIMIDATING BOGEYMAN —
"WE DON'T NEED NO EDUCATION..." (PINK FLOYD)

Many of us carry horrible memories of school. We might remember the humiliating experience of being diverted into the 'slow learner's' group in English, or out of maths and physics altogether because we just couldn't hack the pace. We may have memories of being branded 'dumb'. Plenty of women in their thirties who have excelled in the communication age remember being channelled off into home science, art, biology, home economics, craft. Plenty of men in the same age group will remember being channelled into woodwork or metalwork or out into the TAFE system. They were assessed as 'poor academic learners'. It may surprise many of them now to realise their performance was actually the direct result of inappropriate teaching methods.

Have you ever watched adults come into an auditorium for a seminar or conference? Which seats fill up first? Think about it. The last place in the world we wanted to be was in front of the teacher. Have you ever wondered why? I believe it is a hangover from school days. Up the front, you had to pay attention and stay awake. The front was where the 'nerds' or 'teacher's pets' sat. The cool dudes, the rebellious troublemakers, always sat up the back.

Interestingly, these so-called rebellious cool dudes were often people whose preferred learning style was more active: to learn something they had to *do it* (or a semblance of 'it'). For instance, think of a bottle of blue ink: the 'warning' on the side of the bottle says that it is toxic and will stain material or wooden surfaces. Some kids could read that sign and accept it as truth. I, together with a number of other monkeys, prefer to learn by trying it out on a piece of wood (and, with luck, dab it secretly on one of the 'nerd's' socks)!

Of course, I now appreciate and value academic learning styles which require a high degree of theorising, of absorbing analytically what other people have thought and discovered in the course of their investigations. However, I also now appreciate that a very important component of learning is experimentation — physically getting up and doing something. Learning styles work to complement each other, it is not an 'either/or' scenario.

The memories we have of our learning experiences as children come with us into adulthood and often affect how we see ourselves. If we can't write well or don't read often, we justify our perceived learning inadequacies by saying "I'm no good at reading," or "I don't need to read — I prefer to learn by getting my hands dirty."

Truthfully, however, if we are to make learning as adults enjoyable and fruitful, we have to be aware of our preferred learning strategies. So our opportunities in this extraordinary world are not unnecessarily limited. Sometimes it is essential that we acquire new skills. The skills of our job may change, we might decide to move into another area of business, or we might lose our trade altogether because that field of endeavour has become redundant. Whether we survive change depends on our ability to learn new skills.

Whatever the cause or motivation, learning for many adults might require them to look at themselves differently and be willing to place higher expectations on business educators to deliver the learning in a manner which is both acceptable to and enjoyable for the student.

LEADERS NEED TO BE INVOLVED WITH THE EDUCATION OF THEIR STAFF

Many of the people I have encountered have been frustrated by the lack of understanding demonstrated by leaders about the value of education. Although most managers understand direct capability-based training as it relates to a specific job, many fail to value the long term investment in staff education or, if value is ascribed, it is rarely as high as the demands of marketing, sales, production, administration or finance.

Many people say their requests for further education 'fall on deaf ears' and are always in the 'tomorrow' basket when there will be both more time and more money. Although this is common in many businesses (especially small businesses, where small turnover makes investment in the education of staff more challenging), it is also common in larger organisations and, in particular, among women aged from thirty to forty-five. This is the group that has, in my experience, taken up many of the basic administration, data entry, word processing jobs generated by the information age. These people may have returned to work after getting through the first few years of child raising. They have ambition and intelligence but often lack education. They work behind personal computers, processing information, entering data, performing relatively simple administrative tasks. In their first few years back in the workforce, with still young families, these 'rote' jobs are ideal. They are easy and can be left at the office at the end of each day.

However, with the passage of time, domestic commitments decrease. Women in this circumstance then want the opportunity to improve their knowledge (and therefore their opportunity for advancement). Now, while the issue of women and their approach to their careers will be dealt with in *Myth busters*, it is worth noting here two common complaints this specific group raise. Firstly, despite a company's commitment to education, they often find that their specific managers thwart their endeavours to take up further education, claiming that the department "can't spare them." Secondly, they will be told that the education they are seeking is not related to the work they are doing and therefore the manager cannot justify either the budget or the lost time.

In a younger person, or in a man, the request for further education will more commonly be seen as evidence of ambition. It is also understood that young people, both men and women, will not stay in 'basic' jobs for very long. Men are expected to be upwardly mobile. It is both understood and anticipated in much planning.

I am definitely one of those people who believe that the capacity to learn will become, throughout the next century, the salvation of the human race: it will stop us destroying our planet, it will sustain business, it will feed the curious, it will help us to turn leisure time into personally productive time, it will rejuvenate and inspire people from all walks of life.

Today, more than any other time I know, people are giving each other tacit permission to 'go for it', *irrespective of age*. Fewer people are accepting the old attitude: once a plumber, always a plumber. Hell, if I was a plumber yesterday, I can actually be a vet tomorrow. I will only be limited by my commitment to my own education, my patience (and my family's patience) and the courage to go back to school.

We are inspired by stories of people who have 'reinvented' themselves and we take courage and inspiration from their efforts. I know a forty-five year old businessperson who no longer wanted to sell insurance and decided to go back to university to study physics. He is, today, a fifty-five year old physicist — and loves it. Most of us know people in business who are studying , committing themselves to postgraduate diplomas, masters degrees, doctorates. People are taking up new leisure time skills, adventuring with family and friends.

I remember over a decade ago learning the startling statistic that over the age of twenty-five only 5% of adults acquired a new skill not related to the work they were doing. I suspect that that statistic has already changed and will continue to change even more in the next fifty to one hundred years.

Learning keeps us young, energised, inspired, inspiring. Yes, we acquire new skills, but we also learn to learn and learn to think. Doing this, we can apply our new skills to what we do day by day, but more importantly, apply our ability to think and our ability to learn. It is a cycle that takes us all upward.

In business, harnessing the learning cycle will produce outstanding results. It will generate flexibility, creativity, adaptability. It will give us courage to manage adversity so that the outcomes are useful. It will empower us to harness opportunity so that we beat the odds. It will ensure the 'spread of intelligence' is deeper, wider and more commonly valued.

One last little piece of advice: watch out for people who refer to humans, their motivation and education, as 'soft' issues. This is the rhetoric of a dead era. How on earth did we decide that finance was 'hard' and education was 'soft'? How else do you get to be good with figures except by learning? How do you manage to be a brilliant production engineer, systems analyst, stock market trader, economist, doctor, physicist except through education — formal or informal? People who think that the education of their staff is a soft issue are in for a hard time in the next century, that's all I can say!

Practical help

MENTORING — AN OVERVIEW OF HOW IT CAN BE DONE

MENTORING IS ONLY JUST BEING EXPLORED IN THE CONTEXT OF BUSINESS. THE FOLLOWING ADVICE IS PROVIDED AS A 'BROAD-BRUSH OUTLINE' OF HOW MENTORING CAN BE CONDUCTED. IT IS MEANT TO BE DEBATED.

THE OBJECTIVE FOR DEVELOPING ANY MENTORING PROGRAM IS TO DESIGN A PROCESS WHICH IS FLEXIBLE AND ALLOWS FOR SOME DEGREE OF EXPERIMENTATION IN PURSUIT OF AN AGREED OUTCOME. PARTICIPANTS SHOULD BE REMINDED THAT IT IS NOT HIERARCHICAL OR COMPETITIVE. IT IS ABOUT GENERATING AN ENVIRONMENT IN WHICH INDIVIDUALS ARE ABLE TO GROW AND DEVELOP TOWARDS BOTH COMPANY AND DEPARTMENTAL GOALS AS WELL AS INDIVIDUAL AMBITIONS.

WITH MENTORING, REMEMBER THAT THERE IS NO RIGHT WAY OR PROVEN WAY. WITH THAT IN MIND, HERE ARE SOME THOUGHTS ON THE PROCESS.

PROPOSITION ONE

THE MENTORING PROGRAM FOCUSES MANAGEMENT'S ATTENTION ON BUILDING A CULTURE IN WHICH INDIVIDUAL EXCELLENCE IS BOTH EXPECTED AND DEVELOPED.

PROPOSITION TWO

THE MENTORING PROGRAM IS NOT DIRECTLY GEARED TOWARDS REWARDS, INCENTIVES BONUSES OR SALARY INCREASES, ALTHOUGH ITS RESULTS WILL, NO DOUBT, BE OF VALUE TO LEADERS IN DETERMINING ALL OF THESE. THE MENTORING PROGRAM SHOULD BE DIRECTLY CONNECTED TO THE COMPANY'S EDUCATION STRATEGY. THERE SHOULD BE A CLEAR COMMITMENT TO CONNECT (A) THE COMPANY'S VISION AND BUSINESS PLAN, (B) THE DEPARTMENTAL VISION AND BUSINESS PLAN AND (C) THE INDIVIDUAL'S MEDIUM AND LONG TERM GOALS WHERE THEY ARE RELATED TO MOVEMENT WITHIN THE BUSINESS (THAT IS, IT IS THE PRODUCT OF THE CASCADING PROCESS MENTIONED IN CHAPTER 2).

PROPOSITION THREE

MENTORING IS A TWO-WAY PROCESS. FOR AN INDIVIDUAL TO PERFORM TO THE BEST OF THEIR ABILITY, THEY NEED APPROPRIATE LEADERSHIP. BOTH MENTOR AND MENTORED SHOULD AGREE ON HONEST FEEDBACK.

PROPOSITION FOUR

WITHIN THE CONSTRAINTS OF AN AGREED VISION AND BUSINESS PLAN (FOR BOTH THE COMPANY AND FOR A FUNCTIONAL AREA), THE PROCESS NEEDS MAXIMUM FLEXIBILITY TO REFLECT DIFFERENT REQUIREMENTS FOR DIFFERENT DEPARTMENTS AND INDIVIDUALS.

MENTORING — THE PROCESS

WHO AND WHEN?

(I) INDIVIDUALS, WITHIN REASON, NOMINATE THEIR MENTOR.

IT CAN BE AN EXISTING MANAGER, SOMEONE THEY ADMIRE OR SOMEONE WHO HAS THE SKILLS OR KNOWLEDGE THEY WANT TO DEVELOP. THERE SHOULDN'T BE TOO MANY RULES. TRUST THAT (A) PEOPLE WILL GENERALLY SELECT THE RIGHT MENTOR AND (B) THERE IS RARELY A CONFLICT OF INTEREST. BEAR IN MIND THAT A MENTOR WILL, IN ALL PROBABILITY, BE MENTORED THEMSELVES.

IF SOMEONE SELECTS A MENTOR WHO IS OUTSIDE OF THEIR AREA OR DEPARTMENT, ITS EFFECTIVENESS WILL BE MEASURED BY THE QUALITY OF COMMUNICATION BETWEEN THE INDIVIDUAL BEING MENTORED, THE MENTOR AND THE DEPARTMENTAL MANAGER.

ETIQUETTE CAN BE PRESERVED THROUGH QUALITY COMMUNICATION.

THE OBJECTIVE IS TO FIND A MENTOR WHO IS SUITABLE FOR BOTH PARTIES. NEITHER PARTY SHOULD FEEL INTIMIDATED BY THE CHOICE OF THE OTHER, NOR SHOULD SOMEONE FEEL OBLIGED TO BE A MENTOR SIMPLY BECAUSE SOMEONE HAS SELECTED THEM.

(II) INDIVIDUALS DETERMINE THE FREQUENCY OF THEIR MEETINGS TOGETHER WITH THEIR MENTOR.

LEADERS AND MENTORS SHOULD TRY TO ENCOURAGE A REASONABLE FREQUENCY OF MEETINGS TO AVOID THE REACTIVE JUDGMENT PROCESS MORE COMMONLY ASSOCIATED WITH ANNUAL APPRAISALS. MEETINGS MIGHT USEFULLY BE HELD MONTHLY, QUARTERLY OR SIX-MONTHLY. OF COURSE, AD HOC INFORMAL APPRAISALS SHOULD BE ONGOING. HOWEVER, BY FORMALISING THE PROCESS WITH REGULAR MEETINGS INDIVIDUAL GROWTH IS FOSTERED AND IT DOESN'T BECOME AN AD HOC JUDGMENT TOOL.

HOW?

(I) THE MENTOR AND THE MENTORED SET CLEAR EXPECTATIONS OF ONE ANOTHER.

FROM THE MENTOR'S POINT OF VIEW, THEY COULD REASONABLY EXPECT THE INDIVIDUAL TO COMMIT TO:

— HONESTY;

— OPENNESS;

— A WILLINGNESS TO HONOUR COMMITMENTS;

— A DESIRE TO PROVIDE THE MENTOR WITH CLEAR FEEDBACK;

— A WILLINGNESS TO RESPECT THE COMPANY'S VISION AND PLANS;

— RESPECT FOR THE DEPARTMENT'S VISION AND PLANS;

— SUPPORT FOR THE COMPANY'S EDUCATIONAL STRATEGY (WHERE APPROPRIATE);

— AD HOC MEETINGS ON AN AS-NEEDED BASIS.

FROM THE INDIVIDUAL'S POINT OF VIEW, THEY COULD REASONABLY EXPECT THE MENTOR TO COMMIT TO:

— HONESTY;

— OPENNESS;

— A WILLINGNESS TO HONOUR COMMITMENTS;

— AN INTENTION TO PROVIDE THE INDIVIDUAL WITH CLEARLY UNDERSTOOD FEEDBACK;

— RESPECT THE INDIVIDUAL'S SHORT AND MEDIUM TERM GOALS;

— SUPPORT THE INDIVIDUAL'S EDUCATIONAL REQUIREMENTS;

— A DESIRE TO LIAISE REGULARLY (APPROPRIATELY) WITH THE INDIVIDUAL'S MANAGER.

IF THE MENTOR IS NOT THE INDIVIDUAL'S MANAGER, THEY DO NOT REPLACE OR SUPERSEDE THAT MANAGER. THEY MAY, HOWEVER, ACT AS A CONDUIT TO THE LEADER IF, FOR INSTANCE, AN INDIVIDUAL FEELS NERVOUS OR UNSURE OF THEIR RELATIONSHIP WITH THE MANAGER IN QUESTION. SIMILARLY, THE RELATIONSHIP BETWEEN THE INDIVIDUAL AND THE MENTOR DOES NOT REPLACE THE FUNCTIONAL RELATIONSHIP BETWEEN THE INDIVIDUAL AND THEIR MANAGER.

FLEXIBILITY AND THOUGHTFULNESS IS NEEDED BY ALL PARTIES TO ENSURE INFORMATION DOES NOT FALL BETWEEN KEY INDIVIDUALS. AGREEMENTS STRUCK BETWEEN THE INDIVIDUAL AND THE MENTOR AND THE INDIVIDUAL AND THEIR MANAGER (AGREEMENTS WHICH IMPACT ON WORK PERFORMANCE AND INDIVIDUAL DEVELOPMENT) SHOULD BE RECORDED IN A 'MENTORING FILE'.

(II) THERE IS PRIOR AGREEMENT ABOUT 'JOB ACCOUNTABILITIES'.

BEFORE THE MENTORING PROCESS CAN COMMENCE, ACCOUNTABILITIES MUST BE ESTABLISHED. KEEP THE FOLLOWING IN MIND:

— YOU DON'T WANT TO BOX PEOPLE INTO LIMITING DESCRIPTIONS OF THEIR RESPONSIBILI- TIES IN THE BUSINESS;

— YOU DON'T WANT TO LEAVE THE INTERPRETATION OF THEIR ACCOUNTABILITIES SO OPEN THAT THEY RUN THE RISK OF BEING FRACTIONATED IN THEIR WORK.

THE PURPOSE OF A JOB DESCRIPTION IS TO GET AGREEMENT, IN PRINCIPLE, ON WHAT THE SPECIFIC ACCOUNTABILITIES ARE FOR A GIVEN INDIVIDUAL. SUCH A DESCRIPTION DOES NOT PRECLUDE THEM TAKING ON ADDITIONAL RESPONSIBILITIES OR, INDEED, CHANGING JOB

DESCRIPTIONS. IT SIMPLY ACTS AS A BENCHMARK — IT IS WHAT EVERYONE AGREES IS THE INDIVIDUAL'S PRINCIPAL AREA OF RESPONSIBILITY FOR AN AGREED PERIOD OF TIME.

AGREEMENT ON A PERSON'S ACCOUNTABILITIES NEEDS TO BE 'SIGNED OFF' BY THE INDIVIDUAL, THE MENTOR AND, IF THE MENTOR ISN'T ONE AND THE SAME, THE INDIVIDUAL'S MANAGER.

(III) CRITICAL SUCCESS FACTORS (CSFS) ARE SET FOR THE INDIVIDUAL.

THE INDIVIDUAL, WITH THE SUPPORT OF THE MENTOR, SHOULD DETERMINE THE CRITERIA ON WHICH THEY ARE WILLING TO BE ASSESSED. THESE SHOULD BE SET AGAINST A SPECIFIC TIME FRAME TO HELP BOTH THE INDIVIDUAL, THE MENTOR AND THE MANAGER MEASURE SUCCESS AT THE JOB. THE CSFS MIGHT USEFULLY REFLECT THE FOLLOWING:

— DEPARTMENTAL OR BUSINESS VISION AND PLANS;

— INDIVIDUAL ACCOUNTABILITIES;

— ANTICIPATED WORK IN THE AREA, SAY WITHIN THE NEXT SIX MONTHS (OR UNTIL THE NEXT MENTORING MEETING);

— INDIVIDUAL ACHIEVEMENTS BEING TARGETED (WHICH MIGHT INCLUDE: EDUCATION; UNUSUAL WORK ACHIEVEMENT; GENERAL WORK ACHIEVEMENT; MOVEMENT OF THE INDIVIDUAL TOWARDS A MEDIUM TERM GOAL; MOVEMENT OF THE INDIVIDUAL TOWARDS A LONG TERM GOAL).

IN SETTING THE CSFS THE FOLLOWING SHOULD BE OBSERVED BY BOTH THE MENTOR AND THE INDIVIDUAL:

— THERE SHOULD BE NO COMMENT ON AN INDIVIDUAL'S PERSONALITY; THE FOCUS OF ATTENTION IS ON IMPROVING PERFORMANCE THROUGH SUPPORT AND EDUCATION;

— TARGETS SHOULD BE REALISTIC AND QUANTIFIABLE (WITHIN REASON) AND WITHIN SPECIFIC TIME FRAMES FOR THEIR ACHIEVEMENT (MEASUREMENT CAN THEN, FOR INSTANCE, INCLUDE CERTAIN THINGS DONE BY A CERTAIN DATE TO A CERTAIN STANDARD).

(IV) CRITICAL SUCCESS FACTORS ARE SET FOR THE MENTOR.

ON AGREEING TO BE A MENTOR, A PERSON NEEDS TO CAREFULLY CONSIDER HOW THEY WILL BE ASSESSED. AGAIN, THE MENTOR AND THE INDIVIDUAL WOULD BE BEST SERVED BY DOING THIS TOGETHER. SOME POSSIBLE CSFs MIGHT BE:

— STICKING TO AGREED TIMELINES FOR MEETINGS;

— ENSURING THE QUALITY AND REGULARITY OF MEETINGS WITH THE INDIVIDUAL;

— BEING RECEPTIVE TO THE INDIVIDUAL'S ASSESSMENT OF THE TYPE OF SUPPORT THEY HAVE RECEIVED FROM THE MENTOR AND HOW, SPECIFICALLY, THIS HAS HELPED THEM TO DO THEIR JOB MORE EFFICIENTLY AND EFFECTIVELY;

— BEING CLEAR (PARTICULARLY WHERE THE MENTOR IS A DIRECT MANAGER) WITH SHARED INFORMATION;

— ENSURING THE QUALITY OF PLANNED EDUCATIONAL SUPPORT —— AND FACILITATING ITS PROVISION.

THE APPROACH TO FEEDBACK NEEDS TO BE MANAGED THOUGHTFULLY AND CAREFULLY. A MENTOR WHO IS A MANAGER (AND MANY OF THE MENTORS SELECTED WILL BE JUST THAT) NEEDS TO MAINTAIN THEIR POSITION AND FUNCTIONAL RESPONSIBILITY AS WELL AS ACT AS A MENTOR. HOW LEADERS CAN BEST (OR MOST SAFELY) RECEIVE FEEDBACK IS SOMETHING THAT THE LEADERS HAVE TO SUGGEST THEMSELVES. MUCH DEPENDS ON THE PREVAILING CULTURE OF THE ORGANISATION IN QUESTION. IT IS TOTALLY APPROPRIATE THAT IT VARY FROM PERSON TO PERSON.

A PROCESS NEEDS TO BE PUT IN PLACE TO ALLOW THE INDIVIDUAL AND MENTOR TO PART COMPANY WITHOUT ACRIMONY SHOULD THEIR PARTNERSHIP PROVE LESS THAN FRUITFUL. THE INDIVIDUAL NEEDS TO HAVE THE RIGHT TO SELECT A DIFFERENT MENTOR SHOULD THEY SO DESIRE, PROVIDING THE REASONS FOR THE CHANGE (SUCH AS INADEQUATE TIME AVAILABLE BY THE SELECTED MENTOR OR CONFLICT OF INTEREST) ARE ACKNOWLEDGED AND, POSSIBLY, RECORDED IN THE MENTOR FILE.

(V) THERE IS FEEDBACK FROM THE TEAM.

IN CERTAIN BUSINESSES, TEAM FEEDBACK MAKES GOOD SENSE, IN OTHERS IT MAKES NONE (TEAMS MAY NOT EXIST OR THEIR QUALITY AND DURABILITY MIGHT VARY). HOW THIS IS DONE IS OPEN TO DEBATE BUT SOME IF NOT ALL THE FOLLOWING NEED TO BE CONSIDERED:

— ANY PROCESS MUST BE NON-POLITICAL AND, BY ITS VERY STRUCTURE, AVOID THE OPPORTU-NITY FOR PERSONAL VENDETTA;

— INDIVIDUALS NEED CONSTRUCTIVE FEEDBACK —PRAISE AND CRITICISM;

— INDIVIDUAL PERFORMANCE MUST BE SEPARATED FROM THE TEAM'S PERFORMANCE: AN INDI-VIDUAL'S ACHIEVEMENT OF THEIR PERSONAL CSFS SHOULD BE RECOGNISED EVEN IF THE OVERALL TEAM RESULT IS NOT AS ANTICIPATED; SIMILARLY, EXTERNALITIES THAT PREVENT AN INDIVIDUAL FROM ACHIEVING THEIR CSFS MUST BE ACKNOWLEDGED.

RATHER THAN FORMALISING A PROCESS FOR THE TOTAL COMPANY WHICH DETERMINES HOW TEAM FEEDBACK CAN BEST BE HANDLED, ALLOW FLEXIBILITY WITH THE INDIVIDUAL AND THE MENTOR.

(VI) THERE IS A THIRD-PARTY REFEREE.

THERE SHOULD BE SOMEONE THE INDIVIDUAL OR THE MENTOR CAN TURN TO IF THINGS DON'T GO AS ANTICIPATED. IDEALLY, IF THIS PROCESS IS MANAGED AS IT IS INTENDED, THERE SHOULD BE NO NEED FOR A REFEREE. IN REALITY, IT IS POSSIBLE THAT AN ISSUE MAY ARISE WHICH A MENTOR AND AN INDIVIDUAL CANNOT AGREE UPON. A THIRD PARTY, NOMINATED AT THE BEGINNING OF THE RELATIONSHIP, TO WHOM BOTH PARTIES CAN TURN FOR A 'THIRD' INDEPENDENT OPINION IS THEREFORE USEFUL.

(VII) A RECORD OF AGREEMENT — THE MENTORING FOLDER — IS KEPT.

YOU DON'T HAVE TO BE A GENIUS TO WORK OUT HOW THIS CAN BE DONE. TAKE EVERY ITEM ABOVE AS A 'HEADING' IN THE MENTORING FOLDER — DEVOTE A PAGE OR TWO TO THE ENTRIES. DON'T BOTHER PRINTING UP SPECIAL FOLDERS, THIS IS MEANT TO BE A PRAGMATIC WORKING FOLDER.

KEEP TWO IDENTICAL COPIES: ONE IS FOR THE INDIVIDUAL AND ONE, THE MENTOR'S COPY, IS KEPT UNDER LOCK AND KEY IN A CENTRAL FILING SYSTEM. ACCESS IS LIMITED TO THE MENTOR AND, IN THE EVENT OF A CHANGE, IS MADE AVAILABLE TO SENIOR MANAGEMENT, WITH THE INDIVIDUAL'S PERMISSION.

THE FILES COULD INCLUDE SECTIONS ON THE FOLLOWING:

— SKILLS AUDIT REVIEW —— THE DOCUMENT YOU USE TO CAPTURE (INITIALLY) THE FOLLOWING INFORMATION ABOUT THE INDIVIDUAL:

- THEIR DESCRIPTION OF THEIR JOB;
- SKILLS REQUIRED;
- HOW THEY RATE THEIR SKILLS;
- EDUCATION THEY NEED OR WANT;
- THEIR FUTURE AMBITIONS —— WHERE THEY WOULD LIKE TO GO AND WHY;
- EDUCATION THEY WILL REQUIRE AND POSSIBLE SOURCES;

— A SEPARATE EDUCATION SECTION, LISTING:

- WHAT'S REQUIRED;
- THE SOURCE OF EDUCATION;
- TIMELINES;
- FEEDBACK ON THE WORTH OF THE EDUCATION;

— CSFs FOR THE INDIVIDUAL;

— CSFs FOR THE MENTOR;

— GENERAL AGREEMENTS;

— GENERAL NOTES

- FOR BOTH THE MENTOR AND THE INDIVIDUAL;

— A MEETING SCHEDULE;

— PLUS, OF COURSE, ANYTHING ELSE THE INDIVIDUAL AND THE MENTOR WANT TO INCLUDE.

ACTION FOR EMPLOYEES AND LEADERS ALIKE

DEVELOPING A STRATEGY FOR EDUCATION THAT IS FLEXIBLE AND USEFUL IS USUALLY A MATTER OF TRIAL AND ERROR, ACTION AND FEEDBACK. EVEN IF YOU HAVE AN EDUCATIONAL STRATEGY IN PLACE, ANY AND ALL OF THE FOLLOWING RECOMMENDATIONS WILL APPLY TO ALL INDIVIDUALS.

1. LOOK AT YOUR CURRENT SENSE OF YOUR ABILITY TO LEARN

— DO A SELF ASSESSMENT: ASK YOURSELF WHAT ARE YOU GOOD AT AND WHY, AND WHAT ARE YOU POOR AT AND WHY.

— CONSIDER WHERE TEACHERS HAVE SUPPORTED YOU: WHAT DID YOU LIKE ABOUT THEIR TEACHING SKILLS? WHEN WERE YOU MOST ENGAGED IN THE LEARNING ENVIRONMENT? WERE YOU LISTENING TO OTHER PEOPLE'S EXPERIENCES, HEARING THE THEORY, REFLECTING ON THE INFORMATION BASED ON YOUR PERSONAL EXPERIENCE, OR DOING SOMETHING PHYSICAL?

— SET UP DISCUSSION GROUPS TO COMPARE PREFERRED TEACHING METHODS. FOCUS UPON THE DIVERSITY, NOT THE SIMILARITIES, OF METHODS USED BY THE MEMBER OR THE GROUP.

WHY?

BECAUSE THE FIRST STEP AS AN ADULT IS TO HONESTLY APPRAISE YOUR OWN LEARNING 'PARADIGM'. ONCE YOU ASSESS YOURSELF AS A LEARNER, YOU CAN BEGIN THE PROCESS OF ADAPTING TO OR TAKING ON NEW LEARNING STYLES. A LEARNING INVENTORY WILL ALSO HELP YOU GUIDE A TRAINER TOWARDS A TRAINING STYLE THAT SUITS YOU (INSTEAD OF ACCEPTING ONE THAT DOESN'T).

2. TAKE YOUR INFORMATION TO THE PEOPLE WHO DELIVER TRAINING

— TALK TO THE TRAINERS IN YOUR BUSINESS, SHARE YOUR INFORMATION ON DIFFERENT LEARNING STYLES, FIND OUT WHAT THEY KNOW ABOUT LEARNING DIFFERENCES.

— CREATE A FEEDBACK MECHANISM IN LEARNING ENVIRONMENTS SO TRAINERS CAN IMPROVE THEIR DELIVERY.

WHY?

BECAUSE THIS IS HOW THE TRAINERS WILL CONTINUE TO IMPROVE IN THE DELIVERY OF
EDUCATION WHICH IS, AFTER ALL, FOR YOU.

3. DEVELOP AN EDUCATIONAL STRATEGY

— IF YOUR BUSINESS CURRENTLY HAS NO EDUCATIONAL STRATEGY, CONSIDER A PLANNING
  SESSION WITH STAFF AND MANAGEMENT TO LOOK AT THE FOLLOWING:

  — THE OVERALL VISION AND BUSINESS PLAN;

  — THE RESOURCES CURRENTLY AVAILABLE;

  — THE CURRENT SKILLS OF THE PEOPLE;

  — THE THINGS THE PEOPLE BELIEVE WILL BE NEEDED AND WHY;

  — ADDITIONAL EDUCATION NEEDS AND REASONS FOR THOSE NEEDS;

  — THE COST.

— TAKE MATERIAL FROM THIS CHAPTER, COMMIT TO DEVELOPING A STRATEGY, NO MATTER
  HOW BASIC, THAT WILL MOVE YOUR BUSINESS FROM A 'NO LEARN' ZONE TO A 'LEARNING
  ZONE'.

WHY?

BECAUSE WE ALL HAVE TO BEGIN SOMETIME, WHY NOT NOW? PART OF YOUR STRATEGY MIGHT
BE TO GET EVERYONE TO READ THIS CHAPTER. START SIMPLY BY DISCUSSING THE CONTENTS
AND SEE HOW MUCH IT RELATES TO YOU AND YOUR BUSINESS.

4. COMMIT TO MENTORING AS A TOOL FOR DELIVERING EDUCATION THAT MATCHES BUSINESS OBJECTIVES

— REVIEW THE MENTORING MATERIAL CONTAINED IN THIS CHAPTER.

— HAVE A STAFF OR MANAGEMENT MEETING TO DISCUSS THE IDEAS IN THIS CHAPTER.

— IF YOU DECIDE TO GO AHEAD, DEVISE A TIMETABLE FOR ITS IMPLEMENTATION AND GET
  PEOPLE TO COMMIT.

— BUDGET FOR THIS PROCESS AND, IF POSSIBLE, USE AN EXPERIENCED FACILITATOR TO
  SUPPORT YOU.

WHY?

I DON'T KNOW OF A MORE POWERFUL TOOL TO ENSURE THE EFFECTIVE, TIMELY AND FLEXIBLE MANAGEMENT OF EDUCATION IN SUPPORT OF INDIVIDUAL GROWTH IN SUPPORT OF A BUSINESS PLAN AND VISION. THERE ARE FEW PRECEDENTS TO GUIDE YOU. BE WILLING TO EXPERIMENT AND DEVELOP YOUR MENTORING PROCESS OVER TIME.

Equipment — like it or leave it — it's hard to do the job without it!

Nothing is more time consuming or demotivating than having inappropriate, shoddy, dated or damaged equipment.

I don't know why, but in the context of the work I do I always find it odd that the lack of, quality of or availability of equipment is raised by so many people as a frustration. Increasingly I suspect it is a contextual issue — that is, to really understand it we have to set it into an environment in which much is expected of people. In a demanding, competitive and

 changing world, people will be naturally anxious about their own performance and in order to do their best will, understandably, want the best possible support. That support may come in the form of shared planning, quality leadership, good communication and decent education. It may also be manifested in the standard and availability of the tools of trade.

A FRAME OF REFERENCE

Have you ever gone to do a job at home — maybe mow the lawn, or paint a door, or fix a piece of equipment, or wire up the hi fi, or cut down a tree — and for some reason the piece of equipment you need just isn't around?

I remember one occasion when I decided to mow the lawn. Usually I put this in the 'men's' basket. I don't think I can't do it, it just seems that way. Anyway, on this particular occasion, I was fed up with nagging one of the males in the family to do the job. There had been some reluctance to do the mowing for a while. I wasn't really clear about what the problem was, but there was certainly a lot of grumbling about nothing. I think it boiled down to the fact that the men in my family just wanted another toy — so they were hassling me to buy a new lawn mower. What did they think I was — a money machine? Anyway, the long and short of it was I decided to do the mowing myself, with the old mower. I felt quite bright and perky about the prospect.

It was a lovely day. I went out to our garden shed and got the lawn mower out. Admittedly, it looked a bit dodgy. Part of the casing that protects your legs from being accidentally removed by a rotating blade was missing. I couldn't remember anyone mentioning this to me (not that they would've anyway). I looked at the machine dubiously.

I took the fuel cap off, which was an exercise in itself because the thread seemed to have been unevenly sheared off, and discovered there was no fuel in the tank. That was cool. I jumped into the car and went down to the service station to get fuel... "Have you got your container?" asked a helpful part timer who I knew quite well. "No," I replied, "I didn't know I had to have one." "Yep, that'll cost you $4. But I think you have one, because I sold it to your son about a month ago." "Oh, really," I mumbled. "I'll go home and get it."

Ten minutes later I was back at the station. The young man quickly filled up my container and I returned home. Then I discovered that we didn't have a funnel. I decided to do without one and so got at least half the fuel over the engine and on my feet. Fortunately, I got enough into the tank actually to mow the lawn. Oh, well, only an hour had passed. All was not lost. I pulled out the choke, put the machine in neutral and the gave the cord a tug. Nothing happened. I checked the choke, looked at the engine (looking is a key part of getting anything mechanical to work) and then gave the cord another almighty tug. This time a faint splutter. I went through the routine a few more times. Eventually I called for my husband.

He patiently came to my rescue. He smiled affectionately and asked me if I had primed the fuel line. I looked appropriately baffled. He primed. "Try again," he said, stepping back and waiving at the lawn mower. I did and was rewarded with a mighty roar. He smiled, I smiled.

Happy little vegemite that I was, I then started to mow. About forty-five minutes later, while I was gasping for oxygen, the machine stalled. I was out of petrol. At this point I realised that I had forgotten to put the leaf catcher on the back and, given that I always nag the rest of the family to get rid of the clippings, I couldn't exactly leave the lawn littered. Wanting a break from the mower and not yet willing to drive again to the garage, I went in search of a rake. Twenty minutes later, covered in cobwebs, I discovered the head of one rake and the handle of another unmatchable one in our garden shed. I also discovered the broken leaf catcher.

I took a deep breath and counted to a million. I then got back into my car, went down to the hardware shop, bought a rake, returned to the garage, refilled my container with fuel, bought a funnel, returned home, and started again.

First, I raked the leaves up; second, I refuelled the mower, then I resumed mowing. Another hour and a half had passed. After another forty-five minutes of mowing, I was thinking of taking a break. I paused momentarily and turned around to view the product of my labours. It wasn't too bad, a bit patchy, but hey, I was just learning. It was at the exact point that I was bragging to myself about the quality of my work that I sheared the top off one of my Blundstones. I had accidentally put my foot too close to the unprotected and still-turning blades.

I leapt out of my skin, convinced that I had just removed several toes. I collapsed to the ground, tore off my boot and frantically searched for evidence of amputation. I was still one unit, but I had a sad gaping hole in my pair of favourite boots. It was at this point, I think, that I spat the dummy. I left the mower where it was and stormed up to the house, my shoe making a noise like a wet pancake hitting a surface repeatedly. In the kitchen I found my husband and two sons. They had watched this fiasco from the kitchen window.

"Any lateral damage?" said my eldest, with a glint in his eye. "No," I rumbled. "Having trouble with the fuel?" enquired the youngest son. "No," I grimaced. "Need another pair of boots?" chimed my husband. I looked at all three of them as they looked at me. And then we all burst into laughter.

I looked at my watch. It was exactly 3.30 pm. I thought to myself and then asked aloud: "Anyone want to come and help me choose a mower?" Three males replied with one voice.

TALL TALES AND TRUE FROM THE COALFACE
(Stage is dark, the sound of background drinkers fills the auditorium. As stage lights come up, sound fades into the background. Centre stage, leaning against a counter are two men, obviously enjoying a drink after work. Ties are undone. They look pleasantly relaxed.)

She needed a computer.
Why?
Because she was a data processor.
Why didn't she have a computer?
Because the company had recently merged.
Who did she ask?
Her supervisor
Did he agree?
Yes.
Did he know what to get?
Yes.

Did he know its cost?

Yes, $4,000.

How big did you say the company was?

$500 million in turnover.

Did she get it then?

No.

What happened?

The supervisor put in a submission to his Departmental Manager.

What did he say?

"She."

Pardon?

"She," not "he."

Alright, alright, what did she say?

"Yes, but I can't approve the purchase."

Who approved it then?

The requisition order was signed by the Regional Manager.

So the woman got her word processor then?

No.

What happened?

The Regional Manager had to get it signed by the Managing Director.

Great! That was the end of it, I suppose?

No.

Well?

The MD only headed up one of the business groups in the company. He had to get the purchase order signed by the Group Finance Director.

Jesus! She got it then didn't she?

No.

Go on.

He had to have it signed by the Executive General Manager.

Oh really?

And then the Group Managing Director had to sign it.

Surely there was no one else after all that?

No.

So what happened?

The Group MD said okay and gave it back to the Executive GM who said it was okay and gave it back to the Group Finance Director who said "good" and gave it back to the Business Managing Director who smiled and gave it back to the Regional Manager who grimaced and then gave it back to the Departmental Manager who shook her head with disbelief who gave it back to the supervisor.

Then what?

The supervisor made a report out to the Departmental Manager who passed it to the Regional Manager who passed it on to the Managing Director who passed it on the Group Finance Director who passed it on to the Executive General Manager who made sure the Group MD saw it.

What did the report say?

That the purchase order for the $4,000 personal computer had taken three months to approve and that in the meantime the data processor, a clever and fast individual, had died of old age.

You're kidding me?

Yeah, she didn't die of old age.

What... what happened then?

No, she was poached by the opposition.

What happened to the requisition order then?

Oh, that was interesting: we received approval the day after the supervisor's letter went out.

What, you mean — they got the computer?

Yeah.

So, it all worked out in the end?

No, not really.

Why, what happened?

They never replaced the woman.

So who's using the computer?

I am.

But you can't type.

I know.

So what are you using the computer for?

Well, it's still in the box.

So you're not using the computer.

No, I'm using the box.

What for?

To put my work on.

Why?

Because I don't have a desk.

Why don't you have a desk?

Because I'm waiting for approval from the supervisor to get it.

Oh, don't tell me and he's waiting on approval from the Departmental Manager who's…

Stop there.

What do you mean stop there?

Well, the Departmental Manager can pass requisitions for up to $200.

Not much of a desk for that price.

Oh, don't worry, I've put in two requisitions.

What?

One for the drawers and one for the desk.

Clever idea!

Yeah, it wasn't mine though.

Whose was it?

Departmental Manager's — a really cunning woman that one!

Aren't they all!

(Stage lights darken, sounds of pub can be heard in the darkness.)

This is a true story; only the location has been altered to protect the innocent!

TALL TALES AND TRUE FROM THE TOP

(Stage lights up to reveal the interior of a 'men's' club. Two large leather chairs are centre stage, partially facing one another. A tasteful Persian rug is placed before the chairs, which stands beside a coffee table. Two men are seated in the chairs. They are wearing dark navy blue pinstripe suits, white shirts, ties. Both have their legs crossed. In the background one can just hear the second movement from Vivaldi's Four Seasons. A waiter approaches.)

Can I take your orders, gentlemen.

Whisky on the rocks.

(Exit waiter stage right. The sound of glasses clinking can be heard off stage. Moments later the waiter returns carrying a tray. He places a whisky in front of each man and a bowl of nuts between the two.)

Will that be all, sirs?

Yes, thank you.

(Both men lift their whiskies and take a good, long, hard pull. They both sigh with pleasure.)

Christ Bruce, we're in a mess.

Yes, I know.

We're going to have to do something immediately.

Yes, I agree.

I've given it a lot of thought.

Me too.

In fact, I mentioned it to Hilda last night... I couldn't sleep.
You've got a very special wife, George.
Yes.
Well, what did she say?
Stop the haemorrhaging.
Well, we know that of course.
Yes, well, the trouble is how.
Yes, that is the trouble.
Everyone uses the size of the business as an excuse to purchase anything.
Tell me about it. Bloody Susan in accounts payable put in another request to take her team rock climbing.
Don't these guys understand what's happening?
Obviously not.
Well, that's it, if we wait any longer, we'll all be out of a job.
What are you going to do?
It's very simple — all purchase orders above $500 will be signed by me and all managers between myself and the person who thinks their purchase is so critical.
Christ, that'll slow them down.
Hmm.
Is that the idea?
Maybe it'll stop the bloody leakage all together!
(Both men grin and down the balance of their drinks. Lights dim momentarily. When the stage lights up again it reveals two different men sitting in the same seats. The waiter approaches and offers them drinks. They order whiskies. The waiter exits and returns moments later, places their drinks on the table in front of them and then leaves them to their reverie.)

Christ I'm tired.
Yes, you look beat.

I can't believe what crosses my desk.

What do you mean?

Lucie put a pile a foot high in front of me this morning for signing.

What was it?

Requisition orders.

For what?

Every-bloody-thing.

What do you mean?

Exactly what I said — if anyone wants to purchase anything in this business, I have to sign for it.

You're kidding?

No, I'm not.

Whose idea was that?

Guess.

Not...

Yes.

Why?

One of his ideas for saving money.

Huh?

No, I don't understand either. He seemed to think the company was full of bloody fools. I mean we turnover close to half a billion from eight business divisions and some poor sod in admin in Watson's business still has to put in a requisition for a computer to do the job we employed her for. No wonder he made a bad situation worse!

What are you going to do?

Stop it.

Stop the signing?

Of course.

Are you worried about the level of expenditure?

Who wouldn't be?

What are you going to do?

No, Sammy, it's what you are going to do.

Oh, really, like what?

Well, you are going to take five people from Group Finance and you are going to spend the next five weeks travelling around to all sites explaining what the issues are and how to manage their purchases. If our own people can't think their way through the problem, then we should close up shop tomorrow.

Brilliant but will they remember in three months time?

Yes.

How are you so sure?

Because we will pay them quarterly a dollar for every $10 of their purchasing budget they don't spend. They can work out what is a priority and what isn't.

Let them own the problem you mean?

Yes, that's about it. The last lot talked empowerment, we're going to do it.

Well, I guess Dunno never did believe in that sort of thing.

No, I guess he didn't.

Where is he by the way?

Last I heard he bought an obedience school for dogs in Noosa.

Really... well who'd have guessed.

Yeah, who would have guessed!

(Lights fade. Sound of the third movement from Vivaldi's Four Seasons rises.)

This, also, is a true story — the other half of the equation, if you like. Only the location and gender of the leaders has been muddled up to protect the innocent!

So what's all the noise about?

I know the motivation of many leaders is rock solid when they initiate cost cutting measures in sick businesses. Sometimes, when you face a pending crisis, you do need to take immediate and dramatic action to halt the haemorrhaging of cash. Although I might have hammed it up a bit in the Tale with good old Dunno, the reality is, in many instances, decisions that managers take are generally more thoughtfully considered and have more useful outcomes than Dunno's blanket decision to change the requisition process.

However, I have heard few mindless requests. I haven't heard of any employee asking for the purse strings to be ridiculously loosened. People aren't stupid. As much as managers, the majority of employees would consider it reckless to allow the thoughtless purchasing of anything and everything. The message is simple: we need to genuinely encourage people to consult, listen, pay attention and honourably try and understand why an individual or group of individuals believe that their request for something is, at that particular moment, important.

Most of us accept that sometimes our requests will be turned down. After all, we manage, albeit on a smaller scale, our own purchasing budgets domestically and we understand the danger of spending more than you earn. We understand the danger of not prioritising purchases, we understand the value of quality budgeting. So, we are generally not as silly with money as some would have us believe. No, the real issue in business with regard to demands for equipment — *which drive productivity and profitability* — hinges on the failure of some managers to adequately consult before reaching a decision, or the failure to adequately explain the rationale of a decision.

With all this in mind, read on!

WHAT ISSUES DO EMPLOYEES RAISE WITH REGARD TO EQUIPMENT AND WHY?

HAVING THE RIGHT EQUIPMENT TO DO THE RIGHT JOB; CONSULTATION AND INFORMATION IN THE DECISION MAKING PROCESS

Nothing is more frustrating, time consuming or demotivating than having inappropriate, shoddy, dated or damaged equipment. People everywhere know that competition is hotting up, they understand the push to improve efficiencies. It is then a bitter pill to swallow when you are told you can't have what you need to do the job you want to do to get the results that have to be achieved. It is harder still when you do not understand where the business is heading, have no clear understanding of overall strategy and don't really know why you can't get what you need.

I remember one company I worked for that had an outstanding equipment strategy and had made a decision at head office to spend $4 million per annum to upgrade the group's equipment. Management couldn't understand why there was so much discontent in the business about old, inadequate or damaged equipment when so much was being done to change the situation.

The trouble was that no one knew what management were doing. From across the country, in remote geographic locations, all it looked like was more of the same — "I haven't got anything new yet." "I have no idea of what they are doing at head office." "If there is a strategy, we haven't seen it yet."

If we know about and understand why a decision has been taken and have been told of the outcomes we can expect (and when), if we are consulted in the decision making process itself and have a genuine opportunity to put in our penny's worth, it is easier to be patient and to make do until the new gear arrives.

Consider the following two versions of the same story: Once upon a time, there was a man who was asked by his boss to clean up a storage room. In scenario one, the boss arrives outside the room and simply says to the man: "Bruce, clean it up and I'll be back later." The manager disappears and Bruce enters the room. It's a nightmare, floor to ceiling files, paper, bits and pieces, rubbish. A tangle of history and discarded detritus. Bruce begins the slow task of tidying the room, sorting and organising. By 11.30 am he has made some progress but is tired and thirsty. He's got hay fever from the dust and is wondering if anyone is going to bring him a drink. He keeps going, however, doing the best he can do. By 2.30 pm he is tired and a little angry. He goes to the door of the room and shouts. A deathly silence greets him. He's furious now. He goes back into the room and continues on his now thankless and questionable task. He is rougher with the room's contents, eventually binning stuff randomly without even looking at it. At 6.00 pm he spits the dummy and storms out of the room and into his manager in the corridor. Bruce proceeds to hurl at the manager an earful of frustration, anger and hurt. The manager is taken aback and questions, silently to himself, Bruce's appropriateness to the company — completely failing to understand what kind of day he has, through lack of empathy, inadvertently inflicted on an employee.

In scenario two, Bruce and the manager approach the room. The manager 'pre-frames' the job for Bruce by making sure that Bruce understands that he (the manager) realises that it is an awful job and is grateful to Bruce for taking it on. He explains why it has to be done and apologises for the shortage of help and notice. He then says he will drop in on Bruce regularly, and make sure someone brings him coffee and lunch. If Bruce needs anything further, there is a phone outside in the corridor. "Just ring 999 and my secretary will track me down and I'll ring back!" The manager gives Bruce overalls, bags, bins and hay fever tablets just in case!

Bruce sets himself to exactly the same task as in scenario one, but this time he feels supported and respected. He understands the urgency of the job and the reason for the lack of adequate support staff. As the manager drops in through the day, Bruce is able to get feedback on the job he is doing and, to some extent, vent his spleen about the condition of the room and the laziness of the people who have dumped their junk there over the years. Even though the task is the same, by demonstrating understanding of the task and a willingness to support Bruce, by sharing the purpose and time frame for the task, the manager empowers Bruce to deal with the challenging environment and lack of 'equipment' (in this case, additional support).

Unfortunately, frustration often stems from a lack of understanding as to why our needs are not being fulfilled. Even when requests are excessive, how can we gauge the extent of our excessiveness unless someone bothers to put us straight?

Apart from lacking a context or reasoned explanation for decisions regarding resources, many people are frustrated at the apparent lack of real listening skills of managers. Over and over again I have listened to people say "I'm tired of asking. I've asked so many times over the years I've given up now." This is not useful to the individual or the business.

Sometimes it appears as though managers believe requests are excessive. Sometimes they seem genuinely concerned at the level of company expenditure and they are simply trying to manage cash flow in such a way as to avoid trouble. But sometimes it is simply the result of an arrogance and lack of care — an "I know better" attitude — that diminishes the opinions of the employees when it comes to the question of resource allocation.

MANAGEMENT 'TOYS' AND THE LACK OF PLANNING TIME AROUND HIGH-TECH EQUIPMENT

Although not a major issue, the question of who gets what high-tech equipment (and when) is nonetheless a curious irritant in this day and age and one which will worsen as we progress into the next century. It is often raised in small to medium size businesses.

What happens is this: the Managing Director (or someone in senior management) is responsible for purchasing major capital items. They are also the one to travel to various trade shows, both in Australia and overseas. The MD (let's say of a printing company) heads off to a major industry trade show in South East Asia. While away on his annual purchasing and 'snooping' trip (to find out what the opposition are up to), he sees a fantastic new Gizmo. The Gizmo heralds an extraordinary leap in technology and clearly has considerable advantages for the mixing of dyes in print houses of companies about his size. The salesperson and the Managing Director of the company selling the Gizmo explain to our MD how the machine works. They have devised a measuring mechanism which allows such a refined combination of colours it is almost unbelievable. The actual operation of the machine takes some getting used to but the manufacturers of the Gizmo undertake to send out one of their technicians to Australia for a month to train our MD's staff.

Knowing the benefits to his organisation, our MD makes a tentative commitment. He faxes his Sydney office, explaining the advantages of the Gizmo, the considerable discount if it is ordered at the trade show and the MD's proposed delivery schedule. The Sydney staff are excited — we all like new toys! The Finance Director does his sums, talks to the bank, discusses the Gizmo with head of production and, within twenty-four hours, gives the MD the green light.

The deal is tied up in Bangkok and the MD proceeds on his journey, returning to Sydney some three weeks later. During this three weeks, the print business has been agog with excited whispers, innuendos, guessti-mates and debates. The only person to see detail of any substance has been the MD. Sydney staff have been treated to some broad details. They were unable to give detailed feedback or ask pertinent questions because of the time factor. Additionally, the person who would eventually be responsible for running the new Gizmo was on holiday, camping in the mountains, and incommunicado.

Anyway, the purchase has become a fait accompli. Six weeks down the track, the old paint dispenser is dismantled. Production is held up for forty-eight hours and the new Gizmo is installed. It is a beauty. Everyone is thrilled. It has buttons, lights everywhere, a perspex window to watch the paint being mixed (no functional purpose, but highly entertaining). George, the man who is to operate this machine, is now back and, although excited by the Gizmo, he is a little overwhelmed and not a small amount frustrated that the MD has gone ahead and purchased an item into which George, who has to use it, has had no input. Still, this isn't the time for sour grapes.

George spends the next month working with the technician from Bangkok, and begins to get the hang of the equipment. Production is running behind by three weeks, but that was to be expected. When the technician leaves, George — not the MD — is responsible for keeping things going.

Within forty-eight hours there is a problem. George, cursing that the Bangkok technician is in transit, reverts to the manuals. Twelve hours later he resolves the problem. The factory, which has been at a standstill, grinds back into action, much to everyone's relief. Temporary stoppages of this order, reflecting George's learning curve rather than any innate problem with the equipment, continue for the next three months. Slowly George's skill builds and, in due course, there are few problems George can't resolve without deferring to the now remote and phone-shy Bangkokians.

It has been a bad fifteen weeks for George and a financially nasty fifteen weeks for the business. The company is now running overtime to make up the work backlog, and the salespeople are on a constant rescue-and-save mission with disgruntled customers. However, everyone pulls together (including the very hard-working MD) and, despite the potential for a major crisis, within six months of the Gizmo's purchase, things have settled down and the Gizmo is, indeed, returning the anticipated benefits.

This story is not entirely apocryphal. Many people express frustration about purchases made without the support or input of the people who are to be affected by the purchase. And they rightfully continue with their annoyance when inadequate training time is arranged for those who are supposed to use the new equipment.

It continues to puzzle me why senior management don't make it standard practice to take key coalface people with them on purchasing trips. Businesses that do this not only have the advantage of rewarding an employee with an overseas trip, they also have the advantage of quality hands-on input or observation as they travel around. Such an exercise becomes an invaluable learning opportunity all-round.

RELATED EQUIPMENT ISSUES

WHAT'S IN A NAME?
This problem is surprisingly common in organisations on the acquisition and merger trail. It goes something like this (all names are fictitious):

Johnson Co merges with Actil and becomes Johnson Actil. Later, Johnson Actil takes over Fortnam Ltd. Fortnam Ltd is renamed Johnson Actil. Later still, Johnson Actil (including the old Fortnam) merges with Gordon Smythe & Co. The name, becoming improbably long for the receptionist, is abbreviated to JAGS & Co. Sometime after that, JAGS (as it is known by many who have no idea what the letters stand for) goes public and becomes The JAG Corporation, dropping the S along the way because an advertising company has suggested it sounds better.

Now, the mergers and acquisitions all make good commercial sense. However, one tiny little problem remains. Fortnam, which was based in Townsville, has for the people living in Townsville remained Fortnam because the locals remember Ma Fortnam who founded the company. (Most of the locals think JAG sounds like a yuppie car.) In the accounts department in the Adelaide office, Johnson & Co purchasing forms are still in use because when the company was Johnson & Co somebody put too many zeroes on a reorder of purchasing books and so the company has sufficient stock to last them until 2004. Everyone agreed there was little value in changing the books just because the company's name had changed. In Sydney, just prior to the public listing, all staff were issued with new uniforms which proudly displayed 'JAGS & Co' on the breast which is, of course, out of kilter with all the new Head Office stationery which reflects, as one would expect, the current correct name, The JAG Corporation.

In all, the company is displaying some half a dozen different names in different locations for different reasons. Truthfully, no one has the slightest idea what the right name should be or, if it is right at the moment, for how long it will remain correct. People have developed a laissez faire attitude, frustrated (among other things) by the number of changes in name and sceptical of the future. They wait for someone, somewhere to clear the picture up, but they've been waiting a long time.

This little story is far closer to reality than we care to admit, isn't it?

CONFUSED NAMING OF EQUIPMENT AFTER A RESTRUCTURE OR MERGER

Given the number of mergers, takeovers and acquisitions that happen in today's business environment, this problem warrants mention. I have worked in a diverse number of organisations managing the process and have seen the confusion that arises over the mishandling or time lag associated with handling names on documents, equipment, vehicles and so on. This can become demoralising for staff who are using documentation with an incorrect or outdated name; it can be demoralising for staff fronting customers with vehicles or equipment that display outdated names. These people have to explain to customers which name the company is going to use, why they are using it and when the name change will go through. In the absence of any quality communication from management, I've watched front line staff invent business rationale for customers rather than say "I have no idea what's happening!"

It is always a salutary lesson for managers to remember that coalface staff are frequently closer to the customer than the management and they, better than most people, understand how customers are responding to an unclear corporate identity.

MANAGEMENT DON'T UNDERSTAND OUR PROBLEMS

It must have been at least five or six years ago that I heard the famous Tom Peters tell the story (the detail of which I have forgotten — the moral of which is etched into my brain) of the Managing Director of a large tyre manufacturing company in Michigan who refused to respond to the cries from the factory for air-conditioning in summer and heating in winter. The Managing Director thought the request was excessive and that the investment could not be justified. Staff had repeatedly made requests over the years, complete with costings on installing temperature control equipment. They were always turned down. It was a major bone of contention between staff and management.

When Tom heard about this, he had a bet with the Managing Director. I believe it went something like, "If you can last six months down there in summer, I will guarantee the staff will never raise this topic again." The MD agreed and the next day his desk was moved to the factory floor.

Within two weeks, he had changed his tune and had approved the installation of temperature control equipment. He was both horrified by and embarrassed at his own stubbornness.

The message here is a potent one. Before making a decision that will affect someone else, against the wishes of that someone else, we should all be very careful to 'walk in their moccasins', making sure in the process that we care enough to (a) understand their model of the world and (b) ensure they participate in the decision and understand the reasoning for the conclusion, whether it is in their favour or not.

WHAT ISSUES DO LEADERS RAISE WITH REGARD TO EQUIPMENT AND WHY?

There is only one major issue raised by leaders that is not raised as commonly by employees, and it is a concern that is worth noting, especially in affluent Australia. It is this: too many people justify the quality of their work, their productivity or the business's profitability on either having the right equipment or being located in the right 'office environment'. Implicit in the comment is that more, or bigger, or better is always going to deliver the results. Many managers would suggest that sometimes there is a need to think things through further and come up with lateral solutions that don't cost as much money.

I have facilitated group discussions on solutions to help 'sick' businesses, and see great value in the process. There is often an assumption (particularly when the money being spent isn't theirs) that problems are solved by spending money. Although this may be the case with businesses that need to upgrade both equipment and facilities, there are as many businesses which actually need to upgrade the quality of everyone's thinking.

It is relatively (and I mean relatively) easy to solve a problem if you have an unlimited budget. If sales are falling, increase the marketing budget. If production is behind, improve the assembly line equipment. If the warehouse is distributing too slowly, improve the conveyor system. If this is done concurrent with quality planning, education, systems improvements and is lit by a guiding vision, then no doubt improvements are going to be dramatic.

But imagine you don't have the money. Imagine that you have a great vision, clearly communicated strategy, empowering leadership, participative staff, outstanding education and quality systems, but not a lot of spare cash. What are you going to do? Well, it is possible that the most valuable tool at your disposal, which doesn't cost money, is the ingenuity, commitment and creativity of your people.

One of my favourite activities in business is to work with a group of people to help them solve a problem without spending money. Great satisfaction can come from devising some economical, previously unthought of, highly innovative solution to a problem which initially looked as if it would cost a lot of money to solve.

I start a no-cost problem-solving brainstorming session by stating the problem. For instance, "The conveyor system in the warehouse is unarguably old and nearing the end of its day, but we are not in a position to spend money to replace it because sales are down by ten percent and we want to ensure the business remains liquid if that downturn is sustained." Whatever the scenario, I take care to clearly establish that money is not available and to build in an acceptable rationale as to why money cannot be spent. Then, I begin the brainstorming session with:

"How can we turn this conveyor system to our advantage without investing substantial money in upgrading or replacing it?"

Too many people assume answers are limited — but that's not so! If answers to problems were straightforward or were simply an either/or combination, then I guess we would still be chewing bones in a cave somewhere. Fortunately, human beings are enormously creative and, providing the proposition is clear and members of your brainstorming group are from diverse areas of the business (and include a few teenagers where possible), then, with few exceptions, answers will be generated that people have not previously considered.

I would also like to suggest that 'out of the mouths of babes and suck- lings' come answers that those closest to a problem cannot even guess at. I remember reading a story about a manufacturer of a particular Whatsit — perhaps a refrigerator. The particular item was designed to go into a certain space but designers were having trouble with the handle to the door. One day, when the Managing Director is giving his seven year old daughter a tour of the research and development department, they pass the development site for this marvellous Whatsit with the difficult handle. Patronisingly, the father shows the child the 'fridge' and explains the problem the designers are having. The child looks at the Whatsit, back at Dad and then at the Whatsit, and then says: "Why don't you put a handle on the front of the door instead of on the side?" This piece of advice was followed by a stunned silence and then a barely audible, "What did you say?" "Put the handle on the front," says the youngster. Dad thinks for a moment in perplexed silence. He runs off and gets the designer. They come back to the Whatsit, look at it, talk, argue and bingo! Problem solved. The child's naive observation acts as a priceless catalyst for taking the design in new directions.

I'm not suggesting that genius seven year olds abound in unlimited quan- tity. What I am suggesting is, however, that it is a wise manager who, before throwing money at a problem, encourages a lateral solution. Some of the best lateral solutions in the world have come from people who know little or nothing about the history of or the technology behind a particular problem. Sometimes such people know so little, they don't know why certain things can't be done. Our 'seven year olds' may not always solve the problems, but their line of questioning can certainly challenge the paradigms of the experts sufficiently to point the more informed brains towards new and innovative solutions.

Practical help

THE FOLLOWING PAGES SET OUT AUDIT SCHEDULES FOR EQUIPMENT AND CORPORATE NAMES. I HAVE EXPLAINED IN THE ACTION FOR EMPLOYEES AND THE ACTION FOR LEADERS SECTION HOW TO USE THEM. DON'T HESITATE TO ADAPT THEM FOR YOUR PURPOSES OR, INDEED, TO USE THEM AS THEY ARE.

Equipment – like it or leave it – it's hard to do the job without it!

SIMPLE EQUIPMENT AUDIT SCHEDULE

DEPARTMENT: ....

FUNCTION: ....

....

INDIVIDUAL(S) AND/OR TEAM: ....

ITEM: ....

FUNCTION: ....

AGE: ....

STATUS: POOR...... FAIR ...... GOOD ...... EXCELLENT......

REPLACEMENT/UPGRADE TIMETABLE

REPLACE BY: ....

RATIONALE: ....

....

EXPECTED BENEFITS: ....

....

COST: ....

WRITE OFF SCHEDULE: ....

CONTINGENCY: ....

Simple corporate name audit

Department: ....

Function: ....

Individual(s) and/or team affected: ....

Item: ....

Name that appears: ....

Effect on staff: ....

Effect on customers: Who, when and why? ....

....

Recommended action: What to replace and why? ....

....

....

Date: ....

Initiated by: ....

ACTION FOR EMPLOYEES

IDEAS FOR ADDRESSING PROBLEMS RELATED TO EQUIPMENT.

1. DO AN EQUIPMENT AUDIT

— PHOTOCOPY THE ATTACHED AUDIT SHEET AND DO AN EQUIPMENT AUDIT. INVOLVE OTHER TEAM MEMBERS IF POSSIBLE.

WHY?

ALTHOUGH PEOPLE COMPLAIN THAT THEIR REQUESTS FOR NEW, UPGRADED OR REPAIRED EQUIPMENT ARE NOT MET, IT IS OFTEN BECAUSE SUCH REQUESTS ARE MADE INFORMALLY AND IN INAPPROPRIATE PLACES. A DISCUSSION OVER A CUP OF COFFEE, ON THE WAY OUT INTO THE YARD OR ON THE WAY HOME AFTER A PARTICULARLY BAD DAY IS UNLIKELY TO PRODUCE RESULTS. QUANTIFYING YOUR NEEDS AND COMMITTING THEM TO PAPER IS GOOD PLANNING. IT ALSO ACTS AS A RECORD OF A PLANNED AND THOUGHTFUL APPROACH TO YOUR NEEDS. IT IS THE FIRST PROFESSIONAL STEP TO GETTING WHAT YOU NEED.

2. GET COMMITMENT FROM YOUR MANAGER

— ARRANGE A FORMAL TIME TO DISCUSS THE RESULTS OF YOUR AUDIT WITH YOUR MANAGER. MAKE SURE YOU BOTH ALLOCATE SUFFICIENT TIME TO GO THROUGH THE AUDIT TOGETHER. DON'T GIVE THE WRITTEN AUDIT TO THE MANAGER WITHOUT PRIOR DISCUSSION. AFTER DISCUSSION, YOU CAN LEAVE IT FOR THE MANAGER TO CONSIDER, PROVIDED THAT A SECOND MEETING IS ORGANISED TO DISCUSS CONCLUSIONS.

— LOOK FOR AGREEMENT AND RECORD IT. LOOK FOR DISAGREEMENT, DISCUSS THIS AND REACH A RESOLUTION THAT IS SATISFACTORY TO BOTH PARTIES, MAKING SURE THAT YOU UNDERSTAND EACH OTHER'S PERSPECTIVE. DON'T CLOSE THE MEETING UNTIL BOTH PARTIES FULLY UNDERSTAND THE EQUIPMENT REQUIREMENTS AND BUDGET CONSTRAINTS.

WHY?

GETTING COMMITMENT IS HOW YOU REACH A CONCRETE CONCLUSION. IT IS THE SECOND STEP IN GETTING WHAT YOU WANT OR, JUST AS IMPORTANTLY, SATISFYING YOURSELF THAT YOU FULLY UNDERSTAND WHY YOU CANNOT YET HAVE WHAT YOU NEED. IT IS CRITICALLY IMPORTANT TO DISCUSS YOUR REQUESTS FACE TO FACE IN A QUIET AND TIMELY MANNER. IF THE MEETING IS CUT SHORT, ORGANISE A SECOND MEETING. IF YOU DO NOT REACH AGREEMENT, SUGGEST THE INVOLVEMENT OF A RESPECTED THIRD PERSON.

3. EXAMINE NAMING PROBLEMS THAT ARISE FROM MERGERS OR ACQUISITIONS

— Do a naming audit. Identify, on your own, with your team or with other members of your department, the diversity of names you have identified, where they appear and what impact it has from your perspective.

WHY?

It is often hard to empathise with people's concerns if you don't fully understand what their problem is. When you do an audit of this kind you will alert management to the pragmatic business repercussions of the diversity of names.

4. GET AGREEMENT TO ACT

— Organise a formal meeting to discuss the problems with your manager.

— If you are in a large organisation, ask for this to be formally presented to senior management.

— Ask for a written response.

WHY?

By far the greater majority of senior managers will share your concern. However, during a merger process there are plenty of issues that concern senior management which can appear, at the time, to be more important than your problems. A manager may not give attention to an issue simply because they haven't had it put in front of them. You are entitled to ask for an explanation about when the name change will be formalised across the board.

5. HELP WITH MAJOR CAPITAL PURCHASES

— If you do an equipment audit, many of the problems that you might now experience will be better managed. Nevertheless, be prepared to push your self forward if you know of a senior manager who is considering a capital item purchase that will affect you.

— Commit your thoughts to paper; identify the pros and cons of the proposed purchase.

— Clearly indicate the training requirements that you believe will be required to install or manage the proposed equipment. Consider duration, content, who should be involved and so on.

— DON'T BE AFRAID TO SUGGEST THAT YOU TRAVEL OVERSEAS WITH A MANAGER WHEN YOU KNOW THAT PURCHASE OF A MAJOR CAPITAL ITEM IS BEING CONTEMPLATED. AS WITH ALL THINGS, PUT FORWARD A 'PROFESSIONAL' CASE FOR YOUR INCLUSION: WHAT YOU DO, WHAT YOU CAN OFFER IN THE DECISION, WHAT THE COST OF YOUR TRAVEL IS LIKELY TO BE, WHY YOU BELIEVE THIS IS AN IMPORTANT ACTION ON BEHALF OF THE BUSINESS.

WHY?

IF WE ACCEPT THAT TODAY THERE IS AN INCREASING SPREAD IN INTELLIGENCE ACROSS THE WORKFORCE, THEN THE TRADITIONAL ROLES THAT SEPARATE MANAGEMENT FROM STAFF ARE OFTEN (IF NOT ALWAYS) NO LONGER APPROPRIATE. GOOD MANAGERS WILL HAVE SPECIAL SKILLS THAT YOU MIGHT NOT YET HAVE DEVELOPED; THEY MIGHT INCLUDE FACILITATING EXCELLENCE IN OTHERS OR LISTENING TO (AND HARNESSING) A DIVERSITY OF OPINION. REMEMBER, WITH THE RATE OF INVENTION TODAY, IT IS NO LONGER POSSIBLE FOR ANY ONE PERSON TO KNOW ALL THAT NEEDS TO BE KNOWN ON ANY GIVEN TOPIC. YOUR EXPERTISE IS A VITAL ASSET TO THE BUSINESS. DON'T BE AFRAID TO EXERCISE IT.

6. HELP MANAGEMENT TO UNDERSTAND YOUR PROBLEMS

— IDENTIFY AREAS WHERE YOU BELIEVE MANAGEMENT LACK UNDERSTANDING OF YOUR CONDITIONS OR YOUR PROBLEMS.

— DISCUSS YOUR CONCERNS WITH OTHER EMPLOYEES IN THE SAME AREA AND SEE IF THE CONCERNS ARE SHARED.

— USING THE TOM PETERS EXAMPLE AS INSPIRATION, CONSIDER WHAT YOU WOULD NEED TO GET YOUR MANAGER TO DO — AND PROMISE IN RETURN — TO GET RESOLUTION, ONE WAY OR THE OTHER, OVER YOUR CONCERN.

— USING THE TOM PETERS EXAMPLE, INVITE YOUR MANAGER TO PARTICIPATE IN YOUR 'EXPERIMENT'.

WHY?

NOTHING VENTURED, NOTHING GAINED! NOT INFREQUENTLY IT TAKES AN UNEXPECTED INITIATIVE TO PRODUCE THE ANSWER TO A PROBLEM THAT HAS BEEN NAGGING PEOPLE FOR A LONG TIME. IT IS CALLED 'PATTERN INTERRUPT'. YOU WILL CHANGE YOUR MANAGER'S THINKING BY CHANGING THE WAY IN WHICH YOU ARE WILLING TO TACKLE THE PROBLEM.

ACTION FOR LEADERS

IDEAS FOR ADDRESSING PROBLEMS RELATED TO EQUIPMENT.

1. DO AN EQUIPMENT AUDIT

— GET YOUR STAFF TO DO AN EQUIPMENT AUDIT, BY DEPARTMENT OR FUNCTIONAL AREA. USE THE SHEET PROVIDED AS A GUIDE OR REDESIGN YOUR OWN. KEEP IT SIMPLE AND GET THE STAFF TO DO IT RATHER THAN HAVE IT DONE BY AN OUTSIDER OR BY ONE PERSON FOR THE TOTAL BUSINESS.

— WHEN STAFF HAVE DONE THEIR AUDIT, REVIEW THE AUDIT SHEETS WITH THEM TO GAUGE THEIR THINKING. LISTEN CAREFULLY. IF YOU DO NOT FULLY UNDERSTAND THE PROBLEM TAKE THE TIME TO GO TO THE LOCATION WHERE THE EQUIPMENT IS USED AND HAVE THEM RUN THROUGH THE RELATED PROBLEMS ON SITE.

— GIVE YOURSELF TIME TO GO THROUGH THE AUDIT SHEETS QUIETLY, EITHER ON YOUR OWN OR WITH OTHER SENIOR MANGERS. PREPARE A CONSIDERED WRITTEN RESPONSE.

— GO THROUGH YOUR RESPONSE, ITEM BY ITEM, EXPLAINING ANY CHANGES CAREFULLY. STRIVE FOR UNDERSTANDING OR BE WILLING TO ADJUST YOUR THINKING.

WHY?

THIS PROCESS HAS TO BE OWNED BY THE STAFF AS WELL AS BY SENIOR MANAGEMENT. THE QUALITY OF EQUIPMENT OFTEN BECOMES A METAPHOR FOR THE QUALITY OF TREATMENT THAT STAFF PERCEIVE THEY RECEIVE FROM MANAGEMENT. IF YOU BELIEVE A 'SPREAD OF INTELLI-GENCE' IS AN IMPORTANT ASSET IN YOUR BUSINESS AND IF YOU GENUINELY VALUE YOUR PEOPLE, THEN THIS IS AN IMPORTANT MECHANISM FOR DEMONSTRATING YOUR COMMITMENT.

2. ESTABLISH A PROCESS OF CONSULTATION — ASSIGN THE RIGHT EQUIPMENT TO DO THE RIGHT JOB

— WRITE DOWN ON A PIECE OF PAPER THE CONSULTATIVE PRACTICES YOU ALREADY HAVE IN PLACE IN YOUR BUSINESS.

— WRITE DOWN ON A SECOND PIECE OF PAPER THEIR STRENGTHS AND WEAKNESSES.

— ORGANISE A MEETING WITH STAFF TO DISCUSS HOW THE CONSULTATIVE PROCESS COULD BE IMPROVED, FROM THEIR POINT OF VIEW. ITEMS TO INCLUDE IN THE DISCUSSION WOULD BE:

- ANALYSIS OF CURRENT COMMUNICATION STRENGTHS AND WEAKNESSES;
- REVIEW OF EQUIPMENT AUDIT PROCESS AND DECISIONS THAT HAVE BEEN MADE;
- DISCUSSION OF FUTURE PLANS AND POSSIBLE EQUIPMENT REQUIREMENTS;
- EXAMINATION OF COMPANY EXPERTISE AND HOW BEST TO UTILISE IT;
- IDENTIFICATION OF TRAINING REQUIREMENTS AND TIME FRAME.

WHY?

IF WE AGREE THAT THINGS ARE CHANGING AT AN INCREDIBLE SPEED, THEN IT IS IMPORTANT TO START TO BUILD THE STRATEGIC SKILLS OF STAFF SO THEY CAN ADD THEIR EXPERIENCE AND INFORMATION TO THE DECISION MAKING POOL. FOCUS THEIR ATTENTION ON ONE OR TWO SPECIFIC AREAS TO ENHANCE THE ABILITY OF THE BUSINESS TO ACCESS AN INCREASING EXPERTISE IN A WIDE RANGE OF AREAS. THAT WAY, YOU DON'T RELY SOLELY ON MANAGERS, WHO ARE FEWER IN NUMBER AND MORE GENERALIST IN THEIR KNOWLEDGE. FOR INSTANCE, A MANAGER MAY HAVE A BROAD RANGE OF BUSINESS SKILLS, FAR IN EXCESS OF THE AVERAGE RECEPTIONIST; HOWEVER, THE RECEPTIONIST, WITH SUPPORT AND EDUCATION, WILL BE THE BEST PERSON TO PROVIDE SPECIALIST INPUT INTO THE PURCHASE OF THE APPROPRIATE TELE-PHONE SYSTEM FOR RECEPTION.

3. CONDUCT AND AUDIT OF OVERSEAS BUYING TRIPS

— THERE IS NO ARGUING THAT SENIOR MANAGEMENT SHOULD, IN A LARGE NUMBER OF INDUSTRIES, SPEND TIME OVERSEAS LOOKING AT COMPETITIVE ACTIVITY. IN FACT, IT IS SOMETHING MANY PEOPLE COULD, WITH BENEFIT, DO MORE OF. HOWEVER, INCREASINGLY THERE ARE BUSINESSES CONSIDERING SENDING A 'BUDDY' ALONG WITH THE SENIOR MANAGER ON AN OVERSEAS TRIP. CONSIDER THE FOLLOWING:

- WHY ARE YOU GOING;
- WHAT OUTCOMES CAN YOU EXPECT (BE SPECIFIC);
- WHO ELSE IN THE BUSINESS COULD SUBSTANTIALLY CONTRIBUTE TO THE TRIP;
- EXPERTISE AND ADVICE THAT MAY BE USEFUL;

   – WHO ELSE IN THE BUSINESS COULD SUBSTANTIALLY BENEFIT FROM THE TRIP IN TERMS OF ACCELERATED LEARNING IN THEIR JOB AND INCREASING THEIR CONTRIBUTION TO THE BUSINESS.

— REVIEW BUDGET CONSTRAINTS. BE CLEAR ON YOUR DECISION MAKING PROCESS AND YOUR VALUES IN DETERMINING WHETHER OR NOT YOU CAN AFFORD TO TAKE SOMEONE WITH YOU.

— CONSIDER ALL OF THE ABOVE IN THE CONTEXT OF LOCAL PURCHASES: DO YOU CONSULT AS BROADLY AS YOU CAN?

— LOOK AT YOUR TIMETABLING FOR MAJOR CAPITAL PURCHASES: ARE YOU ALLOWING ENOUGH TIME FOR ADDITIONAL EDUCATION FOR THE PEOPLE WHO WILL BE AFFECTED? ASK THEM TO VALIDATE YOUR TIME FRAMES.

WHY?

THE 'SPREAD OF INTELLIGENCE' IS AN ASSET FOR YOUR BUSINESS. YOU WILL ACCELERATE IT BY SUPPORTING AND EDUCATING IT. THE ROLE OF MANAGERS IS CHANGING DAILY; LEARNING TO MANAGE AN EXERCISE OF THIS KIND EXPANDS YOUR CONSULTATIVE SKILLS. THAT WILL IMPROVE YOUR ABILITY TO LEAD AND WILL INCREASE THE RESPECT PEOPLE HAVE FOR YOU AS A LEADER — MAKING IT, IN TURN, EASIER TO LEAD.

4. ADDRESS NAMING CONCERNS AFTER A MERGER OR TAKEOVER

— USING THE FORM CONTAINED IN THIS SECTION, INVITE STAFF TO IDENTIFY WHERE THE DIVERSITY OF NAMES IS AN ISSUE, WHAT EFFECT IT IS CAUSING AND HOW THEY RECOMMEND IT SHOULD BE CORRECTED.

— IF THE NAME OF THE ORGANISATION IS UNRESOLVED, DEVELOP A SHORT TO MEDIUM TERM STRATEGY FOR MANAGING THE UNCERTAINTY. MAKE SURE THAT STAFF ARE KEPT INFORMED. DON'T UNDERESTIMATE THE DAMAGE FROM A CUSTOMER'S POINT OF VIEW.

— IF FORMALISING A NAME CHANGE REQUIRES AGREEMENT FROM SENIOR MANAGEMENT, MAKE SURE IT IS DEALT WITH AS SOON AS POSSIBLE. SHARE THE RESULTS OF THE NAME AUDIT WITH OTHER SENIOR MANAGEMENT SO THEY FULLY APPRECIATE THE STAFF'S PERSPECTIVE.

Equipment – like it or leave it – it's hard to do the job without it!

WHY?

WHILE APPRECIATING JUST HOW MANY ISSUES CONCERN MANAGEMENT DURING A MERGER OR TAKEOVER, IT IS EASY TO OVERLOOK ISSUES WHICH AFFECT THE MORALE OF AN ORGANISATION. THE REBUILDING PHASE CAN TAKE CONSIDERABLY LONGER THAN IT SHOULD IF MORALE IS LOW. CLEANING UP THE 'CORPORATE IDENTITY' IS ONE ISSUE THAT CAN BOOST IT.

GIVEN THE RATE OF CHANGE AND THE POSSIBILITY (DARE I SAY PROBABILITY) OF ANOTHER CHANGE OF SOME SORT WITHIN THE NEXT TWO YEARS, IT IS IMPORTANT TO FACILITATE CHANGE, WITHIN REASON, AS QUICKLY AS POSSIBLE. NAMING AN ORGANISATION (THAT IS, REDUCING THE NUMBER OF NAMES FROM SEVERAL TO ONE) IS A BIT LIKE REMOVING A BANDAID FROM A HAIRY LEG. THE LONGER YOU TAKE, THE MORE PAINFUL THE PROCESS!

5. UNDERSTAND YOUR STAFF'S PERSPECTIVE

– DO YOU REALLY UNDERSTAND THE TRIALS AND TRIBULATIONS OF WORKING FOR YOUR COMPANY FROM YOUR STAFF'S PERSPECTIVE?

– BE WILLING TO PARTICIPATE WHEN THEY COME FORWARD WITH THEIR 'TOM PETERS' CHALLENGES. PARTICIPATE WITH GOOD GRACE.

WHY?

BECAUSE HUMILITY —— DECENCY, BENEVOLENCE AND KINDNESS —— ELEVATES LEADERSHIP. AUSTRALIA URGENTLY NEEDS HUMBLE LEADERS.

Voices
of the
multitude

*When people speak
so clearly, when the
message is so unified,
when all they ask for
is to be heard; then it
serves us all, leader
and employee alike,
to listen.*

Yes, the voice of the people: the tall and the short, the fat and the thin, the young and the old, the academic and the pragmatic, the carpenter and the physicist, the labourer and the architect, the leader and the follower, the young and the infirm, the men and the women — all have a voice and, if it is not heard, we will all be the lesser for it.

SO, LET'S HAVE SOME BED CHAT...
(A couple, in bed.)

Did the earth move for you too, darling?
Mmmm
Did it hit a few G spots?
Mmmm
Tell me, tell me, which ones?
Oh, you know...
No, tell me exactly
Well, I liked that thing about computers.
Which thing?
You know, the thing about all the information and stuff. It gives me a headache.

Surely not tonight darling?

No, you know what I mean. My brain's not big enough to cope.

But something else is?

Oh, very funny.

What else?

Well, the bit about leadership; I've always wondered why some bosses are pricks and some aren't?

My, we are witty.

No, really. I thought I was on my own. I was the only one who felt inadequate, but now I see lots of other people feel this way.

Yes, I know what you mean.

In my last job, I just gave up, I couldn't give any more because everything I gave seemed to have no value.

Ah, that's when you came to me!!

Be serious. You said you wanted me to tell you what I liked.

Go on then. What else?

I think that thing about the future made sense. It can be spooky. I mean, where is it all going? What is the purpose of it all? Do I count? I could be dead tomorrow — is my life all about doing things that don't satisfy me?

What, are you suggesting you weren't...

God, you're paranoid.

No, I'll be serious. You're right. There are times when I feel insignificant at work, and I'm a manager. I do things I don't agree with because someone else tells me I have to — I always felt obliged to uphold the company politics... but now I feel like I can see how I might change things.

Exactly, that's what made sense in it all — it wasn't just a case of experiencing something interesting, it was about what I should do with what I learnt.

Yeah. This communication thing hit home for me. I mean we can really goof things up at the office by not taking the time to explain things. We are always in such a hurry, but the truth is that being in a hurry is no excuse and in the end, the problems we generate by not explaining what we are doing and why take longer to solve than if we had spent time talking to people in the first place.

Now, haven't I said that to you before... a little talk makes for a satisfying conclusion for everyone?

Now who's joking around.

(Laughter)

> *It's funny, isn't it, how it all seems so obvious but I really thought it was just me. Like when I'm asked to do something and I don't know why I have to do it... I sort of do it like I was a robot.*
>
> Christ, I've just thought of something!
>
> *What?*
>
> You and I do it to each other.
>
> *We do?*
>
> Yeah. You know how when we are driving, you always tell me which way to go, even when I know where I am going.
>
> *Oh, I don't, not really. It's just you sort of turn your brain off when I'm in the car with you.*
>
> That's what I mean. My brain's turned off because you're always telling me what to do in the car. You've told me so often what to do in the car I just sort of expect it now and don't think any more. I do what you've programmed me to do — take your instructions — so I don't pay any attention and I don't use my brain... and that's what I do to you in the garden.
>
> *Explain.*
>
> Well, do you remember when we first got together?
>
> *Which part in particular?*
>
> Not the part you're thinking of! No, I mean when I first stayed at your house.

Yeah, go on.

Well, you had lots of green plants didn't you?

Yeah. So what?

Well, who looked after them?

I did.

What did you do to keep them alive?

Oh... I watered them.

Is that all?

No, I guess I fed them and kept the leaves clean. Oh, I also moved them about and made sure they had sunlight.

Did you re-pot them?

Yes, when they needed it.

So why do you say now that you can't garden?

God, you're right. It's exactly like the car. I don't garden because you make me feel stupid, like I have to do exactly what you say. I felt you knew more than me when we got together... after a while I was too scared to say anything in case you thought I was stupid. I thought it would be better for us just to let you be the boss in the garden.

Isn't that the message in this for us?

You're right — if we rob each other of the ability to think and to be valued for how we do things — no matter how different our ways are, we eventually turn off; stop being interested.

Exactly.

Way to go — that's something to think about.

Yeah.

Jesus, do you think you can keep your mouth shut in the garden. I mean, we do it so differently?

Well, it'll take some time... but why don't we try.

OK, I will if you will.

Well, you'll get tested first.

Why?

Because guess where we are going tonight?
Oh God yes.
You've got it, a nice short drive to your Mother's.
Oh joy, oh joy and she'll tell both of us how to do everything,
won't she!
Yep... but then neither of us takes any notice, do we.
Maybe there's something to think on in that as well...
Mmm...
(Lights dim, muffled sounds of laughter and love making resume!)

A WORD OF WARNING

There are thousands of self-help books for all of us to read; they offer ideas on how to empower ourselves, how to make our lives more rewarding, how to handle stress, how to attain enlightenment, how to become rich and successful. If you're anything like me you will have read quite a few, stolen bits and pieces from here and there, mixed them in with your own unique bag of experience and come up with a recipe which you are now exercising as part of your success strategy for life.

In business, your reading path might be similar: you've read a few 'must-reads' (or you've bought them, read a bit and then put them down because they're too heavy both in weight and style); you've attended a variety of lectures and seminars by a range of overseas 'experts'. Again, you've mixed what you've heard with your experiences.

That's good and as it should be; indeed, you may take this book as another small contribution to your experiences. However, before moving on to Part Two I would like to offer a word of warning, as you formulate your personal responses and consider acting on what you've read.

You have, in large part, been listening to the percolated voices of thousands of ordinary people. They, like you, do not make unreasonable requests. They, like you, ask for respect and dignity. They, too, know they can give more if they feel valued. And they tell us that being valued is measured by the extent of consultation and participation they experience in their day-to-day work.

You don't have to be an Einstein to act on any of this. All you have to be is someone who wants something better and is willing to put effort into achieving it. Anything is possible — all you need is determination and perseverance. The rules are waiting to be rewritten and, if you listen carefully to the voices on the wind, you will know which way to walk. Despite uncertainty as to the specific outcome, you need not be weighed down by adversity.

As you begin to make whatever changes you feel are appropriate, wherever you can, both large and small, watch who responds to your initiative and why. You will find — and of this I have no doubt — that you will be joined in your journey by a surprising range of fellow travellers: a CEO who is no longer satisfied with the way people are treated; a salesperson who recognises she has much to offer; a receptionist who thinks of herself as much more than 'the girl who answers the phone', a forklift driver who has thought long and hard about what can be done to improve business.

In this book I have not touched on many things that would appear in a book on 'How to do business better'. I have not discussed, in depth, how to plan; I have not mentioned the development, installation or maintenance of quality systems; I have not gone into how, exactly, one can implement a participative culture in a business; I have not covered marketing and sales; I have not talked about the place of research and development; and, although they are implicit in much that I have touched on, I have not talked in depth about values and behaviours.

Why haven't I talked about these things? Because people, in large part, already understand them. If they *don't* understand them, it's because there are certain roadblocks. The roadblocks are to do with communication, education, equipment and leadership. They are easily understood and possibly easily changed if we do it together and pay attention to what everyone is really saying, with out fear or favour.

The voices are united in their proclamations and, while that might appear fearsome to some, I think, when people speak so clearly, when the message is so unified, when all they ask for is to be heard; then it serves us all, leader and employee alike, to listen.

I remember one CEO I worked with who argued with me on many of the issues I raised — issues that employees saw as impediments to success in business. He said I was a 'pollyanna' — I believed too much in the potential for good in people. He said there were a lot of foolish, stupid people in the workplace who really ought to be booted out. They were holding the others back. He said I oversimplified things. He said he needed people who were better educated, had a broader understanding of how to run business in the late nineteen-nineties.

It is funny how I think he's both terribly wrong and commendably right. In his judgment of people I think he's operating from a paradigm that's had its day; his opinions more accurately reflect his own lack of flexibility, his own poor communication skills, his own fear of failure, his own lack of education and respect for the people around him than they do anything else. But I think he's right in saying we need people who are better educated and who have a broader understanding of how to run business in the late nineteen-nineties.

The real difference between us is that I would do everything in my power to make sure such people were 'grown' within my business rather than importing them from without because, after all, where did these 'outside' people learn their wisdom in the first place? If we all made the decision that we didn't have the time to help people learn, then who would ever know anything?

Personally, I don't want to think I am surrounded by fools. I don't want to think people aren't capable of greatness in their lifetimes. I don't want to be constantly looking for people who can do this or that better. I want to have the skills (a) to do it better myself and (b) the courage and commitment that it takes to support other people in doing it better — day, by day, by day. It might seem a harder path, but as with so may things that are not just quick fixes, I suspect this is the way to sustain both business and the people in a world gone just a little crazy.

Listening, listening, listening.

Then we see the pattern that connects us.

Then we act.

Part Two

MYTH BUSTERS

Introduction to myth busters

There is actually no certainty other than that which we make.

A TALE
Once upon a time there was a young man. He was, in most regards, no different from many. He was reasonably happy with his life. He was well liked by his friends, respected by work-mates. He loved and was loved by his family. He enjoyed a normal range of life's offerings — food, football, females! He read a little, enjoyed a range of music, went here, went there; lived his life without much thought, effort or complication — or so it seemed.

His flat, perched three floors above a not too busy city road, was comfortable. He lived alone. If you had entered his apartment through the front door, you would possibly have noted to your right a small shelf cluttered with all manner of things a person might collect over time; miscellaneous objects carelessly placed on the shelf as the young man entered his flat. Let's see, what was there? A book on travel to Europe, an old bill, two pens (neither of which work), a magazine on triathlons, a broken fridge magnet, a bottle of correction fluid, a bulldog clip, a piece of wood and a large, heavy metal ball that tinkled when it was moved.

Below the shelf was a large piece of marble, irregular in shape. The young man used it as a doorstop on hot days when he needed a breeze to move the air in the apartment.

Beyond the entrance to the flat was a predictable array of rooms, surprisingly neat considering the haphazard nature of the shelf by the front door; almost as if any purposeless object was discarded by the young man before entering his private world. There was, to the immediate left of the entrance, a small living room which overlooked the road below and beyond, an array of similar terrace apartments. In the living room was an old couch, two comfortable armchairs, a large television and a tangle of sound equipment.

A door on the right as you entered the living room took you directly into a small but adequate kitchen. This also connected the flat to a small laundry on the left. Through the living room and into the hallway, the first door on the right was the young man's bedroom. Second door on the right was the bathroom — old, faded, functional.

In this adequate apartment our young man lived an adequate life. He rose on weekdays at the same time, 7 am. On waking, he stretched, looked at his alarm clock, confirmed it had indeed gone off, and then rose — leaving behind his own body warmth. He would pad slowly to the bathroom, open the door, step through and then close it firmly behind him. Despite living alone, he sought privacy from the flat. We will guess at his activities in the bathroom: predictable and always constant: toilet, mirror, shower and out, all in less than ten minutes.

In his bedroom, he would look through his relatively modest wardrobe and then select pants, white shirt and tie. He dressed the same way each day: underpants, socks, shirt, pants, carrying his tie with him to the kitchen, where he collected his shoes, left there the night before. Draping his tie over a kitchen chair, he would make himself breakfast which was, as with all the young man's habits, constant and unchanging: coffee, cornflakes and toast with Vegemite. Waiting for the kettle to boil, he would eat his cornflakes while reading the unchanging advertising or nutritional information on the sides of the packet. He would eat his toast and drink his coffee while putting on his shoes and tie.

It was the same every weekday morning.

At 7.45 am the young man would leave his apartment without so much as a backward glance. Catching his usual bus, his thoughts would already be turning to his job in the eastern suburbs. The young man tested new computer software for possible faults. He would pretend to be a customer and would run the software through all manner of trial — basically to identify any programming errors before the real release to the real customer. It was a job which required thoroughness and perseverance, of which our young man appeared to have both.

It was not an inspiring job but it paid the bills — and that appeared to be sufficient motivation for the man to stay with the company and to perform his tasks to the best of his ability.

At the end of the working day, our young man would put all his morning systems into reverse. On leaving the office, his mind would already be travelling home. On reaching his apartment, he would open his front door, walk through, turn left into the living room, turn the television on, walk into the kitchen, take off his shoes, take a beer out of the fridge, go back into the living room, check his answering machine, then settle down in front of the TV.

Sometimes the young man would watch the news and then a movie. Sometimes he didn't. Sometimes he had friends over. Sometimes he went out. Sometimes he would cook for himself and sometimes he would have bought something on the way home which he would quietly consume while watching the news.

At about 9.30 pm the young man would make his way to bed. He was careful with his clothing, hanging it up, checking to see if it could be used again, tomorrow perhaps.

Our young man would possibly read for a while, think briefly about his life, observe with curiosity the nagging sensation in the pit of his stomach that told him there had to be more to life than this, and then fall into a relatively untroubled sleep.

The next morning he would repeat all that had gone the day before.

The city sleeps, as does the young man. There is nothing significant about the universe, no portents of change, no witchcraft, no mystery. But then comes one of those strange moments when well laid rituals are turned upside down by a seemingly insignificant event. The deep and quiet, still and dark section of the night is disturbed, irretrievably, by the turn of a screw.

Our young man is jarred from his slumber by a dreadful cacophony of sound. Instantly, he is fully awake, sitting up, alert to the possibility of an intruder. The sound is coming from the hallway just outside his bedroom. First there was a most awful crash, things falling, breaking; now in the dimness of his bedroom, the young man listens to the sounds settle. He is not afraid — alert and curious perhaps — but not afraid.

He gets up and moves carefully to his bedroom door. He stops and listens. Nothing. He turns his bedroom light on and blinks, momentarily dazzled by the light. As his eyes adjust, he peers into the hallway. The light from his bedroom illuminates the mess beyond and offers up a complete explanation for the disruption. There, by the front door, in chaotic disarray, are the entire contents of the shelf that has, of its own accord, come undone from the wall. The large piece of marble beneath the shelf is draped with the magazine on triathlons. The young man smiles. I'll clean it up in the morning, he thinks to himself. With no more concern than that, our young man turns off the light and returns to bed to his deep and now entirely dreamless sleep.

In the morning, apart from a quick tidy up, the young man's ritual is undisturbed. It is only on leaving the apartment that anything out of the ordinary reaches into his awareness. A faint shaft of morning light happens to catch the side of the marble by the front door and, for the most fleeting of moments, the young man thinks he sees the outline of a woman's face, just her jawline, in a new jaggedness in the marble. He pauses a moment but the likeness has vanished and instead, all he sees is the newly removed chip of marble. Must have been the metal ball, he thinks to himself by way of explanation.

Our young man leaves his apartment, the marble and the face gone from his awareness even as the door closes.

The man's day passes the same as all his days. He returns home and his evening, punctuated only by a brief and enjoyable conversation with a friend, is entirely without pause for thought. In a deep sleep the young man dreams of a woman but the dream slips evasively into the unconscious world of non-remembering and so on waking nothing but restfulness remains.

Again our young man prepares himself for his day ahead; bathroom, bedroom, kitchen, coffee. He thinks little on the world or its mysteries, only on the day ahead. Once more, however, as he is about to leave his apartment, the shaft of light falls carelessly across the marble and, in a moment of surprising recognition, the young man sees once more the outline of a woman's jaw, caught it would seem in the solid immovable marble. The young man moves forward to touch the marble and as his hand meets its cool surface, the face disappears. He shakes his head, smiles to himself at the trickery of light and imagination and leaves.

Our young man returns home, thinks nothing of the marble as he passes it, turns into his living room and begins the unwinding ritual of his day.

The third day dawns beautifully. The young man awakens, stretches and checks his clock. Time to rise. He feels good today. Happy. The world is working according to plan and there is nothing to cause concern or discomfort. Over his breakfast he notes, with some humour, that it is Friday already. The week has flown by.

He closes the door to his bedroom, casting a quick and affectionate eye around its order before he does so, and turns, as he always does, to leave for work. Yet again, a soft pale yellow shaft of sunlight cuts across the marble by the door and yet again, as the young man stares, the jawline of the woman appears. He stands transfixed, taking in the line and curve, seeing in that moment all that must lie beneath the surface of the marble. He stands thus for many moments, absorbing a quality in the marble that has previously eluded him. He knows with certainty what lies beneath, the grace and form of the face.

This time curiosity, for once, overwhelms our young man. Without hesitation, he turns back from the front door. He walks purposefully through the living room into the kitchen and then into the laundry. In the cupboard below the sink he finds a hammer, two chisels — one fine, one coarse — and a mallet.

Back at the front door he pauses again by the marble, he mumbles to himself, surprise and pleasure fighting for control of his face. Then, crossing a critical demarcation line, his hesitation is replaced by determination. The young man folds himself down on the floor, one leg under his buttocks, the other, knee up, in front of him, a stable resting surface for the arm that carries the chisel.

And so our young man begins the odyssey of discovery, guided only by an unconscious certainty of the rightness of his action. He begins to chip away, tentatively at first, at the surface of the marble. With time, the hands become more certain, the eye more astute, the mind more at peace. Time vanishes.

At work, people check the clock. Our young man is late. He must be sick. The office hums on, unworried, unconcerned.

In the hallway, dust has accumulated around him. Shards of marble are scattered around his feet, white powder is smeared across once perfectly-creased pants, the tie is on the floor. Still he chips away at the marble before him.

*At the office, people break for lunch. They talk about the young man...
has he rung in... has anyone contacted him... what, just an answering
machine? Curiosity ripples through the lunchroom but it lacks genuine
concern.*

Back in the corridor, the young man works on, oblivious to thirst or
hunger. Even the body, periodically satisfied with the stretch of this or
that muscle, cannot distract the young man.

Over time but outside awareness, the light changes subtly, swinging
from front to back, shadows lengthen, the man works on. Outside the
sound of the world shifts, from the alert, purpose filled activity of work,
to the merging sound of laughter, traffic, unwinding, as the rest of the
world heads home for the weekend.

Still our young man works on, chip, chip, chip.

At one point, sooner or later, he turns on the electric light to work by.
At one point — unremembered, unnoticed — he makes coffee for
himself, grabs a piece of bread to settle the acid in his stomach. But
then he resumes his task.

And at last, sometime later in the night, he realises without question
that he is done. He turns off the electric light in the hall and sits back
on his haunches. The sun, long since gone, is replaced with the more
subtle and embracing mantle of moonlight. As his eyes grow accustomed to this softer light, he looks carefully at the results of this long
day's endeavour. His eye critical and certain, he takes in the every
detail of the work; he is in its thrall. Before him now, where once stood
a meaningless piece of marble, a doorstop in hot weather, stands the
perfect sculpted form of a woman, her face, her body, arms gently
placed around folded knees, graceful and complete.

He looks around him, a little surprised, dazed even. In that moment,
his body claims back his attention. He is exhausted; shooting pains run
up his calf muscles and into his thighs. He rubs his face, stretches his

back and stands. Just once, before stumbling into his bedroom and collapsing, fully clothed, on his perfectly made bed, he looks at the work before him and he smiles.

The certainty that something critical has happened, that the substance of his life has been given weight and purpose, fills his every cell. As sleep claims him, he knows, for the first time, the delight of his own certainty.

And so, in a moonlit corridor, in an ordinary apartment in an ordinary city, our story comes to an end and, dear reader, one might in this moment be forgiven for missing the purpose of it all, thinking perhaps that it is a story about a woman caught in a piece of marble.

But that is not the purpose of this tale.

No, it not about the woman caught in the marble, because, after all, it was just a piece of marble and I, passing in a similar way to the young man, would perhaps have never seen the jawline of the woman.

No, this is not a story about the woman caught in the marble. It is a story about the sculptor caught in the man.

THE PURPOSE OF *MYTH BUSTERS*

It has become apparent to me, after talking to legions of ordinary people, that there are many things we hold to be true and constant in the world around us that require an accident of fate — a fallen shelf — before we realise that there is actually no certainty other than that which we make. Sometimes in thinking this is the way things are, we also think this is the way they will always be. *But this need not be so.*

Myth busters covers an eclectic range of topics, all of which have been consistently raised by many people. The problems they reflect are often generated by assumptions about rules that govern our working lives which we believe are unchallengeable. In this second part of the book, I will try to:

– be the shelf that breaks a shard off the slab of marble;

– offer light on an old topic to suggest a different perspective; and

– place tools in your hands.

Whether or not you create a change, challenge a system or laugh your way to a different conclusion, is entirely up to you.

Rules and regulations

Why do rules remain, continue to have public support even, when their purpose is questionable and their source has been long since lost in the mists of time?

Rules and regulations should serve people; people should not serve rules and regulations. They should be challengeable and flexible. Too many rules, over time, become sacred, untouchable and have inappropriate power vested in them by people who use them as tools for controlling other people. An unchallengeable rule or regulation is fuel for complacency. That's just the way things are — outside our control and not within our power to change. We feel powerless in the face of their apparent immutability. Too many rules dramatically reduce innovation and independent thought.

A STORY ABOUT RULES

That's just the way we do things around here...

I knew him when he was director of Human Resources for a chemical firm. He was smart — very smart. He was also likeable and humble. We became friends. The thing I liked about him most was his clarity of thinking, his ability to sort the good from the bad, the solid from the fragile, the unimportant from the important. I was the revolutionary, the firebrand, the one to whip up the sense of what was possible; he was the strategist, the thinker, the quiet planner, making possible in thoughtful steps what I saw in the round. We learnt a lot from one another.

He was tall and rangy, he had a slightly fey look, either as if he was concentrating on a distant sound or, more likely, thinking carefully about what you were saying. He dressed humbly. He was casual without being neglectful, comfortable without being disrespectful. Sometimes he appeared chameleon-like, taking on the physical characteristics, clothing, voice, language, demeanour, of the people around him. Sometimes he could appear hierarchical, authoritative, business-like, fully the powerful senior executive; sometimes he could appear like one of the lads, sitting on a bale of this or that, talking over a mug of coffee to a couple of forkies having a break. In either circumstance, everyone felt at ease with him. I always believed this was his strength as a leader. It gave him great credibility.

The interesting phenomenon was his clothing. He never dressed differently for anyone, it just seemed that way.

Over time, he was promoted. This was hardly surprising. Over time, head hunters tried to seduce him to this or that job; this also was hardly surprising. Over time, he was finally head hunted to be the executive in charge of strategic planning and human resources for a large mining concern. He accepted. This was surprising to many people, but not to me.

I had lunch with him the other day. It was a chance to exchange notes, catch up on the gossip, learn a thing or two. I went into his office to meet him, up on the twenty-third floor of a city building, into the 'chrome zone'. Behind a marble reception area sat a pleasant receptionist. Behind her in big brass letters was the name of the company and beneath it 'Executive Offices'. Corridors disappeared off to the right and left of reception, quiet, muted, expensive. It was a far cry from his old office at the chemical plant. Was it an improvement? I had no idea. Personally, I felt like a bird in a gilded cage.

I waited while the receptionist paged him. Moments later he came out, smiling from ear to ear. We greeted one another warmly and I remarked that it was the first time I had seen him in a suit. He laughed. I flattered him by telling him he looked good but, truthfully, he looked uncomfortable. Seeing through my dishonest compliment, he confirmed my silent observation. He told me, as we walked to the lifts, that he didn't like the suits, they were uncomfortable and he got a sore neck from the shirt and tie; he felt stuffy in them. "Why are you wearing it then?" I asked. "Because that's part of the culture," he replied. As we travelled down the lift and out into the real world I thought to myself "This is how even senior people lend weight to myths that they don't believe in or want anything to do with."

"The suit is a metaphor for what is acceptable," I said to my friend. "It creates a wall around you. Do you wear it out into the field?" I asked. "Yes," he responded. "Then they will know you are from head office I guess." "Yes," he replied. "Does it make you think any better," I pushed. "No, he answered," a little irritably. He looked at me then, knowing what the implication was. "There are other more important battles to fight," he said, effectively closing the topic.

But it felt to me as if it was an acceptance of an unwritten rule that this is what you look like at the top. And I thought, as I have thought before, about the world of business and the rules that govern etiquette. Who wrote them? Where are they recorded? Why do we all so slavishly adhere to them when few of us like the outcome? Whose power base are we preserving? What weaknesses do we cover with the clothing we wear? What strengths do we exclude because someone does not understand the unwritten code of conduct?

Never mind. This was not the man who would tackle this particular battle and today was not the day to fight an issue such as this.

I changed the topic and we went to lunch.

THE ISSUE DOESN'T GO AWAY

Three days after having lunch with my suited friend, I spoke for a large retail buying group specialising in whitegoods. I don't know how I managed to get the topic into my speech, but I did.

"Hands up those of you who like wearing suit and tie to work?" Fifteen percent of hands went up. "How many of you believe it improves the quality of the work you do?" No hands went up. "How many of you would not wear suits if you didn't think you had to?" Eighty-five percent of hands were raised.

A question I am left with now: Where is the rule written that says business is more effectively conducted by people wearing suits? If it is written anywhere, who wrote it? Why are we sticking to this rule when by far the greater majority of people don't want to any more?

This is the Abilene Paradox at work again.

EXPOSING THE RULES

There is an art to distinguishing between rules that matter, that help, that build, that preserve safety, and those that do nothing or, worse, diminish, stifle, delineate, separate. Does the clothing we wear at work matter? It does, if it serves only to separate us, not out of choice or personal taste but out of status and apparent importance.

If rules lock us in to a specific way of behaving, tell us what we can or cannot do, begin to erode our confidence to think 'out of the mould', then they should be challenged. If rules exist to maintain a status quo with which we are no longer comfortable, they should be challenged. If rules exist the logic of which defies us, the purpose of which escapes us, they should be challenged.

No rule should remain simply because 'that's the way we do things'. Such complacency does little more than spark discontent, feed cynicism and encourage further lassitude!

Why do rules remain, continue to have public support even, when their purpose is questionable and their source has been long since lost in the mists of time? I've thought long and hard on this, so here is what I think:

– The rule has been around for so long we've become used to it.

– The person who controls the rule's power recognises that their own power has become vested in the rule, so to challenge the rule is to challenge to the person.

– The rule has the mandate of the masses — if everybody's following it, it can't be wrong, can it?

– The rule is passed down from some illusive other who is unidentifiable but nonetheless, like God: all-seeing and all-powerful.

– We are too anxious about our own security of tenure to challenge the rule and we fear the repercussions of change more than we want the benefits.

Let's expose them in turn.

THE RULE HAS BEEN AROUND FOR SO LONG WE'VE BECOME USED TO IT

Despite the fact that familiarity breeds contempt, it can also breed acquiescence: "Hey, who cares?" The attitude to what we wear at work might belong in this category. We keep wearing suits — despite the fact that few people particularly like wearing them — because we have always worn them. A change in dress may cause a cascade of changes in other areas; seeing the MD out of a pinstriped suit and in jeans definitely creates a different atmosphere in a business. (But does the business actually perform better or worse? I am sure I can't say. It's unlikely that clothing influences performance one way or the other. However, allowing people to wear what they feel comfortable in — which, incidentally, might be quite formal — will encourage respect for what people *do* rather than what they wear, and that surely can't be bad.)

Some of the 'best' rules in the world in this category exist in government bureaucracies! Think of what it's like to get your driving license renewed, obtain a passport, get a permit to enter another country, move addresses on the electoral role, deal with the lands office, put through a subdivision, build a house, put an extension on an existing house, buy or sell property and so on. I've had some of the most frustrating and some of the funniest episodes of my life in government departments. You know the places — where you have to fill things out in triplicate but no one ever seems to know why. You have to fill out the same information on three different departmental forms and when you ask why the other two departments couldn't get copies of the first form, you're informed that it's just the way they like to do it!

QUESTIONS: **What are the rules that affect your life at work which have been around for so long that everyone just accepts them? Do you know who initiated them in the first place? How do you know the rule is definitely a rule that must be obeyed?**

THE PERSON WHO CONTROLS THE RULE'S POWER RECOGNISES THAT THEIR OWN POWER HAS BECOME VESTED IN THE RULE

This is one of the worst tools for holding onto rules. Ironically, despite a belief to the contrary, the effect of this diminishes rather than enhances leadership. Such leaders, whether they are line supervisors or managing directors, demonstrate their lack of flexibility and their fear of change by vesting rules with their own authority.

You can spot such a rule when you hear managers say things like:

"When you work for me, you'll do it this way."

"This is the way I like to see the job done."

"Look, I've been at this for a long time and I know how to do it."

"You're still wet behind the ears. Do what you're told to do until you've learnt the ropes."

This style of control is one which causes great angst for young people early in their working career. It stifles innovation and diminishes personal responsibility.

QUESTIONS: Do you have a manager who upholds rules this way? What are the things they are trying to control? What do you think is motivating them? Are they afraid of something, if so what are they afraid of? What alternatives do you have in mind and why? How can you lead someone through change with out undermining their confidence?

THE RULE HAS THE MANDATE OF THE MASSES

I love this one; it's called 'social proof'. An action is validated because the masses have condoned it. In this way the Aztecs were able to offer up some 30,000 humans as sacrifices to the gods without overt protest from the general populace. Fascinating experiments have been conducted to see just how far people will go when rules appear to have the authority of the masses behind them. The answer is, they'll go to the very end. We want to belong, we fear rejection, so we uphold rules if we think everyone else concurs.

There is a prevailing sense that if everyone wanted a rule to change, it would. However, as I noted in the discussion of the Abilene Paradox, we are perfectly capable of doing something together without *any* of us wanting to.

QUESTIONS: **How does social proof affect rules in your life? In work, what rules do you accept because everyone else appears to approve? Have you ever tested your assumptions about these rules? Have you asked people if change did occur would they be happy about it?**

THE RULE IS PASSED DOWN FROM SOME ILLUSIVE OTHER

This refers to that 'special elite' of leaders who head some of our largest organisations. Their existence is vaguely comprehended by the vast majority, but they make the many businesses that cascade under them work. They exist on the periphery of our awareness, in memos, on stationary, in annual reports — but we rarely, if ever, actually meet them.

However, their Godly name is invoked to validate all manner of things! Here is a curious thing: having met many of these very senior leaders and, on occasion confronted them with some of the rules that are invoked in their name, they are not only surprised, embarrassed and on occasion horrified, they also admit that their success is based on their ability to bypass such rules! Food for thought.

QUESTIONS: **If you work in a large organisation, can you identify components of the culture that reflect a leadership tradition? From which leaders do the major cultural influences flow? Can you identify apparent rules of behaviour that are part of 'the way things are done here'? Have you ever sought evidence for the substance of these rules? Are they recorded anywhere, in writing? Or are they simply hearsay?**

WE ARE TOO ANXIOUS ABOUT
OUR OWN SECURITY OF TENURE

We are simply too afraid of the potential harm to ourselves that might flow from rocking the boat. I know of a nasty but nonetheless effective game which highlights this particular problem. It goes like this: I place a four metre plank which is twenty centimetres wide on the floor. At one end, I place a five dollar note. I take twenty people and I say, "If you can walk this plank without falling off, you get the five dollars." Everyone has a go and basically everyone gets their five dollars. Nice and easy. Then we hot things up. I raise the plank thirty centimetres and I repeat the exercise. Again, everyone gets across. Then I raise the plank a metre. This time only seventy percent get across, the fear of falling outweighing the gain of getting across. Next time I leave the plank where it is and put twenty dollars at the end. Funnily enough, ninety percent of the people reach the money.

I can go on doing this for some time until the perceived threat of 'death' outweighs any monetary gain I can offer (except for the few mad ones for whom the money was irrelevant in the first place; they were just after the adrenaline fix!).

QUESTIONS: **Are there rules that affect you which you would love to change, but don't, because you feel that the potential risks outweigh the potential benefits? What are the risks that you perceive? Do other people share your concerns? What benefits would have to flow to you to justify taking the risk to challenge the rule? How would you go about securing those benefits?**

There are a lot of rules in business that *just don't make sense* to a lot of people. There's rules about how we dress, how we communicate, how we behave, what we should value, what community responsibility comes with the commercial turf. The rules have held true for a long time and, in some instances, have had great benefits for many of us.

However, things change, and nothing can take us back to where we have come from. As I have said, repeatedly, it is the rapidity of change and the certainty that such change is with us for as far as the eye can see that should fuel our determination to do things differently. Challenging sacred cows is an important place to begin.

In the next few chapters I will try and upset a few applecarts, but truthfully, it is the ones *you* see, where ever you are, no matter what your position and no matter what business you are in that really count. If we all girded our loins and took courage from each other's actions, I suspect we could effect some mighty changes in a very short time frame.

If 'reality is defined by the questions we put to it' then let's start redefining our reality by asking some really hot questions. Remember, nothing ventured, nothing gained!

The quality myth

What else, apart from quality, has ever been measured as successful by a manual and a Government tick of approval?

10

Some people believe quality is a thing that can be encapsulated in a process or a manual. I think quality is an attitude of mind and, as a focus for our actions, comes naturally to people when they feel valued and respected.

A STORY ABOUT QUALITY

I had just been commissioned by a company to do an Honesty Audit. I had spent a great deal of time with the Managing Director and the senior executive team. We had talked about the competitive marketplace, the recent history of the organisation, their ambitions for the future. The MD had been in place for about eighteen months. His principal focus of attention was stated, in no uncertain terms, to be on an abiding commitment to quality and a passion for customer service. These ambitions had been written into the company's vision in as many words:

> "We commit to excellence in our every action and to exceeding customer expectations in terms of reliability, durability and value for price. We value people and take pride in serving."

The problem was that the vision was a figment of the MD's imagination. No one, apparently, shared it with him. He was frustrated and in our first few meetings spent a considerable amount of time complaining to me about the quality of Australian employees: "Good people are so hard to find... young people don't want to work nowadays... people just don't care enough to be careful, check all the details."

My job was to find out why this was so and to suggest some useful strategies for invigorating staff and developing a high degree of motivation for the vision.

Before beginning the Honesty Audit, I was given a tour of several of the company's factories. This is a 'familiarisation' process; the idea is to get an understanding of what raw materials go into the product, how it is designed, manufactured, distributed, marketed. I can then begin the Audit with a basic understanding of the business.

On this particular occasion, the familiarisation process was particularly telling. It was the first time I saw really appalling staff conditions.

In each location, one of the staff gave me a tour. At the first site, I met with local management and saw around the offices. The offices weren't too bad — old but bearable. I asked if I could go out into the factory. The sight that met my eyes caused me a moment's pause. There was rank after rank of machines, poor lighting, dirtiness, age, and a pervasive sense of things having been discarded. There were no staff present. It was 5.30 pm. The factory closed at 4.30 pm.

In the second location, I was able to look around while people were working. They looked tired, harried, a little dispirited. They were working in cramped conditions, and there were no uniforms, despite the dirty conditions.

In the third location, I asked to have a look at the canteen. I was shown into a room in such a dreadful condition that I would not have eaten there had it been my last meal on earth. It was dingy, filthy. There was an old kettle, its lid broken and the electric cord frayed. The tables were worn, many of the chairs were missing backs.

At the fourth location, I saw a similar factory and canteen. I asked to see the changing rooms and toilets. I actually felt ill. They would have done a derelict inner city Brooklyn building proud. Of five toilets in the men's section, only one had a lid. Additional toilet paper sat at the back of the toilets on a filthy cement floor. Windows were grey and smeared. The women's toilets were only marginally better. There were limited changing facilities and no lockers, despite the fact that many of the employees had 'work' clothing (which, I was to find out, they preferred not to wear on the way to or from work).

I think the following pieces of graffiti I found on the men's toilets sum it up:

"A clean hearth breeds a healthy mind."

"No wonder we are so bloody warped."

"Titanium suits recommended when spending time in these premises."

"Contagious diseases have taken the following people: George, Bill, Leigh, Ben, Hocker, Dennis, Woofer and on last sighting, Harry was looking poorly."

"Harry's in here somewhere. If you find him, tell him his friends miss him."

When I asked people why things were not cleaned up and repaired, I was told that the MD was "holding a tight rein" on internal expenditure and that there was never any money to improve things, despite repeated requests to do just that. This led to a 'don't care' attitude which in part explained the grotty appearance of staff amenities. If the company didn't care, certainly the people didn't care.

I also asked if he had ever visited any of the sites. He had, but he spent most of his time in the offices (which were alright), and only a brief moment in the factory. At no time, as far as anyone could recall, had he visited any canteen or made use of any of the factory toilet facilities.

I knew then, before the Audit began, that my biggest challenge would be to help the MD and senior executive team understand that while internal conditions remained unimproved, they would never achieve their external ambitions in terms of quality and customer service.

I wondered to myself what it would be like to work for the business, what would my sense of worth be; I wondered how I would I feel if I did not seem to warrant a decent toilet, canteen or change room. My attitude would embrace many if not all of the following:

I would feel degraded, devalued, cheap;

I would feel resentful, especially since it was common knowledge that Head Office space was clean and new;

I might end up behaving in a manner more suitable to the environment — sloppy, uncaring, disinterested.

In short, if I didn't count, then what was my motivation to care? Leaders neglect others at their own expense.

WHAT IS 'QUALITY'?

In pursuit of improving the professional performance of business we have taken the concept of 'quality' — one of the richest and all-embracing of human pursuits — and shrunk it to a shadow of its former self. It has become encapsulated in a manual; it is now a numbered stamp of approval.

The 'quality' *I* refer to is something much bigger which — when understood and entrenched in the culture of a business — naturally produces all that we might wish to measure quality by today: outstanding product, efficient systems, minimal errors, improved customer relations and, ultimately, improved profitability.

And the driving force of this quality? People — dignified, respected, valued and informed.

THE QUALITY MYTH?

That quality is a thing, an object, a series of manualised documents and procedures for which we get accreditation. That by delegating the process of quality accreditation, leaders will engender a culture that understands quality.

Fascinating, really! I often wonder if the butcher, the baker, the candlestick maker needed to focus attention on quality, or whether it just happened naturally because they were close to the face of their businesses and could measure performance on a daily basis. They might not have had quality systems, but they were, in my romanticised version of history, proud of what they did and genuinely felt valued... Ahh!

There are many ways to treat our fellow human beings — from grandly to abysmally. We can starve them, bomb them, torture them — we can so degrade the body that it seems impossible to think that the human spirit can survive. But it is extraordinary under what circumstances people can and do blossom. I remember a story I heard from a man called Gerry Coffey. He was an American fighter pilot who was shot down during the Vietnam war. He spent seven years in a prisoner of war camp. Despite a severely broken collarbone and arm he received no medical treatment when he was first incarcerated. To the contrary, he was repeatedly interrogated then subjected to severe physical privation in the confines of a six foot by four foot cell.

In the first year the light in his cell was left on for twenty-four hours a day. At random times during the day and never less than once a day, he was routinely hosed down. He was continuously subject to anti-American propaganda. Over time, he was told that the Americans had forgotten about him — that he did not matter.

Despite the conditions, however, Gerry found something to do that gave him the courage to survive. He learnt a form of morse code. This morse code allowed the prisoners to talk to one another, to give each other hope when all else seemed to be failing, to offer succour and love in a place where both were seemingly unattainable.

Despite this severe treatment (which was the same for a range of prisoners), he discovered a richness of spiritual realisation that not only sustained him in his cell but actually gave him a depth of understanding and a greater sense of wellbeing and hope than that possessed by the people he later met in American towns after his eventual release.

I met Gerry backstage at a speaking engagement. I felt humble sharing the stage with him. In a quiet moment I asked him what he had discovered in, of all places, a prison, that he felt was missing from the 'free' people he had encountered on his release. He thought about this for a while, shook his head, and eventually said "Humanity, simple humanity."

I believe he meant the quality of being humane; he was referring to kindness, benevolence, decency. I believe these are the qualities that we should rightly pursue in business, for they are sorely wanting. We still give people mindless, unchallenging tasks, we treat them as if they were our chattels, we withhold information, intimidate, diminish. We justify our actions by arguing that work conditions have improved massively in this century. Unarguably in Australia, we are right. However, our expectations of what is possible have also changed massively and I feel the gap is still substantial. We still have far to go.

QUALITY — DO WE DO IT NATURALLY?

Consider this for a moment: what do you do very well? Is it something you can make — a model airplane, a house, a piece of clothing, a meal? Is it something you can do — ski, rollerblade, play tennis or basketball, make love? Is it something you know — films directed in Hollywood since 1954, how to make a garden grow?

Consider how this knowledge and skill grew: Was it over time? Did you make mistakes to begin with? Did you have to ask questions or experiment? Was it the product of exposure to others? Did you enjoy the journey?

Consider how you feel about your 'expertise' now: Do you have the courage to step outside the so called 'rules'? Do you think you will know more, be better at your hobby, interest or passion five years from now? What about your skill ten years from now? Do you know who does it better and where? Do you know how to get more knowledge?

Chances are that you understand how your specialised ability grew and that you know who is more specialised than you. You know how to access more information if you want it and you know the benefits that may flow from increased skill or knowledge. You exercise personal responsibility in the choices you make and you are rewarded accordingly.

You see, I believe that each and every one of us understands quality. It is in our bones. Producing it has much to do with purpose and outcomes. If you don't know why you are doing something or for whom you are doing it, if your ambitions are thwarted by seemingly insurmountable rules and regulations, by systems and manuals, or by politics and hierarchy, then after a period of time your commitment to doing something better will be worn down or eradicated all together.

Quality and the satisfaction of the people we serve are not fuelled alone by rules and regulations, brilliant systems and measurement. First and foremost, they are fuelled by personal commitment and responsibility, individual skill and imagination, and a desire for undiluted pleasure and personal reward.

These are not the unique fuelling sources for a few high achievers, they are the stuff of life for all people — the very young, the middle-aged and the elderly. To rob a human of these things is to rob them of the essence of life, to take away their dignity, their sense of purpose. They may *appear* to perform well, but something will have been lost on the journey that is hard to replace and whose value is, in this day and age of chaotic and speed-of-light change, inestimable.

Gary B graduated from Law and Economics at university in the top five percent of graduates in the country. Gary was a marvellous character; theatrical, funny, intense — very, very bright. He had applied himself to everything in his life with equal dedication; work, women, having fun. No one was surprised by Gary's graduation results.

Behind the scenes, Gary was a young man on a mission. He had a strong sense of his own purpose in life; he was creative and determined. He felt he had a lot to contribute and that his greatest gift was his ability to find a path in a complex environment that no one else had seen. He had a passionate commitment to excellence and an innate understanding of the value of quality in his every action. Gary was sure that he was going to be successful in business and that sooner, rather than later, he would make his personal fortune.

As is the case for many high performers at university, Gary was quickly head hunted. He had been talking to a couple of companies doing direct recruitment on campus throughout his final year. He had also received support from campus employment councillors who had put him in touch with a number of members of the Australian Association of Graduate Employers. All in all, Gary had some half a dozen job offers when he finally finished his studies.

The company he settled for was a major Australian corporation — a household name, respected and perhaps a little feared in the business world. Gary was thrilled. The pay was good, the opportunities were even better. He finished university in November and started work in February of the following year.

I spoke to Gary about eight months after he started. I asked him what the job was like, how he was proceeding and whether things were happening as expected.

Gary was still reasonably full of life but there was now a brake on his enthusiasm. It was hard to identify, but nonetheless it was present. He talked about how what he was doing was not much of a challenge; he talked about how he was learning 'how things were done' in the business, about what the 'rules' were in terms of doing business the 'company way'. We talked at length about the company's fully accredited quality processes and of how they flowed into every aspect of the day-to-day running of the business. He had met the senior people only fleetingly.

He had, however, met a lot of other graduates. I remember Gary saying neither he, nor they, were entirely sure that they liked what they saw, but nonetheless most remained committed.

I spoke to Gary nearly eighteen months on from this. He was becoming very different from the Gary I remembered. He was sobering up, the roaring fire in his chest had turned into a block of ice. He was angry more than passionate and talked about the company's capacity to stifle real inno-vation. He talked about the prevalence of politics. He talked about the tendency to get rid of anyone who stepped outside the mould. He talked about the daily challenge of maintaining his identity, his instinct for asking how things might be done differently. He talked about the fear that deter-mined many outcomes — fear about doing the right thing, fear about doing the wrong thing. He talked about the sheer weight of the organisation and of the inordinate time it took to get anything changed.

He talked, in other words, about the myth of quality and how corrosive it was to the corporation and its ambitions, to the staff and their contributions, to the individual and their sense of self-worth. I was saddened for him but not surprised by the outcome.

Not long after this I spoke at a conference for an association of graduate employers. The people who attended the conference were predominantly young leaders with an interest in helping their organisations get the best graduates possible. In private, it was astonishing how many shared 'Gary' stories with me; they could cite long lists of bright, enthusiastic, ambitious, clever graduates who got head hunted into large organisations only to spend their first few years having this very energy carefully and systematically extinguished, to be replaced with a mind-set that reflected the organisation's view of what was right and acceptable. And what was deemed 'right and acceptable' was based on the notion of so-called quality processes.

In the words of one particularly frustrated recruiter: "We are given a charter to go out and find the best, and then they spend their first year with us learning 'how things are really done'. If they don't settle down — that is, learn our way of doing things — they either leave voluntarily or we make sure they leave." She shook her head at the madness of the paradox.

You see, innovation and determination, personal responsibility and passion can be extinguished even in the seemingly brightest of people. They and we can be worn down by the apparently 'set in cement' mechanisms that determine the flow of decision making, discourage consultation and inhibit real participation.

In such an environment, 'quality accreditation' makes a mockery of what quality is all about. We are not dignifying the actions of people, valuing

their input. We are setting a standard above which they may not rise —
and this unarguably is the quintessential opposite of quality.

SUBSETS OF THE QUALITY MYTH

1. **THE MYTH:** If we manualise a process, people will read and obey.

   THE TRUTH: We frequently have manuals produced by people
   who don't need them and we give them to people who can't use them.

2. **THE MYTH:** Quality awards make people focus on doing the best
   they can to ensure that quality processes are in place and the company
   is doing all it can to excel.

   THE TRUTH: Quality awards are often seen to be a marketing tool
   for the business; in substance they appear in a number of cases to be
   intrusive and disruptive to the quality flow of business.

3. **THE MYTH:** All it takes to achieve 'quality' is a decision to invest
   in achieving quality accreditation; once the decision is made, the
   responsibility can be handed to a 'quality' co-ordinator.

   THE TRUTH: Leaders fail substantially to understand the source of
   quality; it is an embedded culture of mutual respect, quality communication and comprehensive consultation.

4. **THE MYTH:** Quality is about continuous improvement.

   THE TRUTH: With so many mergers, takeovers, change processes
   continuous anything is almost impossible.

Let's examine each of these sub-myths in detail.

'THE ART OF WRITING MANUALS' — BY PEOPLE WHO DON'T NEED THEM, FOR PEOPLE WHO WILL NEVER USE THEM

Computer boffins should own up to this one. Were you aware that most computer manuals are put together by people who have no use of them for people who find them almost incomprehensible? The same is true for a lot of quality manuals.

Here's my experience; see if yours matches up: it's always an amazingly organised and systematic person who is responsible for producing quality manuals which describe, in minute detail, exactly how we do things round here. They are the sort of person who did well at maths and always looked neat and tidy. Their minds are naturally converted to order. They identify gaps in logic with ease. They look at us mere mortals with the disdain that the chess champion reserves for the checkers player.

We don't really fit their model world but, with much struggling and sighing, they will do the best they can with us. They organise meetings with us, record our comments, look at our paperwork, redesign it to make it simpler, more cohesive with the other departments. They help us understand why our system is mismatching another sector's system. They streamline, order, match and commit information to manuals.

They and we spend a lot of time doing this — months and, in some cases, years.

Eventually, things begin to look good. There are clear, concise, ways for doing everything, from ordering a pencil, to taking a purchase order from a customer. We know who we have to speak to and when, how to record our interaction and why, when to pass the process over and to whom. There are methods for resolving our problems and dealing with customers. When everything is looking shipshape, things are running smoothly, order has been achieved, we finally get that much sought-after stamp of approval. We get this approval from assessors who are very like the people who helped us manualise the universe in the first place.

In the process we have unarguably improved the way we do things, put into place controls for ensuring the maintenance of agreed standards but we have also produced some 'Bloody Big Manuals'. These have been copied out to all departments so everyone has a complete set. In the executive offices there is a special set of 'Bloody Big Manuals'. These look good and are heavy.

There is only one teensy-weensy problem, and it gives the manual writers nightmares of frustration and angst: no one refers to the manuals! What are supposed to be the keys to our success and agreed processes are written by people who don't need manuals for people who can't use them. Things go along quite nicely for a while, but as soon as it gets sticky, the manual writers refer us to Manual B, Part 13, section 2, page 238, paragraph 16... The rest of us break the rules, bypass the system, and go to the human being we trust to get action *now*. We discover along the way that the worst culprits for bypassing the system (actually they didn't really participate in the first place) are the leaders! Their whole modus operandi is one big system bypass.

Remember, however, "do as we say, not as we do"!

All humour aside, we can still fairly ask whether manuals really are useful. One would suspect that, judged by the accumulated dust and rubbish I see resting on many of them, some may not in their current format be as useful as we imagine they should be.

Notwithstanding that some businesses are transformed by committing to quality processes, there are many that are not. Instead of improving performance and creating unity of purpose and process, tracking the processes the company uses, documenting procedures and getting everyone to agree on using them becomes an excuse for not committing to a culture — a care for people — from which quality naturally flows.

The 'systems' people do their job (in truth, a largely thankless task) — they listen, document, streamline and record. Then, in an alarming number of situations, things grind to a standstill. The manuals are relegated to a bottom drawer somewhere and things are pretty much business as usual. People will do what they will do; if the culture supports them they will continue to enhance the quality processes, if the culture lacks values of substance which condone the endeavours of people the quality will go the way of many well intentioned but poorly planned initiatives — into the bin.

QUESTIONS: Do you have quality manuals that few people refer to? Are the processes that are documented in the manuals actually in use? Are they in use in some areas but not in others? What do you notice about the areas in which quality processes work and the ones in which they don't? Could the manuals, which record the processes we are committing to, be designed differently? What would make them readable or useable to the average person? In your experience how important is the culture which supports quality in your business? What do you believe are the strengths and weaknesses of the culture that imposes on you? What would you change if you could?

QUALITY AWARDS — A BONANZA OR A PAIN IN THE PROVERBIAL

Attitudes change. Here's how it goes in relation to commitment to awards. In the first try in the quality award stakes, everyone finds the exercise exciting. They're all behind the idea, which was initially pushed by management. In the second try, everyone finds it hard work but thinks it worth the effort nevertheless. The third try sees most thinking "Oh, Jesus, not again! We've got so much else to do. Whose idea was it anyway?"

A lot of people think quality awards are a very big waste of time. Great if you win — as a marketing tool to the organisations that demand you have quality accreditation before they will do business with you. But why do we do it otherwise? To win takes a lot of time and effort. If getting a quality award has little to do with business and much to do with marketing, why aren't we honest about it? And here's a novel question: If it is about marketing (how to use a public pat on the back to your advantage) what else could we be doing to get the same PR value? Makes you wonder…

QUESTIONS: **Have you or your business ever gone for a quality award? If so, what did it involve? What benefits came from the process? Would you do it again? How can such a process be turned to real benefit for the business? Do you think pursuing awards is a red herring when it comes to pursuing quality? What would you rather do instead?**

DO LEADERS UNDERSTAND THEIR RESPONSIBILITY IN PURSUIT OF QUALITY?

Here's what a lot of people say about leaders and the pursuit of quality:

– quality processes are frequently layed over unhealthy cultures;

– the management of quality accreditation is delegated to someone with no power to affect fundamental change;

– the pursuit of quality focuses on incremental improvement in efficiency without addressing opportunity for innovation.

Leaders are pivotal in all three. Firstly, too many leaders commit to quality processes prematurely. Their organisation has no sense of its own future, what the company is in business to achieve; there is an inherent culture of cynicism, a mistrust of leader-driven initiatives because there have been so many and none have lasted; furthermore, the quality of leadership is seriously wanting. If quality is overlayed over an unstable foundation, the seeds for its failure are sewn before the process has even commenced.

Secondly, leaders fail to address fundamental communication weaknesses that have little to do with process and much to do with tradition. Mature and active politically-motivated hierarchies fall into this category. The political framework is the most destructive of a sustained quality culture. Issues which directly affect quality frequently are manipulated or falsely represented at various levels in order to appear to be doing the right thing. A political environment can stop people from doing the right thing and encourage them to do what seems to be right, according to certain powerful leaders.

Many people feel that in a political or hierarchical environment, strict quality guidelines can lead to a 'witch hunt' mentality. This in turn causes people to buck-pass, duck for cover, avoid the lightening bolts, and wait for the storm to pass. In such an environment, innovation is risky! What if it doesn't work, what if it doesn't deliver the promised results?

One organisation leaps to mind in which this problem was glaringly apparent. The Chairman of the Group was a clever, shrewd but now isolated man. He founded the company some thirty years ago. He had captained its public listing some ten years ago and was now Chairman of the Board and the majority shareholder. The company was successful, in terms of the net return on capital invested.

However, a number of analysts were surprised that it wasn't doing considerably better. It was in a niche market, had an excellent product and was widely respected as a market leader. When I had the opportunity to look inside the business, one problem became apparent — a problem that at first seemed petty and relatively insignificant, considering the size and complexity of the business. Essentially, the problem boiled down to this: the Chairman had, as a young MD, developed a method for weekly financial reporting that enabled him to track his business, day by day, customer by customer, by product category, volume, colour, material and production time from order to delivery. In its early days it was a brilliant system that allowed for extensive incremental improvements in a whole range of business activities.

Over time, however, it became unwieldy and appropriate only at an operational level, at certain factories. Nevertheless, it was still being produced for the Chairman on a weekly basis (all weeks, numbered 1 through 52, starting at the beginning of the financial year). Because he was now removed from the business and not in the operational controlling seat, he used these reports to 'witch hunt' senior management.

Basically, weekly reports were produced on a Thursday and faxed through to Head Office. On Friday, all senior managers were involved in a teleconference the guts of which was a 'why did this happen' debate on the preceding week. The Chairman was always well prepared for these teleconferences and invariably would have questions to fire off at everyone. They were expected to have responses by Monday afternoon at the latest (or sooner, depending on how serious the Chairman felt the problems were).

On speaking to people I discovered that they had been trying to change this process for a long time — years. Without exception, the management team felt that the scrutiny was wasteful, time consuming and of questionable business value. They also thought it cast serious doubts on the reliability of information coming from Head Office (where all financial data was accumulated). I was told, however, at the time of interviewing staff that I had Buckley's chance of getting the Chairman to change his mind.

On looking a little further, I discovered about twenty-five to forty percent of senior and middle management's time was dedicated to resolving retrospective business issues — that is, asking who and what is to blame for what went wrong last week. As one frustrated executive said, "If only we spent half this time looking at business improvements and how to please our customers we would have a very different organisation."

Despite quality accreditation, a clear commitment to quality in the vision and an entrenched culture of 'have a care', the Chairman was unable to lift his head out of his history to observe that the world had changed. He needed fast, flexible and creative managers, yet what he was breeding was a politically intimidated group of fault-finding diagnosticians.

Leaders often don't own the quality process except as a theoretical model the possession of which they regard as commercial necessity. Frequently they don't comprehend the extent to which their actions actually diminish quality outcomes.

QUESTIONS: **Does politics or hierarchy affect the implementation of quality processes in your business? How? What could be done to change this? Why is it worth changing? Who needs to be party to the change?**

THE CHANGE EPIDEMIC PUTS PAID TO QUALITY PROCESSES IN THE BLINK OF AN EYE

Restructures, mergers, takeovers, rationalisations can all have their business value. There are times when they are called for, make commercial sense, are the stuff of legend and survival. However, even when they make sense there are dangers and, as we have already observed, many don't make sense, at least to the people in the businesses concerned.

Achieving quality accreditation or putting into place systems which improve efficiencies takes time — a lot of time. It takes input from a hugely diverse range of people and it costs money — a lot of money. To do it well, people have to work closely together debating every conceivable aspect of business operations, from the simplest to the most complex, often several times over. Then there is a period of trial and error, refining and reworking ideas until eventually, there is a method and everyone signs off on it.

Then along comes the merger or restructure. Given senior management's perspective on commercially sensitive information, one can well imagine that the staff of a business hear about a merger after it has become a fait accompli. They may then be invited in to discuss how to effect the merger as smoothly as possible. Those in the stronger camp are involved in determining who will stay and who will go, what structure the newly merged organisation will have and how the transition will be handled.

Consider a not atypical scenario where the larger of the merger partners does not have quality accreditation, but the smaller one does. Bingo! Accreditation goes out the door and everything is back to square one. If this isn't handled thoughtfully, at least two things occur:

– all the accumulated knowledge and learning from the original quality team is rejected;

– the lack of awareness of senior management for the implications of their decisions feeds the cynicism monster; next time around it is going to be that much harder to get committed people to support the push for quality accreditation.

QUESTIONS: **Have you been through such a change process or know of someone who has? What could be done differently to preserve the experience and the knowledge gained? Should we stop quality accreditation as such and implement a national drive to build 'quality cultures'? How would leaders figure in such a drive? How would staff feature? What are the strengths and weaknesses of the quality accreditation process when it is formalised?**

BETTER QUALITY — THE WAY FORWARD

These then are some of the myths that relate to the quality debate. For many of us there is some scepticism as to why accreditation is being pursued. We may ask whether quality would be occurring without formal accreditation processes; we might wonder whether awareness of the real value of quality and the substance of its fuel has been raised adequately. Perhaps it is time to embrace a broader understanding of quality. The topic and its implementation should be debated so that we might come up with a more flexible, holistic approach.

A friend who I respect greatly and who holds one of the more senior positions in corporate Australia made the following comment to me, knowing my thoughts on this topic:

> *"Quality accreditation can be a trap; in fact is a trap. Nowadays you have to use it whether you agree with it or not. To me, it seems sinister; something you have to do that you frequently don't believe in and which often doesn't add value or substance. You have to commit to it because so many companies demand it before you can do business with them."*

> *"People shouldn't delude themselves; whatever value quality accreditation adds to their businesses, it has little to do with quality."*

I had a particularly interesting experience recently which highlighted this perspective with a company whose standard of quality control was seemingly outstanding. They were ISO 9002 certified in 1987. The business was a specialist precision engineering firm. I had met the Managing Director and principal shareholder at a speaking engagement some weeks before and, during the course of lunch, I had heard a lot about his style of leadership that interested me. Clearly he was a determined individual with a passionate commitment to his business and an ambitious sense of the future. At lunch, after I had spoken, he told me about the company structure, the quality journey they had all been through, their policy of import replacement and their seemingly formidable growth in recent years. He was excited and exciting. We agreed that I should come and visit him and have a look around the business first-hand.

When I arrived, he took me to his office. It was at the front of a rather old but well cared for building, certainly nothing spectacular. We sat down and I asked him about the company's history, the reasoning behind the push for quality accreditation, what it had cost, what impact it had had. He was open with his information, saying that the accreditation journey had taken over two years and had cost in excess of $200,000 (with an obvious ongoing cost). He then noted that it had had very substantial impact on the company's attitudes towards errors and resolving problems.

One example he cited had to do with scrap reduction. Where traditionally a staff member could have lost their job if they identified too many errors, got a 'DCM' notice (don't come in on Monday), now they were rewarded for their commitment to quality and minimising errors. As a result of this initiative alone (where each machine operator was responsible for signing-off work before it moved on to the next process) the business had reduced its 'scrapping' rate (work so unacceptable it had to be scrapped completely) from 7% (which was in its time well below industry standards) to 0.7%. This initiative alone — a direct consequence of reviewing the company's procedures as part of the quality accreditation process — was saving the business many hundreds of thousands of dollars annually.

The MD explained to me that, in the process of getting quality accreditation, everyone had had to think about their role in the business and how it interacted with everyone else's. His perception was that overall, standards of production had improved dramatically and individuals now accepted their responsibility in the process. Supervisors were removed from the hierarchy altogether and team cells were set up, each of which had a team leader appointed by management (although selected with input from the teams).

I asked to have a look at the factory, at which point his eyes lit up. At speed and with considerable pride, he took me for a tour. The factory was clean, well ordered, humming with activity. We passed design centres, production scheduling offices, the quality assurance department. Everything looked well used, well planned, orderly. We walked down row after row of sophisticated machinery, each worth in excess of half a million dollars, each with its individual operator, all computer run. The MD explained to me that many of the operators were paid in excess of $70,000 per annum, reflecting their expertise and their knowledge of the systems which drove these enormous machines.

He asked a range of employees questions, appeared to know their names and have an interest in them personally. About two thirds of the way through our journey it became apparent that we were running late — he was running late. He didn't say anything, simply moved along more quickly. We parted company at his reception in a flurry and as I left I sensed I carried more with me about the business than this particular successful and doubtlessly determined MD would have liked me to take away.

Here are observations I made which led me to believe that quality, even in this doubtlessly successful and highly motivated organisation, was only understood in part:

– The Managing Director, together with three other key executives, was responsible for the strategic planning of the business — something he revealed in the course of our discussion in his office. When I asked him why this was so he was puzzled — it hadn't occurred to him, even in this highly skilled organisation, that strategic contributions could come from a range of staff.

– All innovation came from the MD; he saw that as his job. Why? Because it was the part he loved, he liked the research involved in searching out new equipment, both in Australia and overseas. He said that he used input from staff on an as-needed basis, at times sending staff overseas. I asked him if staff had ever initiated a purchase or directed him to a source; again he was puzzled — clearly, staff were not in a position to do this.

– In the factory, all operators sat quietly by their machines, their principal responsibility being to ensure the computer operated equipment didn't malfunction. They were also (I assume) responsible for setting up the original program and for tooling changeovers. I had the opportunity (when the MD was some distance ahead of me) to quickly ask one of the operators if he enjoyed his work: he looked shy and said that he did; I asked him if he ever got bored and he said that that happened too, but that when someone was sick or away, he might get the chance to try out on another piece of equipment. Clearly, multiskilling was evident in the business, but not, perhaps, job sharing.

– The MD repeated to me several times that he made it clear to staff that he only wanted people in the business who wanted to be there and if anyone didn't like the work, then he would help them to find another job. It became clear to me as I walked around the factory that there was one extended shift: all staff were expected to work that shift, and Saturday, too. There was some flexibility subject to the level of business being put through, but clearly there was a high work ethic. Who drove this work ethic? The MD. Was an alternative possible or even desirable? I don't know, but I got the distinct impression that anyone suggesting an alternative would be told "if you don't like working here…"

– I asked the MD about regular staff get-togethers; he said that they happened on a monthly basis. I asked him what they did at these monthly functions and he said that he told them about the business's performance and upcoming developments. I asked if this was also a time for feedback and work improvements; he said it was not, but that once a year they went out to a restaurant together and he had a major Christmas function. As there was no relationship between my question and his answer I gained the impression that there was no vehicle for staff to put in anything other than basic operational suggestions.

– I asked the MD about his own education; he stressed the importance of his coalface experience. He had risen up the ranks and knew everyone's jobs as well as they did; he told me that he was a member of half a dozen key industry bodies and that he regularly advised some of these bodies on international trends in his area; he felt that he understood his people well and had good rapport with them. What I noticed was substantial deference on the part of the staff. They were shy: he asked questions on our walk-around and on at least two occasions talked over staff as they started to respond; they shut up, and I wondered about the quality of his leadership skills.

I was left with the impression that this leader understood only one dimension of quality, and personally, it reflected not so much an *innate* understanding of quality as a learning curve on how to be professional in his business. The systems I saw — which undoubtedly impacted on the quality of the product — were pragmatic solutions to quality manufacturing. Many of the improvements were about becoming a highly professional and well planned business.

Were they about quality? For me, only in part — and a relatively small part at that. Nothing in the systems elevated the intrinsic value of the humans who worked in the business; no system sought to capture their intelligence except in direct relationship to their principal accountabilities; I was shown no process which harnessed the capacity of these highly educated and experienced people to think creatively about their jobs, the work process, the business. I was left with the impression that what I had seen was an immensely well oiled machine of which the humans were a critical part — but *a part of,* not *apart from,* the real machines.

I was sure it was all more efficient and indisputably more profitable, but was it more rewarding for the people? I really don't know. I am sure they all earned more money and felt secure because they were part of a successful business, but it seemed to be the first part of a journey which was far from complete. If it represented all that could be achieved under the mantle of 'quality', then I think we have missed just how much reward the pursuit of quality can really bring to human beings who understand its power.

Quality is, more than anything else, a state of mind. We can become so caught up in the parry and thrust of day-to-day business that we forget what quality really means. We measure it only by improving efficiencies, diminishing errors and by the increasing profit we generate. However, I believe quality can be measured by many things: it can be measured by wellness, by the sense of having done something worthwhile in a day, contributed something of value to the whole. It can be measured by the satisfaction people reflect, their humour, their openness, their respect for one another, their capacity to listen.

Quality can also be measured by people's curiosity, their innate willing-ness to learn and improve, and their ability to accommodate innovation and change. Quality can be measured by the response we get from each other, and from the paying recipients of our efforts — the ultimate measure of our commercial worth.

Quality can uplift us all. It gives us a sense that what we do, who we are, has substance, purpose. Our sense of personal worth grows and we become empowered to think more effectively and create with greater vision. This strikes me as a worthwhile focus for everyone's endeavours.

The myth of customer service

To offer outstanding customer service, any human being has to feel valued, worthwhile, self-responsible, empowered, dignified.

11

It's true, you know. Mushy as it might sound, it is true. If we really care for someone it is apparent to them and to us. If our actions are motivated by our care, the quality of our service is exceptional. The substance of our reward always more than we expect.

Do we confuse 'service' and 'servility' in pursuit of customer service? I think many of us do.

Service can mean many things. Simply put, I mean the act of providing a service or a product to someone in such a way that they are entirely satisfied by the outcome. The service is given by a human being able to choose to provide the service. We give service because we can, we want to, we know we do it better than someone else, it gives us pleasure.

This is very different from an act of servility. To be servile is to be obsequious, behaving in a manner more suited to a slave; a servile person has to do what they do, they do not choose to do it. It is motivated by the fear of the repercussions of not doing some act; punishment, loss of financial reward, loss of job, death even!

To offer outstanding customer service, any human being has to feel valued, worthwhile, self-responsible, empowered, dignified. If the giver of a service does not feel this, the act of service becomes an intellectual exercise lacking any real care or it degenerates into obsequiousness. Either way, guess who is the first to sniff a rat? The customer.

MYTH BUSTERS: CUSTOMER SERVICE

MYTH ONE

The right remuneration to staff will produce outstanding customer service.

If paying adequate salaries is our measure of the justification for performing a certain task, we are in trouble already. Remuneration is the lowest form of motivation for a human being. If money is how we hold people to a commitment then we will never have their loyalty; they can be bought for a higher price by someone else.

Money won't buy commitment, responsibility, imagination, thoroughness. Only a sense of our personal worth will do this and that is measured by the respect we are afforded by people who count.

QUESTIONS: **What is the standard of customer service in your business from your perspective? Could it be improved? How? What will drive these improvements? How important is it to you to feel valued and respected? What impact does it have on your performance, your ability to think and act creatively, to provide outstanding service?**

MYTH TWO

Stating our intent to have outstanding customer service in our vision and or business plan will focus people on producing the desired outcomes.

Too many businesses put the delivery of outstanding customer service ('We will exceed customer's expectations') into their vision and then fail to develop adequately a strategy to address how this will be done. Business plans cover marketing, product development, distribution, production and customer service. However, they not infrequently gloss over or leave out altogether the question of the development of people within the business or the quality of leadership required to achieve the stated outcomes. Yet clearly, above all else, the quality of leadership and the extent to which people are educated and supported will have a greater impact on producing major strategic outcomes than almost anything else.

QUESTIONS: **Is customer service included in any of your company's visionary or strategic planning processes? If so, does it have credibility to the people of the business? Do customers believe they are getting outstanding customer service, exceeding their expectations? Do staff feel more could be done? What stops them from doing more?**

MYTH THREE

Training people in 'how to give outstanding customer service' will produce outstanding customer service.

In so many businesses, management perceive that people simply do not understand what quality customer service means. In some organisations, they may be right. In some organisations, quality educational programs are developed and attended by staff. For a period of time, customer service improves, but often the improvement is not sustained or is not as all-embracing as it needs to be.

Why? Because there are a range of cultural issues that are undermining the company's external face from inside: it could be the quality of staff facilities, the approach to remuneration, the absence of quality communication or consultation or the absence of a sense of the future; why exactly are we doing what we are doing?

Whatever the source, in order to deliver outstanding customer service externally, first we have to be sure that we are doing everything internally to dignify and respect people. A process that starts with a committed and caring leadership finishes with a loyal and satisfied customer.

QUESTIONS: **Do you believe your business is doing all that it could to engender an attitude embedded in the culture which is supportive of the delivery of quality customer service? If not, what improvements could be made? Of these improvements, what lie in the hands of leadership and what lie in the hands of staff?**

The quality of customer service we deliver is one more indicator of how we feel about ourselves and the place we have in the universe. As with quality, we have clutched at the customer service straw, thinking that if we focus our attention here we will produce the results we hunger after. I don't think we will.

If the product or service we have developed lacks the quality our customers are seeking and if our customer service fails to meet or exceed their expectations, then the greatest gift we can give our organisation is to relentlessly focus our attention on the care of the people who make the business tick. These people should know what to do. We have to be sure that people are motivated and educated to do all that can be done — not through fear of the repercussions that will come their way if they get it wrong, not by the financial rewards offered by way of palliative for their efforts but by the certain and widely held sense of value that everyone places on their individual contributions.

A THOUGHT TO LEAVE YOU WITH —
A McDONALD'S STORY!

I acknowledge that McDonald's is one of the enormous, extraordinary success stories of the late twentieth century. I accept that my children will, much as I fail to comprehend why, choose above all other options to eat McDonald's when I say... "I don't want to cook tonight, let's eat take away!"

Be that as it may, I still don't like McDonald's food and I especially can't stand their style of customer service. It is robotic, meaningless, too nice and makes me feel like pulling out a bazooka and levelling the place! I admit my reaction is a tad over the top but it happens every time I pull my car up in front of the plastic speaker, in front of the plastic menu, and I give my order to a disembodied voice.

They're just so damn nice, clean and smiley! But do they give a great good-God damn about me? No; I don't think so. At least that's how I feel until they make a mistake — and I have to say I look out for McDonald's mistakes the way other people check for typos in the newspaper! As soon as they make a mistake I am down on them like a tonne of bricks, testing to the limit their commitment to pacify me: "I did *not* order two small fries, I ordered two large fries," or "I have *two* Cheeseburgers and I ordered *one* McFeast." Pity help them!

What I notice is that when they are delivering the script according to some service guru in the States, their performance is robotic and dead. When they make a mistake and are required to use their own initiative, demonstrate their own sense of humanity, they behave, surprisingly, like human beings. It is at these times that one senses the quality of the McDonald's educational initiatives. Staff are obviously empowered to use their own nous to manage unhappy customers in whatever way seems best at the time (with, I assume, the proviso that the customer must leave happy).

There is only one reason I continue to pour money into McDonald's: when they stuff up, they look after me as if I mattered. I just wish they would be like that all the time.

Customer service is ultimately measured by the very last interaction that occurs between us (in the form of our product or service) and the customer. It strikes me as self-evident that this then should be the focus for all our attention — how can we make that contact point more rewarding, satisfying, dignified and exciting for all concerned. We spend money and time focusing on product, facilities, marketing, distribution and pricing but ultimately every element is made to work by people. People who know they count care more — it's as simple as that.

Meeting madness

Don't you feel sometimes that you'll die in a meeting, or waiting for someone else to get out of one?

Meetings don't have to be a pain in the proverbial. Done well, they are a refreshing and intelligent way to gather and disseminate information, to communicate and consult.

12

THE MYTH

We have developed a mania for meetings! There are just too many.

THE TRUTH

The volume of meetings is not the problem, it's the people calling them and the lack of planning going into them.

A CAVEAT ON THIS CHAPTER

The content of this chapter may seem inappropriately simplistic to some people. You may already believe you conduct effective, timely and productive meetings. However, if like me, you are either tormented by your own poor meeting skills or by the quality of meetings conducted by others, read on.

A FRAME OF REFERENCE

(Ring, ring... ring, ring... ring, ring.)

> *Good morning, Mr Sheen's office, how many I help you?*
>
> Could I speak to Bob Sheen please.
>
> *One moment... I'm sorry, Mr Sheen is in a meeting, can I ask him to return your call?*
>
> Yes, thank you.

(Ring, ring... ring, ring... ring, ring.)

> *Good morning, Abbott & Costello, how may we help you?*
>
> Can I have your service department please?
>
> *Certainly, who would you like to speak to?*
>
> Ms Armadillo.
>
> *One moment... I'm sorry, Ms Armadillo is in a meeting, can I get her to return your call?*
>
> Yes, thank you.

(Ring, ring... ring, ring... ring, ring.)

> *Good evening, Pearly Gates Incorporated, we can always help you.*
>
> Yes, I'm sure you can. Can I speak to God please.
>
> *One moment... I'm so sorry. God is discussing infinity with the Arch Angels, can I have Him return your call?*
>
> No, it might just be faster if I wait until I'm dead.

THE REAL AGENDA

People (yourself included?) always seem to be in meetings. Don't you feel sometimes that you'll die in a meeting, or waiting for someone else to get out of one?

On the face of it, we might complain that we just have too many bloody meetings. However, dig a little deeper and I think we may have to own up to the fact that the problem is a little more personal. Truthfully, I think the real problem is that *most people manage meetings appallingly.*

There is no clear purpose to the meeting and no agreed time frame. The person in the chair can't chair; there is more joke-telling than anything else. We don't have the facts and figures we need, so someone rushes off to get them halfway through the meeting. We don't have the people we need to conclude the meeting, so a second and sometimes third meeting has to be called. People bring their mobiles and take important calls halfway through the meeting. Important people unexpectedly leave early, so the entire meeting begins to wander off course. We waffle, exchange gossip, eat sandwiches, drink coffee, head off to the toilet, take smokos. All this behaviour spells the end of the meeting for you!

Every now and then we have a fast, efficient and to-the-point meeting which satisfies everyone and produces a clear, crisp outcome. Invariably, we're all absolutely blown away. How amazing! So, *that's* how it's meant to be done. I wish Sasha chaired all our meetings!

Many of us have gone into denial about the cause of the problem. It's as though we are members of a really bad footy side who won't accept the need to improve! We continue to grizzle about the number of games we play and lose, yet at the same time we refuse to change our bad habits. We sort of hope that the problem will go away of its own accord.

Well, it won't. Meetings are not going to go away. They are a product of the information age and, fortunately, they are one way we get to see each other face to face (except, of course, when we are not talking via the Internet or via a teleconference). Done well, meetings are the ultimate tool for quality communication and consultation. Recalling that in this book one of my loudest cries for change is for quality communication and decent consultation, it might serve to provide a very simply recipe for making meetings work. So, here it comes!

Simple recipe for quality meetings

OUTCOME: ASK YOURSELF WHY YOU ARE CALLING THE MEETING

The outcome describes not what the content of the meeting will be but what you can expect as a result of the meeting. This requires thought *well before* the meeting. It's like going into the kitchen to cook a meal. First you have to know what, exactly, you want to cook, what it will look like. You make your decision based on your competency and who you are feeding. When it comes to determining an outcome for a meeting, it is no different. Whether or not you can produce the desired outcome depends on whether you are the person to call the meeting. If the meeting is not within your domain and you are not confident that you can produce the outcome you are after, someone else should call the meeting.

Write down your desired outcome in a couple of sentences.

PEOPLE NEEDED: DECIDE EXACTLY WHO NEEDS TO PARTICIPATE

Select only those who have critical information or expertise or who will have to manage the repercussions of the decision. You don't want a small army attending your meeting, but to ensure that the outcome is achieved fluently, cleanly, you have to have everyone present who needs to be present or, at the very least, their nominated delegate.

Think about appropriate attendees before the meeting. Write the list down and work out why the people need to be there and whether or not they can actually delegate participation to someone else. Time spent considering who should attend will save an enormous amount of time during the meeting because you are less likely to be missing critical people. Inclusion of the right people at the right time also demonstrates a commitment to quality communication and consultation.

AGENDA: SET THE PROCESS
BY WHICH YOU WILL ACHIEVE YOUR OUTCOME

Many people confuse an agenda with the outcome. They are different. The outcome is your destination, the agenda is how you get there. Circulate your outcome and proposed agenda not less than two days before the meeting. This ensures that participants:

– are prepared;

– can bring any material to the meeting they think will be required;

– have the opportunity to add to the agenda items (which can then be adequately planned into the meeting);

– can double-check the attendees list to ensure all key players are present.

It is courteous to circulate an agenda. It makes good sense and it saves a lot of time.

NOMINATE A CHAIRMAN:
DON'T CHAIR IF YOU CAN'T!

Just because you are calling the meeting doesn't mean you are the best person to chair it. In fact, chances are you aren't! There is nothing more frustrating that having someone sit in the chair who cannot control the meeting. A good chairperson will:

– ensure broad participation;

– stop waffling, joke telling, time wasting;

– keep people focused on the agenda items;

– hold participants to the agreed time frame for agenda items and the meeting.

Frequently, items will come up during a meeting that were not on the original agenda. A good chair will ensure these are deferred to the end of the meeting and are addressed, time permitting. (Not withstanding the odd occasion when something unforeseen but critical arises.)

MINUTING: DON'T DO IT!
RECORD DECISIONS TAKEN AND ACTIONS REQUIRED

I think there is something vaguely ludicrous about recording the entire proceedings of any meeting, as if the meeting itself were of critical importance. If a meeting has been called for a purpose, surely it is the decisions that have been made and the actions that arise from the meeting that need to be recorded? Politicians and bureaucrats are good at recording processes — but then they might not be so good at precipitating action! In business, time is of the essence and for someone to spend time taking shorthand during a meeting is pointless.

However, I strongly recommend recording the decisions and proposed actions in *all* meetings, no matter how small. I recommend this because we all experience 'reality' differently. We may think we have come out of a meeting with a clear understanding of what's next, but I think the 'X Factor' overrides our intentions! The X Factor is this: the interpretation of decisions, actions and responsibilities arising from a meeting, multiplied by the number of people present. The outcome is all too frequently self-evident.

DON'T BE A SCHOOLMARM!
IF THE GROUP IS FADING, DO SOMETHING!

Don't treat adults like children. Stop the meeting if people are fidgeting, yawning, doodling, gazing with rapt attention at a print on the wall, checking their message bank, gazing lovingly at the sandwiches, tapping their packet of cigarettes, going to sleep or staring at you without blinking.

There is absolutely no point pushing to the end of a particular agenda item because you want to finish it before lunch, or time is running out. You might want people's minds focused on the topic, but if they are hungry, thirsty or tired, they will be paying attention to basic human need instead.

If you are really short of time, break the meeting and get everyone to get out of their seats and, at the very least, move briskly for a couple of minutes.

If two people are talking and it looks like they are the only ones who are needed for a particular agenda item, either get them to reconvene a 'sub-meeting' at another time or get them to leave the room. Don't waste everyone's time sitting around listening to one or two people hold forth.

WATCH OUT FOR CONSTIPATION: WEED OUT TIRED AGENDA ITEMS

We've all seen it: that frustrating, not-so-important item that just won't go away and die somewhere. It keeps turning up at the bottom of the agenda and we just don't seem to get around to it, do we? Delegate it, defer it or destroy it *but don't keep typing it up* on the agenda.

Put the following question to the group: "This item has come up before. What do we need to do differently to make sure it doesn't come up again?"

REPORTS OUT; ACTION IN: REPORTS SHOULD BE READ BY PEOPLE, NOT TO PEOPLE

Don't use meetings as a vehicle to deliver reports. It is a chronic waste of quality time. Reports should be given to people in sufficient time in advance of the meeting so they can read and digest their content. The meeting time can be used to check items, seek clarification or debate content.

Tabling a report at a meeting is a brilliant strategy for ensuring people don't debate the content there and then.

GASTRIC REFLUX: SAME PEOPLE, SAME PLACE, SAME AGENDA — BORING!

Assuming there is value in having people's creative and thoughtful participation in a meeting, consider where, when and how you conduct your meetings. Meetings that occur in the same place, at the same time, with the same people to discuss remarkably similar agendas end up being rote performances with little if any quality activity.

Again, we've all participated in such meetings. Typically, they're the death throws of an idea which started off with lots of oomph. If they need to be given the death knoll, do it honestly and honourably.

On the other hand, there are certain meetings which do need to happen regularly, involve basically the same people and are generally on the same topic. If this is the case, consider changing any or all of the following on a regular basis:

– location;
– dress;
– catering;
– time.

This is called Pattern Interrupt. People tend to do things the same way — it is easier. However, it also means you don't have to put in as much thought, and that isn't good. Pattern Interrupt is a technique for keeping people on their toes, interested and involved.

HANDY HINTS: HONOUR YOUR TIME COMMITMENTS

It's bad enough that we waste our own time; it's criminal if we waste someone else's.

HANDY HINTS: WARM PEOPLE UP TO A MEETING

When people join a meeting they are bringing all sorts of baggage with them; they are worried about or preoccupied with what happened just before the meeting or what will happen just after the meeting. Warming people up can be done in thousands of different ways but at the very least, get people to arrive ten minutes early, give them coffee and biscuits and use the time to exchange gossip and check up on everyone's wellbeing.

HANDY HINTS: TABLE THE MINUTES OF THE PREVIOUS MEETING

Quite apart from anything else, previous minutes are evidence of progress, that things are being done. They show that the system you are using is working.

HANDY HINTS: GET FEEDBACK

While you are experimenting with the best way to conduct your meeting, get feedback from participants. Ask whether the meeting format is working, whether you are achieving your stated outcome, and what you could do differently.

Meetings are not going to disappear. If anything, they will probably increase in scope. They are part of the times in which we live and we can help make everyone's lives at work more enjoyable if we concentrate on conducting them more professionally and with greater awareness of the impact they have.

So what if you have to attend someone else's meeting and they are no good at it? Have courage and tell them (and maybe everyone else attending) to read this chapter. If we assume the meeting has a purpose, sooner or later the people calling the meeting have to learn to do it better.

Managing change — doing it honourably

By treating people inappropriately, we so harm the substance of the culture that it may take many years to recover.

13

Because so many of us have been affected by change processes, mergers, acquisitions, takeovers and the like, I suspect this chapter will be relevant to every reader. However, it will be most powerful in the hands of leaders responsible for such events. They are, after all, the ones who might benefit from knowing there are more ways than one to skin the unfortunate proverbial cat and, despite popular myth, you don't always have to hurt or even kill the beast in the process!

THE MYTH

Changes (including mergers, restructures, takeovers, acquisitions) are most effectively and professionally managed by maintaining secrecy, limiting the number of people involved in discussions, acting swiftly, with little or no consultation and by dispassionate retrenchments. The primary focus of attention is on the business justification for takeover, measured only by the synergy of business activity, the dollar savings by merging functions and the rationalisation of competition. People are represented in terms of numbers and functions in the change process.

THE TRUTH

Change seems rarely to deliver the promised advantages. The most effective changes occur with broadly based consultation and a policy of honesty. The management of people during a change process is the most important and frequently most neglected key to success.

THE HEART OF A GOOD MERGER

There has to be a better way of managing mergers, takeovers, downsizing, restructuring, change. I don't like much of what I have seen and experienced in recent years and clearly many, many Australians agree with me. For fear of stating the obvious, I am going to offer some thoughts on how change could be managed with less harm to the majority.

This is not a technical guide on how to run a merger or a restructure; it is a guide to managing and caring for the people in the process. It is a reminder to those of you upon whom the responsibility of a merger or restructure falls that there is nothing more important in the process than the people your actions affect.

The viability of the organisation and the continued profitable performance of the business should not be used as smokescreens for behaving without heart. By treating people inappropriately during a change process we reduce the opportunity for success, harm the organisation and, in some instances, so harm the substance of the culture that it may take many years to recover.

Issues which need to be considered are as follows:

– Planning the process: who to involve, when and why.

– What to tell the masses and when.

– Who to keep, who to shed, and who should make staffing decisions.

– Management of retrenchment: doing it with heart.

– Style of communication: visibility of leadership.

– Staying in touch with issues that affect the people.

– Don't use shareholders as an excuse.

– Hold true to your core values.

Each of them are considered in detail below.

PLANNING THE PROCESS: WHO TO INVOLVE, WHEN AND WHY

Usually, the plans for a merger, takeover or restructure usually occur many months before they become confirmed knowledge. However, they have been unconfirmed common knowledge for as long as they have been the subject of executive discussion. Gossip, insidious and determined, finds its way into canteens, production rooms, factories, accounts departments, retail floors.

The motivation or cause for the change is also usually well understood by staff, particularly if the reason for change flows from poor performance. After all, staff can see the repercussions of a downturn in trade every bit as intimately as can the leadership.

So, the first thing to do is to decide who to involve in the planning process and when. To begin the planning process you have to tell people that a proposed restructure or merger is under consideration. Traditionally business leaders hold such discussions close to their chests, assuming that their staff, competition or customers will react badly or would be anxious if they were to hear the truth.

Well, you don't need to be an Einstein to understand such a reaction. The question is, which is more harmful? The inevitable gossip which does occur and over which no one has control, or straight facts from responsible people?

PROPOSAL ONE: Tell all the people affected, especially staff, the truth. Explain why the issue is under consideration and the extent of consultation that you will commit to. Be sure to elevate everyone's education; make sure they understand the commercial significance of the proposal. Don't treat people like idiots. If you really don't want the opposition to know, ask for support from your staff.

Don't keep critical information from the ninety-eight percent that matter for fear of the harm it might do in the hands of the two percent who are going to hear about your intentions anyway.

The next step is to determine who to involve and why. Let's start with the 'why'. You would chose to involve people in the feasibility phase to ensure the final decision is informed, from all levels of business activity (and not just the accountants!). Remember, an alarming number of mergers, takeovers and change processes fail to deliver the promised efficiencies. Why? Because too much importance is placed on the isolated calculations of number crunchers who do not adequately understand the implications of their paper changes.

PROPOSAL TWO: Involve a cross section of people from all areas of the business or businesses. Let them bring a diversity of opinion to the discussions. Don't isolate decision making or input to management. No one will understand the potential problems you might encounter in merging two production facilities better than the people who work hands-on in these areas. By the same token, no one will be able to identify the benefits as quickly.

Coalface staff bring a pragmatism to strategic discussions that is frequently missing during mergers, takeovers and restructures. Even in a very large organisation, looking at an allied acquisition, staff from another business can alert senior executives to some of the more

telling structural problems the business has that will be exacerbated after an additional acquisition.

If it is an acquisition, let a vertical slice of staff meet and discuss the idea, the benefits, their fears, the opportunities. Let them brainstorm the pros and cons with management.

Assuming the decision is to proceed with a change process or a takeover, the next decision is to determine who should participate in the detailed planning of the process.

Again, the first step is to identify the areas that have to be addressed and in what order of priority. In my experience this is an area in which management isolate themselves to their own detriment.

PROPOSAL THREE: Once you have decided to proceed, make sure there is a clear representation of staff to help work up the strategic plans for implementing the change. In identifying the range of areas to be addressed, the group who have worked with management to determine the viability of the proposal are an obvious and immediate resource.

Once the list is identified, teams should be created from many areas in the business or businesses. Rather than tell people they have been selected, invite appropriate areas in the business to nominate representatives. Explain the purpose clearly.

Unarguably, poor communication and inadequate education will diminish both the confidence and the extent of contribution from a spread of staff. However, people are frequently capable of contributing more than they are credited with. There is only one way to improve their level of contribution, and that is by involving them more. Management's track record for producing sustained results following change doesn't stand the testimony of time, so there is clearly value in experimenting with an alternative.

WHAT TO TELL THE MASSES AND WHEN

Generally, the masses — the bulk of staff — are the last to formally hear about change, but the first to actually talk about it publicly. The whispers begin early, around the canteen, in the change rooms, over the machinery, outside during smokos. Staff know something is happening when executives are closeted away for hours on end in unusually exciting or serious discussion. You can be sure that at least one or more staff have a close personal relationship with one or more executives and they are the first to unearth the truth as soon as the top secret meeting is finished.

Despite exhortations to confidants to "keep it to yourself," within twenty-four hours everyone has the gist of what's been talked about. Unfortunately, however, because the information has come via the gossip chain, it is embellished by storytellers who, lacking accurate detail, make up part of the picture. From person to person the story changes and, before you know it, a thought expressed by the CEO that there might be benefit in discussing a merger with major competition has turned into fully-blown confirmation that (a) the merger is going ahead, (b) forty percent of staff will be retrenched as a result and (c) the reason for it going ahead is because the company is about to go belly up!

PROPOSAL: **Tell people the truth as soon it has moved past the stage of pure executive speculation. If the decision is to do a feasibility study, senior management should make a verbal and a written presentation to staff stating clearly the purpose, the process, the time frame and the possible outcome of the change. Written detail is important because it avoids the trap of individual interpretation which frequently occurs when the source of information is only verbal.**

Explain to people the process of consultation.

WHO TO KEEP, WHO TO SHED, AND WHO SHOULD MAKE STAFFING DECISIONS

Assuming the process of consultation has been effected in terms of how to proceed; the structure that should be put in place; what systems should change, merge or be deleted; and so on, there will often be the hard decisions to do with managing workforce rationalisation. Many change processes move on the basis that functions can be merged and costs saved by reducing duplication of effort. This may or may not be true depending on who has been involved in the feasibility and planning stages.

Assuming that some rationalisation of staff is necessary, unions are usually called in for negotiations fairly early on in the process. In fact, union negotiations on retrenchment are generally handled efficiently (if not heartlessly). However, given that union membership is small compared to the number of people who work, the recommendations that follow are for small businesses or for non-union staff.

P R O P O S A L O N E : Explain to the people working in specific functional areas (a) what the plan is and why, (b) how it was arrived at and with what consultation and (c) what now needs to be done. Keyed into a humane retrenchment process — which should be explained at this point — should be invitations to functional areas to manage staff reduction. It is highly likely that they will require management support if they have limited team experience, but let people own the process rather than be on the receiving end of it.

It is important when managing the reduction of a workforce to care not only for the people who will, often through no fault of their own, be asked to leave, but also to look after those who will remain. None of us feel good about seeing mates lose jobs; a lot of us have had first-hand experience of the pain associated with losing a job. Confidence and motivation can be lost all round — is lost all round — if there is a lack of quality, compassionate management of the process.

PROPOSAL TWO: Make sure everyone, including those remaining, understand fully the retrenchment process, payouts and on-placement facilities. Manage retrenchment with heart (see next point), and make sure justice is seen to be done by everyone — not just those on the receiving end of it.

If the company purports to have values which embrace integrity, honesty, consideration, then the way in which redundancies are managed will be the ultimate test of the voracity of these values.

MANAGEMENT OF RETRENCHMENT: DOING IT WITH HEART

Few people today would run the risk of retrenching people without the correct financial remuneration. Challenges to unfair dismissal and union retaliation have put paid to unjust behaviour. However, there is much more to consider in the retrenchment process that most people realise. We can make people redundant according to the letter of the law yet in the process do immeasurable harm to the people concerned and to the organisation. I do not have industrial relations expertise, but I do understand the lasting damage we are capable of inflicting on one another in the name of commercial rationalisation. From a purely pragmatic point of view, I think we can conduct ourselves with greater wisdom and produce quality business results in the process.

PROPOSAL ONE: Pay a little more than people are due, not a little less. Be seen to do the right thing and the message to the organisation is "we do care." This builds loyalty from those remaining and ensures that the motivation to rebuild is not corroded. Pay less, and the staff remaining quickly perceive that there is a lack of moral substance on the part of leadership; this corrodes commitment at all levels.

Never, never retrench people at holiday times. This should be a criminal offence; its harm is immense. How can we justify laying people off at Christmas? No matter what dollars we think we are saving, the real, fundamental loss of human commitment is incalculable. It is a practice that appals me. A leadership that behaves so callously can hardly expect remaining staff to commit to the idea of customer service, of a commitment to quality, of the importance of values.

Kindness and compassion, partnered with quality planning and good business nous inevitably improve rewards. No amount of good business know-how will secure the future of an organisation if it is led by managers who have a disregard for people.

PROPOSAL TWO: Be very careful about the timing of redundancies. Act in the interests of the business, certainly, but make sure that it is not just the number crunchers determining the timing. Listen carefully to Human Resources people: what repercussions do they see? The long term benefits of a slight delay may far outweigh the short term gains of retrenching at an inconsiderate time.

If people lose their jobs through no fault of their own, as a direct consequence of a downsizing, a restructure or a takeover which you initiate, look after them. If you don't, who will? Outplacement, the appointment of a company or internal person responsible for finding these people work is an indication of the values of the business and the genuine measure of just how important leaders think people are. Outplacement should not just be offered to executives. (Ironically, they are often more familiar with finding jobs than are staff.)

PROPOSAL THREE: Before publicly announcing redundancies or inviting functional areas to suggest people who would be willing to take voluntary redundancy, investigate the choices you have in managing outplacement. Research your options and, having selected

one, make sure you clearly commit to paper how it will work. Call a meeting or series of meetings and openly discuss the process, how it will be handled and why. Be willing to take questions and, if you don't have the answers, commit to getting back to staff.

Don't, no matter what the accountants say, retrench people who have been working for the business for a long time. If they are not as physically able, are part of 'the old guard' and appear to be recalcitrant in the face of change, put the effort in to re-educate them. Manage them in the change process — don't punish them for the change you are leading.

Long serving staff speak much for the history of the business. Their network of contacts, their experience, their sense of history have a value, irrespective of their standard of work. You might indeed need younger, more educated, enthusiastic and ambitious people to fuel the future of your business, but those who have served their time also have a place.

I wonder how one rationalises the retrenchment of a fifty year old who has served a business for thirty years. They are too old to learn? They fear change? They are blocking other people? They belong to an old culture? Do we think that dollar signs will make the retrenchment bearable? Should that make it acceptable to the business?

I don't know, but it just doesn't feel right to me, no matter what the economic rationale. It feels ugly and without integrity. I think to myself that this person might have only had five or so years before they could retire with dignity. Considering the payout that was required, what did the business *really* save? More to the point, what did it lose in terms of lost credibility at the coalface?

P R O P O S A L   F O U R: Don't retrench people who have served the business for a long time. Re-educate them, find alternative positions or tolerate their continued presence on the basis that it is an investment in maintaining continuity between the old and the new.

STYLE OF COMMUNICATION: VISIBILITY OF LEADERSHIP

Many leaders underestimate the pragmatic business value of staying in regular quality contact with the people of the business. It is something executives say is important yet strangely never manage to find the time. In my opinion, during a major process of change, leadership simply cannot spend enough time out with the troops. The more visible management are, the more supported and supporting staff will be. Questions can be raised, spontaneous discussions can occur, previously unthought of concerns can be debated, gossip can be quelled, speculation can be put to bed, feedback can be taken in abundance. This all is of value to the business and improves the quality of the change.

PROPOSAL ONE: Look at what you have to do, your real time commitments in the process of change. Determine what is more important than spending time with staff and why?

Plan your time so you have a regular period in each day that is set aside for 'staff time'. Make sure you or your secretary avoid making other appointments for this time.

Spending time with staff should not appear as a token gesture, it should have substance and purpose. Often the capacity of a senior executive to talk to staff is measured by how well they know their staff's work. The more you talk to staff the more you will know.

PROPOSAL TWO: Before heading out for time with staff, consider what you want to discover, talk about, explore or get feedback on. If you are going out to maintain contact and friendship, do that! Develop a genuine interest in what staff are doing and what they have to say.

STAYING IN TOUCH WITH ISSUES THAT AFFECT THE PEOPLE

During the strategic planning of a major change process many senior managers become disassociated from the concerns of staff. They are preoccupied with 'global' or broadly based planning issues, sometimes involving the survival of the business. Given these distractions, the concerns of staff can appear trivial by comparison.

The best way I can illustrate the importance of avoiding this pitfall is to draw a parallel with what not uncommonly occurs during divorce proceedings. Men and women are so embroiled in the trauma of the event — the legal wrangling, the anger, the vitriol, the blame — that they completely overlook how children are responding. They offer token gestures of understanding or appeasement but truthfully, they are so wound up in the emotional demands of their own situation that they are unable to experience the world from the children's perspective.

The problem comes home to haunt both parents when distressed and troubled children become yet another concern in divorce proceedings. Had the children been respected, their needs elevated, had they been involved in the discussions and quietly and without prejudice guided, then those problems might never have arisen.

Now, while the control necessary by parents to afford the children this level of wisdom might not be present in many divorce proceedings, the equivalent 'parenting' should be present on the part of leaders during major change processes — particularly if the leadership in question genuinely subscribes to the belief that people are and will be important contributors to the success of the business.

Concerns may appear trivial comparatively but life is a relative experience. Good leaders judge people's concerns according to those people's model of the world and not from the leader's perspective.

PROPOSAL: **Take time to think carefully about concerns raised by staff. Try to understand them from their point of view. Consider what staff know as opposed to what you know. Does the quality and quantity of information empower you to manage the process with less heartache? What are the real concerns that staff are expressing and how best can you support them at this time?**

DON'T USE SHAREHOLDERS AS AN EXCUSE

I think there are a lot of Australian shareholders who would cringe at the things that have been perpetrated in their name. I would like to suggest that the majority of shareholders would uphold acts of decency and that far from diminishing trust in the leaders who are managing their investment, such acts will elevate it.

PROPOSAL: **Don't use shareholders as an excuse for inhumane behaviour. If you are in doubt about how shareholders will respond to an initiative and your reasons for it, ask a sample of shareholders for a response.**

HOLD TRUE TO YOUR CORE VALUES

Sustained business success is measured by the quality of the organisation, the business structure, its methods, processes. It is also about the core culture and the values that are held by all people, despite the ebb and flow of business, the coming and going of leaders, the exigencies of the greater economic climate.

Decency is its own reward. If you value courage, be courageous; if you value integrity, act with integrity; if you value compassion, be compassionate; if you value truth, be honest; if you value growth, create an environment in which people can grow; if you value learning, let people learn.

PROPOSAL: Think carefully about your core values. What do you hold to be important above all else? Why are these things important? What behaviour supports these values? What business activities are you engaged in which reinforce these core values? What business activities are you engaged in which undermine them? How do you make the distinction between when it is okay to live up to your values and when it is okay to undermine them?

By managing change processes with compassion and decency, leaders help build organisations in which change is a dynamic and healthy part of growth and development and not something to be hated and feared. They reinforce the values which sustain the people and they ensure that their brief period of tenure is genuinely adding value to the business, to the people, to the customers and to the community.

If the alternative is a disenfranchised and angry workforce who feel that change has reached terminal velocity and who respond to leadership-driven initiatives with cynicism and mistrust, it would hardly seem to be a choice at all, would it?

The long term picture — 'profit' is not a dirty word

There are other ways to measure profit in business apart from our net return on turnover or capital invested.

14

Idealism without pragmatism, vision without planning, innovation without thinking, purpose without profit, leads to imbalance instead of balance — certainly in business. The imbalance is frequently measured by the debt to equity ratio of a business, which, when out of balance, translates into the nightmare of excessive borrowings (relative to the capital base of the business), increasingly tight cash flow (incoming dollars from revenue) and reduction of cash (either in terms of revenue or borrowings). It is a downwards-spiralling catch 22. The imbalance produces less turnover, lower profits, higher borrowings, reduced resources, increasing anxiety and, at the end of the whole process, closure.

THE MYTH

There is only one way to measure profit in business and that is in terms of the dollars made, net, on turnover. Pursuit of profit is somehow a low-order pursuit.

The truth

For better or worse, dollar profit fuels much that people delight in and take for granted. However, there are many other ways to measure profit; money, despite its importance, is both the shortest lived and the most fragile.

No one wins when a business goes under. People lose their jobs, good products or ideas are lost, founding entrepreneurs — the very people whose innovation and courage fuel the growth of new business — lose everything they own. Many do not get up again. When a major business goes through, we all shudder, feeling the vulnerability of our system and the danger of a capital structure built, not infrequently, on promises and illusions, sleights of hand.

So, let's agree on one thing: while we can debate the appropriateness of growth for growth's sake, especially in the commercial sector, few of us would disagree that, for better or worse, the world's economy is built on profit that is measured in monetary terms. If you have it, you can move forward, if you don't, you can't. It doesn't make life better, it doesn't make you or me happier, it doesn't generate love, security, friends or even real wealth. It just makes the commercial world turn over.

This books aims to bring dignity and compassion, integrity and honesty, back into the workplace, to elevate our vision of the business domain and to embrace not only the generation of profit, but also the elevation of human endeavour within the business world. In this chapter I encourage people to pursue a higher order of business activity, to find a way to reconcile the need to produce a dollar profit with the desire to enshrine a different order of activity — one which can work in harmony with the pursuit of profit.

'PROFIT' IS NOT A DIRTY WORD!

Growth for growth's sake is mindless. Our world cannot sustain indefinite growth. We do not have the physical resources; the natural environment is already groaning under the pressure of human excess. We all know that. We do not have to be told any more by people like Professor Suzuki or organisations like Greenpeace. Even Blind Freddie can see it.

However, we shouldn't confuse profit with growth. It might fuel growth but it also does much more. Profit fuels reward for individuals who put in the extra effort and innovation, and come up with ideas that take us forward. Profit enables us to clean up the mess we have made. Profit provides food, clothing and houses, better education, greater care for the sick and the needy. Profit funds parks, national wildlife reserves, research and development in a million different areas. Profit provides workers compensation, funds traffic accident compensation, unemployment benefits.

Unarguably, profit allows the Western world to enjoy high standards of living. It doesn't, however, make all that we are doing right, not by a long shot. If profit simply fuels endless growth and such growth is how we measure success then we are heading towards an awful precipice indeed!

PROFIT — A WIDER CONCEPT

THE PROPOSITION: The dollars made, over and above the costs of running a business, are only one measurement of profit. Profit can also be measured by how we add value to the people who work in the business, the community, the environment. This measurement of profit is long term; it represents an investment in the future and, without such a measurement, profit, measured in dollars, becomes illusory. We are talking here of a second bottom line — the second tool for measuring the profitable performance of a company. The first is the percentage return on turnover, after interest, before tax; the second is the achievement of stated objectives with regard to people and the environment. Both are equally important.

Affluence in the West has brought a greater sensibility towards our fellow human beings. We now look at business practices in developing countries and although we recognise our own origins, we don't like what we see: child labour, subsistence salaries, women in sweatshops, hazardous work conditions, unequal and frequently inaccessible education. It is hardly surprising that in these countries, basic human rights are the principle issues; in the West, however, we can now set ourselves outcomes that are generated by higher expectations of what is achievable in life for the individual. It is not appropriate to compare ourselves to developing countries, to justify not changing based on what we've got, the privileges we enjoy. We recognise that survival depends on our ability to move forward, but we must ask ourselves, in what direction? with what values guiding us?

We need to expose ourselves to the idea that there are other ways to measure profit in business apart from our net return on turnover or capital invested. We can put these other measurements into business plans and so begin the process of legitimising what we are all thinking about. This appears to be simplistic, that's because it *is* simple: consider the way your business might quantify the following measures of success over a twelve month period:

– how value is added to the quality of life for staff, customers, the community;

– what environmental initiatives were instigated and what were the benefits to the business, the staff, the shareholders, the broader community; and

– what community projects was the business involved in, with what benefits.

These are not soft issues. They represent a 'second bottom line' measurement.

Think for a moment of a board meeting of a major Australian corporation. Think on the issues that pass through a typical meeting: quarterly financials, prospective takeovers, mergers, acquisitions, forthcoming marketing initiatives, research and design developments, senior executive recruitments and so on. We expect these issues to be reviewed strategically by senior people. They look at the broad picture, knitting together the activities of many. Why not then add in a regular review of environmentally smart activities, value-adding strategies being implemented by the organisation, measurements for how staff feel about working for the organisation, how the business is seen by the broader community?

What would the outcomes be for all of us if business accepted that these were reasonable and responsible issues that warranted regular review? What impact could we have, and in what time frame, if we elevated such outcomes and put behind them the quality of strategic thinking, of innovation and envisioning, that goes into the planning of the traditional business streams that occupy the thoughts of senior management?

Business is a powerful tool for change. Enshrining a higher order of behaviour, recognising the advantage, commercially, of value-added activities — to staff, customers and the community — strikes me as a very worthwhile pursuit as we approach the twenty-first century.

We certainly can't lose with such a focus and, conceivably, we may gain a great deal.

Surviving business into the twenty-first century will, beyond a shadow of doubt, have much to do with the survival of people on the planet. We shouldn't forget that in Australia we are in an immensely privileged position. We are an essentially safe, clean and affluent society. Relative to many parts of the world there are few seriously disadvantaged people and, although that should not drive us to complacency, it should help us appreciate how lucky we really are.

Good women are hard to find!

We are wired to work together, each sex offering something to the other; whatever the benefit of our union, it is for all of us and for all time.

15

I have shilly-shalleyed around this topic while writing this book. I almost came to the conclusion that the topic was too hot to handle — for me anyway. I am not at all sure that I can be dispassionate, and probably risk prose-lytising — preaching the gospel of conver-sion, despite a strong wish not to do this. What I really want to do is to offer feedback which is simple and to the point, doesn't duplicate what has already been written, doesn't antagonise either men or women and is of use to both.

This chapter does not pretend to be definitive on the issue of women in business. The purpose of including this highly risky topic is very simple: to expose a range of commonly held myths about women, their style of behaving or emoting, and to then invite you to consider (a) whether the myths have ever (be honest here!) crossed your mind, (b) the potential damage these myths cause and (c) how we might actually approach these myths differently.

The myths do not apply to all women. They don't even apply to most women. They simply apply to some women — enough, that is, to warrant exposure in the context of the *Myth busters* section of this book.

Some of the comments offered could as well be said about men. I will leave that for you to extrapolate. This chapter is not about men (to be honest, the myths that could be said to be directed exclusively towards men have been well and truly been dealt with elsewhere in the book).

The issues raised in this chapter are women's issues, about women. However, bear in mind that their resolution lies in the hands of both men and women. Similarly, our failure to deal with the issues has repercussions for all of us.

THE MYTHS IN SUMMARY

MYTH ONE

Women are selected for positions according to their capacity and not because they are women.

TRUTH ONE

It depends on who's doing the selection. If men are selecting, chances are they are operating from a paradigm which excludes many of the skills and natural abilities that women can offer, so they fail to identify 'good' women. It's a case of not knowing how to look, rather than not being able to see.

MYTH TWO

Women are too emotional. They are often unable to take the tough decisions and they allow their emotions to interfere with the quality of their thinking.

TRUTH TWO

The gift women bring to much decision making is the extent of their emotional interpretations. Men and women not infrequently have different priorities in the process of decision making.

MYTH THREE

Some women are moody and unpredictable, especially at that time of month, and this can make them a liability in terms of the quality of their work and the reliability of the decision making.

TRUTH THREE

Some women do experience emotional ups and downs (don't we all), but that may actually be an asset in terms of their work and their decision making. Quite possibly it gives them the emotional flexibility and experience to reconsider decisions that yesterday appeared clear-cut. This might add a dimension to thinking that is possibly missing in business.

MYTH FOUR

Some of women's worst enemies are other woman who are competitive and ruthless. They, more than men, contrive to limit the growth of other women.

TRUTH FOUR

Women can thwart other women (as men can thwart other men) but it is frequently the product of a conditioned sense of scarcity — a perception by women that senior positions open to women are scarce and competition will therefore be much tougher than it is for men.

MYTH FIVE

To be successful, a woman must be ambitious and single-minded, prepared to sacrifice traditional family responsibilities, her femininity (whatever that is) and her role as a mother in pursuit of her chosen career.

TRUTH FIVE

Successful women come in all shapes and sizes. Women can and do integrate their success in business with motherhood and femininity — (whatever that is) provided the environment and the prevailing business paradigm allows it.

MYTH SIX

Good women are hard to find, but we are looking.

TRUTH SIX

Good women are everywhere; where exactly are you looking and what are you looking for?

UNQUOTABLE QUOTES

In front of me now I have a very good dictionary of quotations. It is the *Home Book of Quotations, Classical and Modern*, selected and arranged by Burton Stevenson; a vast and weighty tome which has stood by me through many hours of writing. Today I looked through the section on women to see if I could find something apt. I often look for a quotation which succinctly focuses my thoughts — a few words to encapsulate what I am going to say. Today all that happened was that I felt enraged and then saddened and then overwhelmed. Here are some of the headings I discovered in the book. You try them on for size and see how you react:

Women: Her Creation (quotes on our true source)

Women: Good and bad (good refers to our soft, beautiful and engaging nature)

Woman: Saint Abroad, Devil at Home

Woman: A blessing (usually because of our grace and beauty)

Woman: A Curse

Woman: Her Nature (all about our fickle emotions and daft intellects)

Woman: Her Mind (and its inconstancy)

Woman: Her Power (and you'd better watch out because it's awesome)

Woman: Her Advice (given too often and frequently unsought)

Woman: Her Falseness

Woman: Her Fickleness and Inconstancy

Woman: Her Tongue

Woman: Her Untruthfulness

Woman: A Woman's "No" (which everyone understands as "yes")

Woman: A Woman's Reason (or its complete absence)

Woman: A Woman's Vengence (which is swift, mighty and bloody awful)

There are a couple of supportive sections: about woman's love, her ability to nurture, to build a nice home, to provide comfort in the dead of night... and that's about it. To try and get some balance, I decided to have a look at the headings under 'Man'. The headings are equally enthralling:

Man: Definition (largely biblical although acknowledging the full range of human emotion and endeavours reasonably fairly)

Man: An Animal (appealing to our sense of the nobility of the beast)

Man: A Child (every woman knows this)

Man: The Image Of God

Man: His Growth

Man: His Virtues

Man: His Faults

Men: Most Men Are Bad (about four quotes)

Man: Great and Small

Man: His Inhumanity (couple of columns)

Man: His Life Span

Man: His Misery

Man: The Study Of Man

This topic ends with a very lengthy section called *Man And Woman* which finishes with three quotes from Oscar Wilde:

Women are never disarmed by compliments. Men always are.

(*An Ideal Husband*, Act iii)

Women represent the triumph of matter over mind, just as men represent the triumph of mind over morals.

(*The Picture of Dorian Gray*, Ch. 4)

I like men who have a future, and women who have a past.

(*The Picture of Dorian Gray*, Ch. 15)

Now, not withstanding the wit of Oscar Wilde, let's face it, these lists are far from fair! *Man*, despite his occasional fall from grace and his proclivity to violence and certain shameful acts is, essentially, a noble, honourable, courageous and intelligent beast. *Woman*, on the other hand, despite her occasional elevation through intellect, skill, courage and achievement, is essentially a fickle, silly, shrewish, gossiping, mindless, forgetful and vainglorious afterthought!

So much for the weight of history. If it doesn't bear down on your shoulders, it certainly bears down on mine. My edition of this dictionary is dated 1967 and, to be fair, represents collected thoughts from many, many hundreds of years, some predating the birth of Christ, some as recent as the nineteen-fifties and early sixties.

Whatever else that can be said, the *Home Book of Quotations* is as interesting an example of where we have come from as any I can think of. In a few short pages we can get a quick insight into the evolution of thought on a whole range of topics. In this instance, we can see how far we have come this century in liberating men and women from a limited model of the worth of women. Today I don't think too many people would openly talk about the fickle nature of women, their dullness, their stupidity, their lack of intellectual substance. We no longer think that the worth of a woman is measured by her physical beauty and her charm, her sweet and compassionate nature and her capacity to offer comfort. We no longer worry about her idle hands turning her spirit to gossip and meanness, devilry and destruction.

No, to all intents and purposes, women and men regard each other as equals and we are generally increasing our understanding of our differences and improving our tolerance for each other's apparent madnesses.

Or so it seems. Realistically, however, who really knows? Different men and women report different perceptions, have different experiences, are more or less sensitive to certain innuendos. Truth and fiction have blended so it is sometimes hard to tell one from the other. Perhaps we have talked so much about equality, as with enlightened business practices, that we are in danger of believing our own rhetoric. In reality, it may be that we are as far from equality of the sexes in business as we are from true empowerment.

So, as you read on take into account that these myths and truths are all perceptual; they are based on how, it seems, a large number of men and women see these issues. I am only interpreting what I have heard, looking for the 'pattern that connects people', but, to the best of my ability, I will try to present as unbiased a perspective as is possible, notwithstanding my obvious bias!

Whatever else you do, keep smiling for the balance of this chapter and remember this is a relatively hot issue for all of us and one where, as far as I know, no one has absolutely got it right yet. As long as we all keep trying, we will move forward.

THE MYTHS IN DETAIL

MYTH ONE
Women are selected for positions according to their capacity and not because they are women.

TRUTH ONE
It depends on who's doing the selection. If men are selecting, chances are they are operating from a paradigm which excludes many of the skills and natural abilities that women can offer, so they fail to identify 'good' women. It's a case of not knowing how to look, rather than not being able to see.

Many women believe that the process of selection, especially for senior positions, is biased in favour of men. Their perception is that the recruitment is often done by men and the outstanding qualities women possess — which would be an asset in the most senior positions — are qualities that men have inadequate skills in assessing. The skills being assessed are limited to the skills that men understand; almost by definition, they are predominantly 'male' skills. For instance, assuming common industry skill, a man may be chosen for a senior position because of his 'leadership skills' which manifest in his authority, ambition, perseverance, ability to make 'tough' decisions (that is, hiring and firing), his entrepreneurship, determination, 'presence' and power. A woman going for the same job might not have any of the above skills or not have them in comparative depth or quantity. This may be an active choice; she might not value these attributes. Does this make her a poorer choice for the employer? It depends on whether you are a man or woman making the selection based on 'traditional' (male) criteria or whether you are asking yourself the following liberating question: If men and women ruled in equal part, how would leadership be done? What attributes would be commonplace and why? The criteria for selection to senior appointments should be drawn from the list that comes from such a question. While a woman with equal industry skill might not have an authoritative nature, or bear herself with charismatic determination, she may have any and all of the following qualities in abundance:

– compassion;

– tolerance;

– capacity to teach;

– capacity to communicate and consult;

– capacity to support and nurture;

– capacity to listen;

– capacity to mentor;

– natural inclination to network and establish friendships with
   working companions.

Many of the qualities listed above are seen as 'soft', lacking real substance in the hard, cold world of commerce. However, I suggest that our world is sorely lacking these qualities. Nature enjoys balance. Our decision making in business appears to be out of balance. I certainly wonder, if women and men were in equal number in senior leadership positions, what questions would be raised, what debates would be co-joined, what outcomes we would produce that are different from today. If nothing else, in the words of Geoffrey Miller, a research scientist at the Max Planck Institute for Psychological Research in Munich and an evolutionary psychologist who's provoking some interesting debate on the differences between men and women (Writing in *New Scientist*, 23 December 1995, p 31):

It's just much more fun to live in a world where everybody is producing interesting things than in a world where one sex with one viewpoint produces the great majority of public culture.

PROPOSAL: **Look a the process of promotion in your business. What are the unwritten rules that are at work? Do you believe they advantage either sex? Have you asked the women of your business how they feel about promotion? Do they see their natural attributes as having a value? Are their natural attributes taken into account in the selection process? Have you ever conducted a serious meeting to discuss a critical topic with an equal number of men and women? Try doing this and see if the outcomes are different in substance from those you could reasonably expect if the majority of decision makers were male (say 92% male, 8% female — to be in keeping with current middle management distribution).**

MYTH TWO
Women are too emotional. They are often unable to take the tough decisions and they allow their emotions to interfere with the quality of their thinking.

TRUTH TWO
The gift women bring to much decision making is the extent of their emotional interpretations. Men and women not infrequently have different priorities in the process of decision making.

I am not sure that women are more emotional than men. In fact, they prob-ably aren't. What they appear to do, however, is (a) demonstrate their emotions more easily and (b) place a higher value on them than men do. Personally, I find it very hard, despite many years experience as a senior leader, not to place greater importance on my emotional response to some-thing than on my intellectual response. I trust my emotional response to have greater integrity. Intellectually, I can be too cold, too calculating, too considered, and although this unarguably has value, if it dominates my thinking, I end up walking over other people or missing critical human issues. After the event, this adversely affects the outcome of the work I am doing. I think this is a common experience for business leaders.
Emotions allow us to express our humanity. In the workplace they allow us to bring colour to what might otherwise be a monotone environment. Humans respond to emotions, they are elevated by them, motivated by them, moved by them. No matter how brilliant the intellectual appeal of a proposal, it will be regularly one-upped by a passionate and emotionally laden call to action.

The benefit to all of us of valuing both styles of thinking —intellectual and emotional — is the balance it brings to the way we act. An emotional response, without thought, can be irrational, untimely, ill considered and powerless. An intellectual response, without emotion, can be cold, inhu-mane, hurtful and destructive. Together, however, the two responses bring balance.

We value intellectual rigour in many human endeavours, but think a moment on where we value emotional input: at home, between friends, in families, in leisure time activities, on holiday, in community aid, in art. Why is emotional input so poorly valued in business?

P R O P O S A L : Either consider individually or arrange a brainstorming session to debate the following: Where in your organisation could you benefit from emotional input? Consider some of the 'tough' decisions that have been taken recently. How might they have been handled differently if quality emotional decision making accompanied intellectual rigour? Do you use your emotions in decision making? How? When? When push comes to shove, which do you value more greatly — your intellectual response to a problem or your emotional response?

MYTH THREE
Some women are moody and unpredictable, especially at that time of month, and this can make them a liability in terms of the quality of their work and the reliability of the decision making.

TRUTH THREE
Some women do experience emotional ups and downs (don't we all), but that may actually be an asset in terms of their work and their decision making. Quite possibly it gives them the emotional flexibility and experience to reconsider decisions that yesterday appeared clear-cut. This might add a dimension to thinking that is possibly missing in business.

Not all women get premenstrual. Not all women experience an 'emotional cycle'. Not all women wake up one morning during the month thinking that doomsday is upon them, disaster is imminent and suicide is a preferable choice to getting out of bed!

For women who are regularly or (according to some) excesssively emotionally cyclical, managing their emotional upheavals can be a nightmare. It can also be a nightmare for the other women and men around them who are not on the roller-coaster ride with them. For some women the ride is mildly irritating, amusing, discomforting or just curious. For others it can be a torment. Whatever the case, a woman doesn't choose to menstruate or be the one to go through the agony of childbirth, she also doesn't choose to be on this monthly roller-coaster.

I believe that in the majority of instances (not withstanding the benefits that might come from appropriate therapeutic or medical support), the deciding factor between benefiting from the state or drowning in it can often hinge on how such women are treated by the people around them.

In the average sort of family with the average sort of woman I suspect there is acceptance and understanding, if not a modicum of ducking and weaving, during these times. While fully expecting to be misunderstood or to misunderstand the needs of the person they love, a loving husband or child or friend will see a woman's need for comfort and support and will offer it without qualification. If we care for someone, we take the good, the bad and the ugly. We don't discriminate and say "you're only part of this family when you are dolled up and your tiara is in place."

We value emotions and we understand that from emotional change can sometimes come inspiration. When our moods change we see the world around us differently, rethink decisions and sometimes come to conclusions that yesterday might have appeared far-fetched or impossible.

In business, we hardly acknowledge this emotional flux. Women who are emotional in excess of the accepted 'norm' go into hiding or denial when the cycle is in full swing. They can be the butt of unkind innuendos. Jokes can abound around the photocopier, coffee machine or smoko room... "Jesus, Mary's a livewire today!" "God, it must be that time of the month again for June, she looks like she ran over a black cat!" or "I can't put a foot right with Sally today, she's as mad as a hatter." or "You can't trust bloody women, they're all over the place emotionally!" or (and I had this one given to me by one of the most senior corporate executives today in

Australia, who shall remain nameless) "The trouble with women is they are cyclical!"

Prejudice towards any group of people diminishes all of us. When it is a form of prejudice that embraces so many, there is no excuse for its continuance. So, to begin the process of elevating a state which is natural for a large number of people, here's a thought to ponder: being cyclical is natural. Our world is cyclical. Seasons come and go, weather patterns change, all things cycle through life, from birth to death, all matter cycles, the universe is a series of cycling patterns, chaos is simply a series of cycles, from infinitely small to infinitely large, changing, evolving. Men and women are part of the cycle and are themselves cyclical. To punish a woman for being cyclical, moody, changeable, unpredictable, is to punish her for being part of the natural world. She can no more help it than she can help being hungry or thirsty. All of us experience emotional cycles. If some people experience these cycles more than others, perhaps tolerance and compassion, respect and support, space and understanding are called for. It is not appropriate to suggest cyclical behaviour is unprofessional or unbusinesslike. It just is.

One man I spoke to about this made the following observations.
"Recognition of the cyclical nature of humans, regardless of sex, is fundamental to men parting with their fear of and competitive response to women. Many men are frightened of women and in the only way they know they react by ostracising women — seeing them as a real threat to their [men's] survival. In other words, they become the enemy."

Sooner rather than later I trust we will cross this particular bridge together. If our emotional differences divide us now, there may be a time when they will bring us together and, rather than resenting one another, we will see value in harnessing our diversity.

PROPOSAL: Take time to consider the following: Are you emotionally cyclical? Do you experience a certain time in the month when emotions change? Are the changes disturbing to you or to others? Does your emotional state affect how you work or your relationship to other people? How would you like to be treated differently? Are there people in your work environment who appear to be emotionally cyclical? Do you find it disturbing or difficult to deal with? Have you spoken to this person when they are their 'normal' selves? Why don't you try doing this and see if between you can't work out a strategy for looking after everyone concerned. What benefits flow from changes in emotional states? What are you able to do better, understand more fully as a result of a changed emotional state?

MYTH FOUR

Some of women's worst enemies are other woman who are competitive and ruthless. They, more than men, contrive to limit the growth of other women.

TRUTH FOUR

Women can thwart other women (as men can thwart other men) but it is frequently the product of a conditioned sense of scarcity — a perception by women that senior positions open to women are scarce and competition will therefore be much tougher than it is for men.

Women can be their own worst enemies. I have, together with many people, experienced that peculiar 'bitchiness' that women can show one another in a competitive environment. I am not sure that I know the male equivalent. Maybe there isn't one. Dare I say it, but despite politics and hierarchy, in many instances, men in a competitive environment can play a cleaner game than some women.

I don't pretend to understand this behaviour. It goes against everything I understand and value as a woman. It serves no one and diminishes everyone. It is mean-spirited in the extreme and, given the incredible paucity of women in senior positions, it is downright puzzling.

Perhaps the behaviour is ancient, a biological response to being 'chosen' by the dominant males? Maybe women think "I am important, I have been selected, I will make damn sure my place is secure by not letting any other females in on the turf." Somewhere deep inside, unable to be substantiated intellectually, I sense the motivation is an intuitive response to the notion of scarcity — the thinking is more like "there are very few senior positions available, I'm on my way, I had better keep the competition out of the way." Women do not understand, despite the apparent clarity of selection criteria, how or why people are selected to senior positions. Especially in larger organisations, most women feel they are at a disadvantage in the recruitment stakes, compared to men. Most women are aware that, to a large extent, their appointment to senior ranks will rely on their hiding of many female traits and their ability to show they can 'play the game' with the boys. And you don't have to be an Einstein to realise that there are very few women appointed to senior positions, so scarcity for women is a reality.

Whatever the motivation, the behaviour is counterproductive. We have to ask ourselves — men and women — how we should challenge this type of behaviour and what, in our structures and promotion selection criteria we have to do to change in order to remove the notion of scarcity.

PROPOSAL: **Set up debating teams. Agree that the debate is not a forum for making personal attacks. Pose some or all of the following questions: Has any of the group experienced the 'bitchiness' referred to in this chapter? How does it show up? What are the repercussions of such behaviour? How could it be challenged with out being unkind to the individual or individuals in question? Do you believe there are a**

paucity of positions at senior management level available to women?
How does this affect the performance of women in general? How would
you encourage the appointment of more women to senior ranks?

MYTH FIVE

To be successful, a woman must be ambitious and single-minded,
prepared to sacrifice traditional family responsibilities and a sense of her
role as a mother and feminine woman in pursuit of her chosen career.

TRUTH FIVE

Successful women come in all shapes and sizes. Women can and do integrate their success in business with motherhood and femininity (whatever that is) — provided the environment and the prevailing business
paradigm allows it.

We have a long heritage that suggests that women were at their best at
home, beside the hearth, in the kitchen, in the bedroom, in the laundry,
adorning an arm at a ball. They were admired for their beauty, their grace,
their kindliness, their charm, their maternal fortitude. Now, while there
might be value in some of this, we have unarguably made substantial
strides forward in the last hundred-odd years. We have achieved useful
changes to predictable stereotypes. We have expanded our model of
'woman' to embrace all manner of activity; in theory, few (if any) doors
remain closed to the ambitious and determined female.

Now, at the end of the twentieth century, we need to learn to incorporate,
without judgment, traditional feminine ideals with ambition and
achievement. They are not mutually exclusive. It is possible to have a
family, be a loving mother and wife and still aspire to the heights of any
chosen profession. There are increasing numbers of role models who are
doing just that — Managing Directors of businesses that run with the children in the background; Chief Executive Officers who take a couple of

days off because an elderly mother is ill or a child is starting school. There are Board Directors who have to leave early from a meeting in order to cook dinner and there are Executives who have to attend a Little Athletics Meeting to see Johnny or Sally run.

Instead of saying these people are demonstrating a lack of professionalism, we admire them for their flexibility and time management skills. Perhaps some of us even envy what appears to be a more holistic approach to life — their life appears more fulfilling than ours. We are increasingly putting a comparative value on home activities with respect to business, and when someone makes a choice to place home demands over business, we respect their decision.

PROPOSAL: Are you married or single? How do you value business compared to your private life? Which is more important? How do you relate to the responsibility of family? What about the elderly and the young? What changes would have to be made in your working environment to accommodate more sympathetically the needs of families, of working men and women? Are women supported in their commitments to children or are they judged as less able to take up senior appointments? What would have to change in your workplace to elevate the importance of family and to diminish or eradicate altogether the judgment that says women who have families represent a poor investment in the future?

MYTH SIX
Good women are hard to find, but we are looking.

TRUTH SIX
Good women are everywhere; where exactly are you looking and what are you looking for?

Generally, women rarely get head hunted and, with some high profile exceptions, they aren't approached, despite their skill, experience and general know-how, to join boards of companies. The result is that it appears that the same women turn up time and time again, as representatives of women in general, in the media, on boards, heading up research projects on behalf of a variety of organisations and on behalf of both federal and state governments. One could reach the conclusion from this that, indeed, good women are hard to find; efforts are being made, but really the selectors (whoever they are) are battling the odds!

To find more good women, we need to look in a variety of different places and we need to use more enlightened criteria. Look for them in:

– schools (principals, deputy principals, administrative executives);

– hospitals (Directors of Nursing, senior nursing and administrative staff);

– community projects (welfare initiatives for the poor, sick, young, homeless, disadvantaged);

– direct marketing companies (senior branch managers, executives for direct marketing companies, where the senior branch managers are frequently in charge of businesses in excess of a million dollars);

– small businesses (home-based businesses — look up listings from the federal or state offices for small business);

– the service sector (especially plumbing, electrical and housing; many of the million-plus businesses started as family businesses and, indeed, the General Manager is often the wife who started off as the bookkeeper);

– the entertainment industry (music, theatre, film);

– marketing (many of the senior account executives, creative directors and public relations specialists are women);

– journalism (television and print);

– fashion (manufacturing and retailing).

In many of these industries there are women — clever, experienced and creative women — in very senior positions. They either never or rarely get head hunted for specific jobs or to join boards.

PROPOSAL ONE: Is your organisation looking for women? If so where are you looking and what criteria are you using to select your proposed targets? List the criteria for selection and, against your list, make a second list of qualities that you believe women specifically will bring to the job. Ask yourself or the team searching whether they are biased towards men when they set their selection criteria; it is likely that they are using a more 'traditional' model. Ask yourself or the selection team what their attitude is towards promoting women. Do you believe that jobs should be offered to the best people, irrespective of sex? If you think so, ask why it is that only 1.7% of very senior positions are taken up by women and, in the general work force, only 8% of management positions are occupied by women.

PROPOSAL TWO: In searching for senior women to join executive teams or boards or to act as advisers, where else could your organisation be looking? Make a list of possible sources. Are you looking for industry expertise or a broad executive capacity?

THE WAY FORWARD

These, then, are just a few observations that I think are worth throwing into the fray. They stem from conversations I have had with both men and women in a variety of settings but, of course, we each of us have our own life experiences to draw on, our own well formed opinions based on what has worked for us and what hasn't. As well, there are countless books on the subject. Take your pick!

However we construct our sense of what is true in the world, especially as it affects women in business, we could benefit by reminding ourselves that it is just our perception; it is not an objective reality (despite our best efforts to make it seem that way!). It isn't necessarily the objective truth; in fact it might not even be a widely held perception. Whatever else happens, I think it is essential that we continue the dialogue — that we look to increase our flexibility, embrace the opinions and perceptions of others — resolving the level of discrimination that women feel still prevails in the modern workplace. The most hurtful thing is to deny its existence. Platitudes such as "women have the same chance as men in our organisation" can often be discredited when looking at senior management statistics. If opportunities are equal, why are so few women turning up in senior positions? If they are choosing not to take the positions up, it's worth asking why!

In my voyage so far I have, by choice and by accident of fate, not had a great deal to do with the debate concerning the liberation of women (or men, for that matter). I have, for most part, been so busy doing things that I haven't really had time to discover what might be obstructing me on my journey. There have been times when I have felt a little ashamed by my lack of participation but there also have been times when I have been grateful for the distance between the recognisable agitators and myself.

Be that as it may, I cannot deny that in the last two years, more than at any one time in my career, I have become increasingly aware of how ingrained our prejudice towards women in business remains in Australia. There is a slightly ockerish quality to a fair quantity of corporate leadership — a boys' club, a network of very male contacts that is closed to women not because competent women are in short supply but because they are not welcome. We excuse our behaviour, saying that qualified women are few and far between or are hard to find, but who are we really fooling?

In a world marketplace that is increasingly allowing for the development of women (especially in the West), making space for them to take up their rightful place as partners in the management of the planet, Australians would be parochial indeed if we didn't change our recruitment practices and dismantle many of the myths that surround women in business.

We can't deny that women constitute an enormous percentage of the work-force — up to a certain level. Learning a great deal about their various businesses, their skill sets *must* be developing. Where are they all disap-pearing to? Are they all leaving to have children? Are none returning? Or if they are returning, is their knowledge so profoundly devalued that they are unable to subsequently take up more senior positions?

We all lose in the end. There seems to me to be a terrible loneliness to leadership which is predominantly male. Emotions are devalued, a strongman hierarchy frequently prevails; a softer more compassionate, more sensitive manner is missing, not because men can't express it, but because women are not there to encourage and validate it. We are wired to work together, each sex offering something to the other; whatever the benefit of our union, it is for all of us and for all time.

Governments can legislate for change, activist groups can agitate for it. Ultimately, however, *fundamental* change occurs when the majority of us take up the call, personalise the mission and decide to take responsibility for specific and measurable action in our own lives. In this way, even stagnating ideas that once mobilised thousands to passionate demonstration, turn again into unstoppable revolution.

I ask you, without such a movement, knowing what we know about what isn't working, what makes us think that business will work well for us all and for our planet? What makes us think that balanced decisions will flow from the hallowed halls of decision making when they bear principle witness to the solid footfalls of men and not to the faster, lighter sounds of a woman's tread?

Are we not now on very thin ice?

Busted!

Sometimes, we don't need to see the end, merely the beginning.

In *Myth busters* I have tried to suggest ways for the silent majority to find a voice. Practices abound in business which many of us don't like but which

16

continue because we think we are alone in our opinions or experiences. Even when we don't agree with a commonly accepted practice, we go along because everyone else does. We assume that we must be wrong, that what we see happening around us must be the truth. However, such a reality has little foundation in anything other than habit — if we keep doing something for long enough we begin to think it is the only way it can be done.

To change we must first see a better alternative. Then we have to identify the real benefits that will flow from the change. Finally, we have to be clear on how we can begin the process of change.

Sometimes, we don't need to see the end, merely the beginning.

PILLOW TALK
(A darkened room.)

> Christ... what was that.
> *What was what?*
> Can't you hear?
> *Hear what?*
> Jesus... listen... there...
> *I don't know what you're talking about. Go back to sleep.*

(Deep silence, ink blackness.)

There it is again. For God's sake wake up!
I am awake, thanks to you.
Can't you hear it?
Hmm... yes... now that you mention it.
Well...
Well what?
What are you going to do?
Nothing.
Don't be ridiculous.
Look, if you're worried, you do something.
No way, what if it's an axe murdering rapist?
Jesus you're a dramatist.
I'm not kidding, there's something there.
Okay, okay, I'm getting up.

(Silence.)

You said you were getting up.
I am.
When?
Now.

(Sounds of man stumbling out of the bed, heading for the door.)

Christ, don't go like that.
What are you talking about?
Put something on.
I'm okay.
What if someone's down there?
I'll give them a bloody big fright.
I'm serious, put something on.
Okay.

(Time passes. The person re-enters the room.)

There's your culprit.

Where?

(Plonk on the bed goes a soft heavy object... loud purring can be heard.)

Oh, Sammy darling, my poor pussy, were you locked out in the horrible old cold.

I tell you what, if that cat gets me out of bed one more night, something a lot worse than being cold is going to happen to him.

Yeah, sure.

(Silence descends and, the cat being the wiser of the three, artfully inserts itself under the bedding and firmly and warmly tucks itself into the small of his master's back. The sounds of deep breathing soon fill the room. The drama in the night unfolds, but not in this room.)

(Next morning over coffee in bed.)

You shouldn't be scared of the dark.

I'm not.

Well, why didn't you get up last night?

Men's work.

Oh, yeah, great excuse.

It's not an excuse.

Yes it is.

No it is not. What if there had been someone downstairs?

But there wasn't.

That's not the point. There might have been.

Yeah.

It's all a matter of what you think is possible.

You mean what you think is possible.

Yes, that's what I said.

No you didn't.

It's what I meant. If I think there is someone downstairs then I'm too scared to go down and let the cat in.

So, you know it's the cat!

No I don't.

You just said you did.

No, I said if I think there is someone downstairs, I can't get up and let the cat in.

God, I will never understand women.

No, me neither.

(Laughter and the sound of rustling paper.)

By the by, I guess that's what it's all about.

What?

Perceptions — if you think something is real, you act that way. Like you hear the cat but you imagine there is someone downstairs and that's more real to you than the cat trying to get in at the window.

Yeah... but I can't help myself.

I know — that's what I mean — that's what we have to challenge.

What, our own fears and stuff?

Yes, in a way. The point is that we make our own reality and sometimes it works and sometimes it doesn't.

Go on.

If we don't challenge the way we see things, then we'll never know whether we could see it differently.

If you're working your way towards persuading me to get up in the night, forget it!

No, that's okay. I'm just thinking there are things that we should challenge. You know... the whole idea that there are rules we have to live by, that can't be challenged. For instance, I've always worn a suit to work because everyone else does, but it's stupid. I hate wearing suits and I feel like I am being strangled by my tie.

So what are you going to do about that? What can you do about it?

(Pause)

Well, what do you think of this idea... on Monday I'm going to take a poll at the office to see who wants to change.

I bet your boss will be the first to agree!

Actually, I think he will be. The whole thing is worth discussing.

Hmm... actually, I think it's a great idea. If we think about perceptions, there are so many things that we could do differently. Like, I know it sounds stupid, but I've just thought about how many women in our office get PMT.

What on earth is PMT? Sounds like a vitamin.

Oh, you know, they get moody and stuff in the middle of the month. Do you know we had a woman in our department last year... Annette or something... we all thought she was dippy and I remember Andy, who was Divisional Manager, giving her hell. Do you know what we found out yesterday?

What?

She had some sort of hormonal imbalance but she thought she was going crazy. It was only after Andy fired her that she went to a doctor who put her on some tablets. Apparently she's in charge of McNairs Marketing Division now.

Really. Well she must be good.

Yeah, she was, we really lost someone special. I feel awful for not having helped her.

Next person, hey.

Yeah. I tell you, perceptions really affect everything, don't they? We're considering merging with Mastersons but Andy was saying today that we have to keep it top secret. Just before I left the office, I overheard the guys having a smoko by the back door; they were already talking about the so-called secret! Andy thinks it has to be kept top secret but I don't think it is possible. God, the gossip in our place is so fast.

So what can you do? I mean if everyone is already talking about it?

Well, that's the problem. They'll get it wrong if Andy doesn't come out with the truth. When we merged with Alpine everybody panicked. We all thought we would lose our jobs, but we didn't. We just had months of being miserable.

Maybe if Andy told everyone what you were planning and why, you could avoid distressing everyone this time.

That's what I was thinking. Maybe I'll talk to Andy and see what he says.

Yeah, good idea. Gutsy move on your part. I hope he understands your intentions.

Well, isn't that what you were saying?

What do you mean?

Not to be scared and stuff. I think the thing we have to really concentrate on is what we can do. We can't always just wait for someone else to do the hard work, getting others to see value of doing things differently.

Yeah, although that's easier said than done.

Why?

Well people have to want to change.

I think people do want to change — it's just that no one makes the first move or, maybe like Andy, they just don't know how to do things differently.

Well, even though I said I would like to see how many guys would like to get out of suits, I still wonder why I should be the one taking the risk.

Well, I guess it is the same for me. But if I don't take a risk, get Andy thinking about other ways of doing things... who will...

Yeah, you are absolutely right... We are always waiting for someone else to make the change... but if you and I don't do something, who will?

Let's shake on it.

You're on.

Monday — it's a deal.

Bet I do it and you don't!

We'll see, we'll see!

(Silence)

So...

So what?

So what about the cat...

So what about the cat?

So what about the cat at night time...

So what about the cat at night time?

So what about the noise the cat makes at night time...

So what about the noise the cat makes at night time?

So what about you getting up and letting the cat in at night time next time?

No way, Jose!

So, some things will never change.

Not in my lifetime honey bun, not in my life time.

I guess I can cope with that one.

(Sounds of laughter and rustling of bed clothes.)

DIVINE DIVERSITY

Consider this: in Egypt, the colour of mourning is yellow, yet in some cultures yellow is the colour of cowardice. In China the colour of mourning is white, yet in our own white is the preferred colour of the bride. In Iran (once Persia) the colour of mourning is the colour of withered leaves, a pale brown, and yet to us, it heralds autumn. Humans are infinitely inventive and the mixture of cultures on our planet today stands as testimony to our innate diversity.

Our inventiveness, however, is also matched, culture by culture, individual by individual, by our natural tendency to find patterns, to rely on repetitious ways to get things done. Such patterns make life easier; we have less to think about. We understand what is acceptable, we know what to do to belong. Foreign practices are mysterious and less meaningful. Before the world's varied cultural practices became as integrated as they are today, it must have been confusing to a young Chinese bride to accept that a European bride was expressing joy and innocence in wearing white to her wedding. For the Westerner white at a funeral might have appeared to be inadequately sombre.

If something is familiar to us, it seems right: we can draw upon prior experience of the outcomes. It is our sense of the outcomes, our personal history, that gives meaning to our world.

While certain practices represent 'laws' which govern our behaviour, sometimes over time they become no longer appropriate. Unfortunately, despite this, despite the fact that certain practices may no longer be working for us, neither we nor our practices change easily. We like to settle into an acceptable form of behaviour and stick to it — and preferably without much thought.

Until, that is, someone shows us another way of 'seeing' reality, of interpreting what is around us. The extent of our motivation to change will be measured by our perception of the potential benefits versus the potential risks. If we think the benefits outweigh the risks, over time we might change.

Myth busters is designed to give an alternative view on a range of issues which many people hold to be important and, by demonstrating that this alternative view is held by many, to provide motivation to change.

Admittedly, some perceptions will stay constant. Some perceptions will be seen as absolute truths and some lies may go unchallenged. We are, after all, human, and there is much that is crazy, irrational, illogical and hard to fathom about people and the way we live.

If *Myth busters* seeks to achieve anything, it is to invite more people to question and to think, to challenge and debate, to consider alternatives and to act, where and when appropriate. The issues are an eclectic bag but they are commonly raised by people in a diversity of businesses and, as such, deserve an airing.

Having read this section, I trust you feel empowered to explore not only the myths exposed here but, indeed, the many, many more that you may have experienced in your own work or daily life. Take little for granted and assume there are no sacred cows. We are born to challenge and change and ultimately we can only benefit from the process.

And remember, if you don't, who will?

To every-thing a beginning and an end

I trust that one day we will learn to work together with less personal vested interest and a greater respect for and appreciation of the cumulative efforts of people.

In essence, this book is really all about 'scenario planning'. It is an honest exposé on where we are now, based on where I believe we are going, taking into account events that are occurring around us at the moment. The content has been determined by many thousands of employees and many hundreds of managers — the subject matter is the 'pattern that connects' them. All

I have tried to do is gather the information into a readable whole and to share with you the insights that these thousands of people have offered.

A THOUGHT ON A SHOWER

I moved house recently. The hardest thing to deal with was the shower. In my old house the shower was part of a modern bathroom; two walls were glass. In the shower I had a sense of spaciousness, of being able to see beyond the shower, of being in touch with the world, of hearing the people who matter in my life pass by. Some people thought that the shower was too exposed. It made them feel naked before the world. Of course, they *were* — but for me the shower just felt unfettered... like a camp shower in the bush.

In the house we are in now, built at the turn of the century, the shower is more like an old sauna box. There is one glass door, opaque glass at that. Three walls are heavy ceramic tiling. The shower hose is set into a solid roof. When the door closes, you are in a coffin. At least, that's what it felt like to me at first. I was sure I couldn't breath. I panicked to begin with, felt claustrophobic with the door shut.

For the first couple of months in the new house, I showered with the door partly open. The result was a mini flood every time I showered. Despite the adverse results of my showering technique, I decided the benefits outweighed the consequences. I didn't like the shower; it was okay for the shower not to like me. It demonstrated its frustration with my stubbornness by filling the bathroom with shower water. I demonstrated my stubbornness by mopping the water up daily.

But time passes. The door closed a little more each day, without my really noticing. Then one day, without thinking, I closed the door completely. The draft, which I had become accustomed to, disappeared, and the shower closet sighed with relief. The shower whispered, "Let me show you how to have a shower now... the way it can be!" I stayed in until the water ran cold.

Thereafter, I enjoyed the pleasure of an old-fashioned shower closet — its warmth, its intimacy, its privacy. I delighted in the space for thinking I found in the shower, with my thoughts turned inwards. I played in the shower, discovering another reality that I had not previously enjoyed.

This place is now my favourite of all in a house full of wonderful places.

THE SHOWER SCENE

'Scenario planning' — it has a nice ring to it. Dr Terry Heng, Vice
President and Director of External Technology Planning for Chicago based
Motorola Inc lays claim to its coining. Motorola is one of the most
successful and fastest growing companies in the United States today —
apparently.

I read about this individual in the 2 October 1995 issue of *Business Review
Weekly*. He is quoted as saying:

> *there will be many issues that will effect our lives in the future, things
> that today we would not normally take into our planning in business;
> human rights, the rise and rise of women in third world countries,
> conflict between Islam and Christianity, possible changes in China's
> ruling powers. These things, any one of them, can change the world's
> marketplace, the global economy overnight.*

Reading between the lines I can hear a broader discussion about the challenge of making predictions in a world which can change so rapidly, about
the importance of gathered intelligence and of education; a conversation
with Dr Heng might roam onto the nature of leadership and danger of
certainty which excludes alternatives. Together, these represent the skills
and behaviours that we may or may not have at our fingertips — to call on
when the world we take for granted is turned upside down by any one of a
thousand possible scenarios.

I wish change was easier, more straightforward. I wish that we could
operate together with less personal vested interest and a greater respect for
and appreciation of the cumulative efforts of people. I know we are slowly
drawing closer to a time when we take for granted the outcomes of
synergy — of the whole amounting to more than the individual parts —
but it is a long road with an irregular surface, and not all travellers on the
road are interested in the same outcome.

I think there is much about business which is like my shower. We may not want to change because what we are doing now is producing the results we want — the profit that we have aimed for. We might feel too much is at stake — our own reputation, shareholder's money, our market share. We are not motivated to change because where we are is just fine.

But then, something will come along when we least expect it, and what we had will be no more. I moved house because I loved the house. I never thought about hating the shower.

A PARTING OF THE WAYS

Every issue raised in this book reflects the comments of many people who each believe that their ability to maximise opportunity is clearly limited by either one or all of the problems covered. How on earth can this be ignored? Why would anyone, sound of mind and body, choose to ignore it?

There is a voice of iron here and I trust that you can hear it, join it and act on it because there is one thing of which I am absolutely certain: the winners in the future will be the people who listen and learn and, having learnt, act.

I hope that somewhere along the line this book has struck a familiar cord. I trust you know the truth of what is said, or have experienced problems similar to those written up here. Perhaps you have seen the repercussions of similar idiocies in your own work life. Perhaps you, like me, have been the perpetrator of some of these so-called idiocies and are on the challenging and sometimes painful road of self-realisation.

It's fearful territory, isn't it! If you take up the challenge, you face tough questions: "Can I make the change? Will it work? Will people respect me afterwards? What if I'm wrong? What if others don't see the point of the change?" Well, you'll never know unless you try.

The future is not for the faint-hearted, it is for the bold. It is for people who are not afraid of trying, of being wrong, of learning and of trying again. It is in the hands of wise people, *and people learning to be wise.* There will come a time when both are rolled into one — all of us wise, all of us learning.

For myself, I now quite enjoy that feeling of uncertainty in my gut that I know marks a period of learning. I am in water a little deeper than I would like, learning to swim in a way I have not swum before. Although I think I can make it to the other side I cannot be absolutely sure. The uncertainty motivates me, makes me try harder, pay closer attention to the details, ask more people along the way how they would make the journey. In the process, I discover how to swim better — day, by day, by day.

There is great strength in learning and great danger in complacently deciding we know it all. I have decided I don't want to be in a position ever again where I think I know it all. I want to listen, learn, experiment and move forward, because one day I will be dead — and truthfully, there are many ways to live a life, aren't there?

All things turn, by and by. What we like today may not please us tomorrow. What we are certain about today may seem impermanent tomorrow. What we swear by today we may have forgotten tomorrow.

Nothing is certain, fixed, absolute. Everything can be built or destroyed, challenged, improved, developed, changed. We live during a time of immense learning — learning about simple things like showers and about complex things like business and world economics. And in it all, the difference is how we think about what we do and how we act on what we discover.

I don't pretend that change of substance is necessarily easy, but I do believe in the weight of human opinion and in the power of people who act on dreams. In my heart I believe in decency and compassion and I believe in treating people with dignity and respect. There is too much uncertainty in life for us to make it harder than it needs to be.

This book owes much to the people from all over Australia who so willingly told me their stories, who shared their ideas. It is indebted, too, to the leaders who had the courage to let their people speak freely.

This is really their book and it is certainly their story. May it inspire all of us to speak openly and to act with courage.

Fabian Dattner

Fabian Dattner is the Managing Director of a consultancy specialising in strategic leadership initiatives, rebuilding cultures post-merger/takeover and the design of curriculum based business education. She is well known to many Australians for her accomplishments in the business sector and for the work she has initiated as the founder of The Second Chance business register — an organisation that assists people with a record of offence to find work.

Fabian is a much sought after speaker and an advocate of leadership development and education in business. In 1992 she wrote the best-selling Nothing Ventured, Nothing Gained (Penguin) where she shared her personal approach to the challenge of change. In 1993 she was included in Susan Mitchell's Tall Poppies Too!, seven essays on well known Australian women (also published by Penguin).

As a leader in the Australian business and working community Fabian specialises in alleviating tension between leaders and employees. Her extensive knowledge of business practices and her commitment to innovation enable her to help leadership teams develop flexibility and openness in managing people and developing an exciting sense of the future.

Fabian can be contacted at:

Cherry Trees
32 Kent Hughes Road
Eltham, VIC 3095

Phone: (03) 9431 2602
Facsimile: (03) 9431 0842
Email: f.dattner@pgrad.unimelb.edu.au